CW00959181

SHAHJAHANABAD

THE LIVING CITY OF OLD DELHI

Also by Rana Safvi

*Where Stones Speak: Historical Trails in Mehrauli,
the First City of Delhi*

The Forgotten Cities of Delhi

SHAHJAHANABAD

THE LIVING CITY OF OLD DELHI

Book Three in the
Where Stones Speak trilogy

RANA SAFVI

HarperCollins *Publishers* India

First published in India in 2019 by
HarperCollins *Publishers* India
A-75, Sector 57, Noida, Uttar Pradesh 201301, India
www.harpercollins.co.in

2 4 6 8 10 9 7 5 3 1

Copyright © Rana Safvi 2019
Photographs courtesy the author
Maps courtesy Shubham Mishra 2019

P-ISBN: 978-93-5357-347-8
E-ISBN: 978-93-5357-348-5

Rana Safvi asserts the moral right to be identified
as the author of this book.

The views and opinions expressed in this book are the author's own
and the facts are as reported by her, and the publishers are not in any
way liable for the same.

All rights reserved. No part of this publication may be reproduced,
stored in a retrieval system, or transmitted, in any form or by any
means, electronic, mechanical, photocopying, recording or otherwise,
without the prior permission of the publishers.

Typeset in Adobe Garamond Pro 11.5/16 at
Manipal Technologies Limited, Manipal

Printed and bound at
Thomson Press (India) Ltd.

For Subuhi Safvi

Tu shaheen hai parvaaz hai kaam tera
Tere saamne aasmaan aur bhi hai

You are an eagle, keep on soaring (higher and higher)
There are many skies beyond this for you

—ALLAMA IQBAL

Ye shehr buland aalam-e baala se thha
Humshakl gharaz jannat-e maawa se thha
Ab kya hai ik aabaadi-e registaan hai
Dehli ko sharaf qil'e mualla se thha

This city was higher than the heavens once
In beauty, it resembled the paradise once
Now it's nothing but an inhabited desert
Delhi's soul was its exalted fort.

—GHULAM MAULA QALAQ

CONTENTS

PREFACE

By the time Emperor Shah Jahan ascended the throne of the Mughal Empire in February 1628, the empire had expanded and the *darbar* (public court) was attended by many rajas and *umara* (nobles and grandees). Two factors influenced his decision to shift his capital from Agra: one was that the Agra Fort, from where his father and grandfather had ruled, was too small for his needs, and the other was the unsuitability of the narrow lanes and ravines of Agra for his ceremonial processions.

Thus he decided to shift his capital. Lahore was considered, but the existing fort was also small and the winter climate was harsh. One of the main requirements of Emperor Shah Jahan was that the place should have a moderate climate and be near a river so that water could run through the palaces, thus a river flowing just below the site chosen for the Qila was ensured.

According to Shah Jahan's biography *Padshahnama*, after consultation with his engineers, Hindu astrologers and Muslim *hakims*, an auspicious location for the Qila was chosen between Firozabad and Salimgarh on the banks of the River Yamuna. Emperor Akbar and Emperor Jahangir had often come to Salimgarh, the island fort built by Salim Shah, son of Emperor Sher Shah Suri.

In his twelfth regnal year, Emperor Shah Jahan, corresponding to twelfth Zil-Hajj 1048 AH[1] (29 April 1639), gave orders to start the digging of the *Buniyad-e Mubarak* or the auspicious foundation. This is recorded in gold on the arch in the royal *khwabgah* or personal apartments by Sa'adullah Khan.

The architects chosen had already proved their mettle in the construction of his beloved wife's mausoleum, Taj Mahal.

The auspicious time decided by the astrologers for commencing the construction work on the foundation was Friday evening of the ninth Muharram, AH 1049 (12 May 1639), and at that auspicious time, Ustad Hamid and Ustad Ahmed laid the foundation. Both these architects had no parallel in their field and their intellect and expertise attracted great envy.

The emperor had given strict orders for the Qila to be completed as soon as possible, and therefore experts in the field of construction were called from every corner of the empire. Very soon, talented and famous *miamar* (architects), *sang-tarash* (sculptors), artisans, *munabatkar* (embossers/carvers) *parchiin saaz* (those who do inlay work on stone) assembled, and working their magic, took the Qila to its ultimate conclusion.

The Qila-e Mubarak or 'Auspicious Fort' was finally ready. At that time, Emperor Shah Jahan was in Kabul. Makramat Khan, under whose supervision it was completed, sent a message to the emperor that the *Daulatkhana-e Badshahi* (royal palace) and *Diwan-e Hazrat Zill-e Ilahi* (Palace of the respected shadow of God on earth) had been completed, and that the Diwan-e Aam and Diwan-e Khas, the *hammams* and canals, were waiting to be blessed by the fall of his footsteps and his noble self should sanctify this piece of heaven, which is the envy of heaven itself.

The emperor himself was very impatient to see the fort and gave orders to leave from Kabul for Agra and reached as soon as he could. On 24 Rabi' al-Awwal AH 1058 (AD 18 April 1648), he entered the fort he had ordered to be built on the banks of the Yamuna in Delhi, and 'illuminated' the new Qila with his 'blessed presence' and celebrations began.

The Qila-e Mubarak was indeed like an octagonal flower in full bloom, and had taken nine years to build.

The master architects Ustad Ahmed and Ustad Hamid had envisaged it as a piece of paradise, and perhaps that is why the famous Persian couplet was inscribed here:

Agar firdaus bar ru-ye zamin ast
Hamin ast-o hamin ast-o hamin ast

If there is Paradise on earth
It is this, it is this, it is this

This was in keeping with the paradisiacal theme with rivers and gardens that were laid in the Qila by the architects. A *Nahr-e Bahisht* or stream of paradise originating near Shah Burj and designed to flow into the row of palace buildings, in beautifully carved channels, connecting them to the gardens, further heightened the effect. This was interspersed with marble fountains of outstanding beauty, inlaid with jewels and inlay work[2] in the palace complex and silver fountains in the gardens.

The fate of the Qila-e Mualla/Qila-e Mubarak also varied with the fate of its royal inhabitants. In 1803, Emperor Shah Alam signed a treaty with Lord Lake, giving the British [East India] Company all powers and basically becoming their pensioner.

It was famously said of Emperor Shah Alam (1759–1806):

Sultanat-e-Shah Alam Az Dilli te Palam

The kingdom of Shah Alam is from Delhi to Palam

However, the decline of the Qila-e Mubarak as a political power saw it become a new intellectual and literary centre. The famous poets Mir Dard, Mirza Rafi Sauda, Mir Taqi Mir all lived in Delhi. Emperor Bahadur Shah Zafar presided over a literary renaissance with some of the most famous Urdu poets adorning his court. Sheikh Ibrahim Zauq, Hakim Momin Khan Momin and the unparalleled Mirza Ghalib were all jewels shining in his court.

Music received impetus, and *dhrupad* and *khyaal gaayki* flourished in the court, with famous proponents like Tanras Khan practising their craft under royal patronage. Miniature painting was also revived, with famous painters such as Mazhar Ali Khan and Ghulam Ali Khan receiving patronage from British officers posted in the court.

As in my previous books in this trilogy, I base this book on my own visits, as well as contemporary accounts, while the base of the descriptions come from both volumes of *Asar-us-Sanadid* by Sir Sayyid Ahmad Khan, *Waqiaat-e-Darul Hukumat Dehli* (*Accounts of Delhi, the Abode of Governance*) by Bashiruddin Ahmad Dehlvi, *The Archaeology and Monumental Remains of Delhi* by Carr Stephen and *Monuments of Delhi* by Maulvi Zafar Hasan.

Even though this city bore the brunt of the Uprising of 1857 and the Partition of India in 1947, Shahjahanabad, now called Old Delhi, is a living city. Many of the residents are fourth- and fifth-generation residents. They describe a Delhi that no longer exists – their beautiful city has been vacated by many old residents who moved to more open areas after Independence for ease of living. The narrow lanes of Shahjahanabad are not conducive to vehicular traffic, built as they were for horses and buggies. The havelis there have been rented out and have become warehouses...

I have tried to describe these changes, and reconstruct the city as it was before.

I have also included in my account of Shahjahanabad's monuments outside the walled city, such as those outside Ajmeri Darwaza, Kashmiri Darwaza and on the Ridge, and from some of the suburbs of Shahjahanabad, such as Paharganj, Jaisinghpura (now part of Lutyens, Delhi), Rakabganj (near Parliament House), and Shalimar Bagh, Roshanara Bagh and Mahaldar Khan ka Bagh in north Delhi.

It is a vast area and a throbbing city with a palpable past. I hope the reader will excuse me for any exclusions or mistakes.

I

A QILA IS PLANNED

Ye qasr dheh nahi sakta ke iski
haakim ne
Zameen ke saath dilon me bhi
neev daali hai

Till eternity this palace will
proudly stand,
Its foundation firmly laid in
hearts and land.

—Ajmal Siddiqui

From ASI Archives

In this book, we will go on a journey into the Qila and the city that was and now is.

But first let's go back in time.

In your mind's eye, come for a walk with me in the Qila that was.

The Diwan-e Khas with its pillars of inlay work of precious stones and gilded walls is glittering – brocade curtains, rich Kashmiri and Persian carpets piled on the floors under which flows the Nahr-e Bahist, adding to the opulence. The Diwan-e Aam with its grandeur is a symbol of power and stands grandly testifying to the might of the Mughal Empire.

Near it the winter sun is pouring in and this is just the right time to walk in the Bagh-e Hayat Baksh or the Life Bestowing Garden. The bagh was planted with fragrant and colourful flowers, flowering bushes and trees.

The dew is still damp under our feet and the flower buds are slowly opening up giving out their fragrance. I can imagine what went through Sir Sayyid Ahmad Khan's mind when he described it in his book on Delhi's monuments, *Asar-us Sanadid*:

> This garden is a sign of God's Divine Grace and rejuvenates the heart of the onlooker and makes him ecstatic and cheerful.
>
> The gardens of Heaven come up in front of the eyes. The height of the trees can make men envious of its stature and every flower can make a fair maiden blush and its tendrils put to shame the beloved's curls.

The sound of water running gently, the flow of a thousand fountains and the heady smell of camphor incense used to be rejuvenating, when the *Nahr-e Bahisht* flowed over the marble niches in the two identical pavilions built facing each other in the Bagh-e Hayat Baksh. The northern pavilion is Sawan, and the southern one is called Bhado'n. They were so named because they recreated the effect of the monsoons when the Nahr-e Bahisht flowed through them and on to the gardens.

There are small arched niches made in the pond and the chutes of this building in which, during the day, flower bouquets were placed, and, at night, camphor candles would be lit. The cascading water over these candles and flowers created an unbelievable feeling.

Let's keep walking, and enter the Mahtab Bagh or Moonlit Garden. It was for enjoyment in the heavenly evenings and nights when the scent from the flowers overpowered the senses, the camphor lamps and candles from the Sawan and Bhado'n pavilions made one dreamy and languorous. This was planted only with those flowers, bushes and trees, which had white blossoms. They enhanced the effect of the moonlight.

Perhaps the Badshah walked here with his begums, while the prince and princesses dreamt of crowns and palaces.

I am rudely awakened from my dream by loud voices. Who are these people shouting and disturbing the emperor's entourage in the bagh? Oh! It's a group of tourists, and I am back with a thud in the twenty-first century. There is no Mughal bagh – just some very English-looking manicured lawns and shrubs.

During the Uprising of 1857, this Qila saw much action by the Indian sepoys who had revolted against the East India Company rule. As a result, once the British crushed what they termed as a mutiny, they exiled the Mughal emperor.

In 1902, the remnants of Bagh-e Hayat Baksh were found buried deep in debris: that is, those portions that had not become part of the roads the British had built for their convenience inside the Mughal Qila.

Ugly army barracks replaced the Mahtab Bagh, and its fountains were silenced forever. Eighty per cent of the original buildings in the Qila were destroyed to accommodate the new British rulers.

Its nahr, waterfalls, water channels, flower and footpaths for roaming in the garden were all destroyed. Whatever we see today are the portions that were preserved and repaired by Lord Curzon. He replanted lawns and trees in the portions not occupied by the barracks.

Despite the vagaries of fortune, it still remains an icon of power, and the Qila-e Mubarak is now the Red Fort, a symbol of India's independence, from where the Prime Minister addresses the nation every 15 August.

Qila-e Mubarak/Qila Shah Jahan/Lal Qila

Emperor Babur (1483–1530) founded the Mughal Dynasty in 1526, after defeating Sultan Ibrahim Lodi. He ruled for four years from Agra. His son, Emperor Humayun (reigned 26 December 1530–17 May 1540), who succeeded him, shifted his capital to Delhi and started to build his palace there that he had named Din Panah. He could not complete it and had to flee India after Sultan Sher Shah defeated him. Sultan Sher Shah expanded Din Panah, which he renamed Sher Shah Garh, today known as Purana Qila.

Emperor Humayun did win back the crown of Delhi (22 February AD 1555–27 January 1556), but died soon after, and his son, Emperor Akbar (reigned AD 1556–1605), and grandson, Emperor Jahangir (reigned AD 1605–27), chose to rule from Agra.

Emperor Shah Jahan came to the throne in AD 1628 and found that the Agra and Lahore Fort were not spacious enough to accommodate the retinue of the dignitaries attending court, and decided to shift his capital to Delhi.

He made several visits to the area himself and finally, on the advice of ulema, saints and astrologers, he finalized the present location, between Firozabad and Din Panah, for his Qila and laid the foundation.

Naqqarkhana

The city of Shahjahanabad, now called Old Delhi, was built around this Qila.

In the thirteenth century, before Sultan Firoz Shah Tughlaq (reigned AD 1351–88) built the fifth city of Delhi, named Firozabad then, the area where Shahjahanabad was built was a wilderness, and that is why the 12th century Sufi saint Sheikh Shams-ul-Arifieen Bayabani, known popularly as Shah Turkman, had chosen to live here. He was a contemporary of Sultan Qutbuddin Aibak and Sultan Iltutmish, and belonged to the Bayabani sect, who, as per their name, which means wilderness, lived in uninhabited places. His dargah is in present-day Mohalla Qabristan (an area in Old Delhi, near the Turkman Darwaza).

Near Shah Turkman's dargah is Sultan Raziya's (reign AD 1236–40) grave. She was buried according to Sir Sayyid by the saint himself in his *khanqah* (hospice). Today his khanqah is reduced to just the area of his shrine and Sultan Raziya's grave is close by in the area known as Bulbulikhana.[3]

Thus the location where the city was being planned was not uninhabited as part of it had been included in the city of Firozabad, built by Sultan Firoz Shah Tughlaq. There were pockets of previous habitation in the area near Shah Turkman's khanqah and Chitli Qabr. Many pre-Mughal buildings such as mosques and tombs existed, though most of them have been completely renovated and now look modern. The only exception is a mosque built in Firoz Shah Tughlaq's reign known as Kalan Masjid,[4] which still stands tall within the walled city, near Turkman Darwaza. It is more or less in its original form and, unlike other mosques of such antiquity, is still in use.

Another Sultanate-period mosque known as Hafiz Daud ki Masjid exists in Mohalla Qabristan, but when I visited it, I found that it had been completely rebuilt in 2010 and is now called the Chand Wali Masjid. There is nothing left except local memory (that too will not last beyond the older generation) to show that it is a medieval mosque.

The thirteenth-century saint Syed Roshan Shah's dargah (famous as Chitli Qabr near Matia Mahal) was also present before Shahjahanabad was built. That area too had some pre-existing structures, one of them Syed Rafa-e Sahib ki Masjid. This too has been renovated in recent times and looks modern.

This area also housed Salimgarh Fort built on an island in the River Yamuna by Salim Shah (AD 1545–54) also known as Islam Shah, son of Sher Shah Sur. Salim Shah had also built a *baoli* (step-well) known today as Khari Baoli, Asia's largest spice market, and some *sarai*s (inns) for travellers.

The Naqshbandi saint Hazrat Baqi Billah had come to India during the reign of Emperor Akbar, so that area in Paharganj must have been well-inhabited.

The Neeli Chhatri (blue umbrella) on the Nigambodh Ghat, which is said to date back to the legendary Pandava period, had a pavilion made by Emperor Humayun to which Emperor Jahangir added a verse. The Mughal pavilion doesn't exist any more, but the temple famous as Neeli Chhatri is very popular today.

The Qila was planned to be double the size of Agra, and many times the size of the Lahore Fort.

According to Muhammad Waris's *Padshahnama* (translated by Prof. S. Ali Nadeem Rezavi), the foundation was marked on 29 April 1639, and the foundations of the fort were laid by expert diggers (*beldar*s) after five astrological hours (*sa'at*) and twelve minutes (*daqiqa*) on the night of Friday, 9th Muharram, 23 *Urdi Bihisht*[5] (12 May 1639).[6]

It was done under the supervision of Izzat Khan, who later became the subedar of Sind.

Ustad Ahmed Lahori and Ustad Hamid, two expert architects who had been involved in the construction of the Taj Mahal, were called.

Izzat Khan had the foundations dug up in five months and two days. Allah Vardi Khan replaced him. Allah Vardi Khan took two years, one month and fourteen days to construct a 12-yard-high wall all around the Qila. He was then appointed as subedar of Bengal, and Mukaramat Khan took over from him.

Mukaramat Khan took nine long years to finish this task. In the twentieth year of Emperor Shah Jahan's reign, the Qila was complete.

Emperor Shah Jahan entered the Qila for the first time through the Khizri Darwaza (he had come by the river route) on 18 April 1648.

Muhammad Waris writes in the *Padshahnama*:

> The designated hour, which was 16 and a half *ghari*, as calculated by the astrologers, was communicated to the Emperor. The appointed time was wide enough for the Emperor to leave Kabul and reach the capital city of Delhi.
>
> When the auspicious hour neared, His Majesty left Kabul and reached the capital city (Delhi). And thus the hidden became apparent to the intelligent. It is difficult to narrate the grandness and beauty of this Mighty Fort, its palaces, bastions and heaven-reaching arches…
>
> … There can be no other such strong fort on the face of this universe – probably there is no such fort underneath the sky which glitters such as the sun and the moon in the firmament. Its structures are beyond imagination. Its every corner is dazzling

and every direction full of heavenly gardens. It is in the form of heavens.

What should I say about the design of this building?

That the tongue gets tied by its very vision?

The qualities of these buildings are so high that none can elaborate on them!

In them the crafts are such that even the craftsmen are themselves over-awed.

The builders of the present age have embellished this edifice in such a way that its design is envy for all![7]

According to Muhammad Waris in *Padshahnama*, the total expenditure on these buildings was ₹60 lakh.

Faiz Nahr

Water, an essential prerequisite for a city, was also available, as Shah Jahan had given orders for the canal built by Sultan Firoz Shah Tughlaq to be revived. This canal, which took water from the River Yamuna, had fallen in disuse. It was extended to from Safidon (in present-day Haryana) to Khizrabad (present-day Defence Colony) under Emperor Akbar, and rejuvenated and brought to Shahjahanabad under Shah Jahan's orders. It was completed by Ali Vardi Khan at the same time as the Qila.

One branch flowed down to Chandni Chowk and then Faiz Bazar (modern-day Daryaganj), and the second branch came into the Qila at its northeast end through a mechanism known as *shuturgulu* (camel's neck) as the level had to be raised.

The branch in the Qila was known as Nahr-e Bahisht, and the one in Chandni Chowk as Faiz Nahr.

As Sir Sayyid Ahmad Khan wrote in Volume 1 of *Asar-us Sanadid*:

There was no building in the Qila where the Nahr did not reach and there was no alley or street in the city it didn't flow into. It even went into the royal kitchens, making the task of cooking easier.

By the reign of Alamgir II this nahr had broken and been choked with mud, thus preventing the flow of water. The city lost its freshness and attraction.

When the British government gained control over the city, once again spring came to the city and they had it repaired and even improved it. Now it once again flows into every building and alley of the Qila and city.

Inspired by the success of this canal, the British government even made provisions for water to rural areas, and it now flows into most *pargana*s and districts.

There are two branches of this canal, one that flows to the west towards Sirsa and Hissar, where it ends, since there is a desert beyond it.

Another part flows via the city of Shahjahanabad into its *bazaars* and the Qila, towards the southern direction of Karnal, Ambala and Panipat. Once again the buildings of the Qila have been refreshed and rendered attractive.

The canal then flows into the River Yamuna.

The Structure of the Qila

The Qila is an irregular octagon with two major sides, one side facing the river on the east and one facing the city on the west. The other six smaller parts are on the north and south. It is 1,000 yards long and 600 yards wide, with an area of 6 lakh yards. The walls of this fort are 25 yards high and its foundations are 11 yards deep. The width is 15 yards at the bottom and tapers to 10 yards on the top.

The eastern side, towards the Yamuna, was on a plinth of 12 yards. The river used to flow to the east of this fort, and on the other three sides a 3,600-yard-long, 25-yards-wide and 10-yards-deep moat was dug, which was kept filled by the water from the river. Today the river has shifted – to be replaced by the MG Road. The moat can be seen near the Delhi and Lahori Darwaza and is dry, with grass growing in it.

The walls and bastions of the Qila were built of red sandstone.

All the buildings of the north – that is, Hayat Baksh Bagh, Hammam-i Athhar, the Shah Mahal, which is famous as Diwan-e Khas, the Aramgah-e Muqaddas (private apartments), Burj Musamman, Imtiaz Mahal, Khwabgah, the aramgah of the ladies, the palaces belonging to the chief consort – were built in such a way that the river was on their eastern side and gardens on the west.

The Nahr-e Bahisht flowed from the north and wound its way through the buildings to the south.

The Qila Is Ready

Phir zabaan-e Khuda pe lafz-e kun
Jashn ka ehtimam ho jaaye

Once again the divine utterance of 'be'
Come one, come all, celebrate with glee!

—Hashim Raza Jalalpuri

Mir-e Imarat Mukaramat Khan informed Emperor Shah Jahan who was in Kabul in those days that the Qila was finally complete, and invited him to come and grace it with his blessed presence.

On 24th Rabi Awwal AH 1058 (AD 18 April 1648), the Badshah entered the Qila in an open sedan chair from the riverside and after inspecting the splendid palaces and other buildings proceeded to hold his first court in the Diwan-e Aam.[8] He used the Khizri Darwaza, and ironically this was the same gate that was used by Emperor Bahadur Shah Zafar when he exited from the Qila on the night of 17 September 1857. It is the gate that is under the Musamman Burj, and was used only by the emperor.

Emperor Shah Jahan entered in a grand procession with his eldest son and heir apparent, Prince Dara Shukoh, showering gold and silver coins till he reached the Diwan-e Aam.

The Qila was an octagonal flower all ready to be enjoyed with its attractive buildings, refreshing gardens and streams. Orders were given for celebrations. A darbar or public court was announced in the Diwan-e Aam. A huge gold embroidered tent (*shamiana*) was put up outside the Diwan-e Aam, which was named *dal badal* (cluster of clouds). It had especially been prepared in the royal *karkhana* (workshop) in Ahmadabad at the cost of ₹1 lakh. It was supported by four silver columns, each measuring two and one-fourth yards in girth and surrounded by a silver railing. It covered an area of 3,200 square yards, and 10,000 men could stand in its shade. Three thousand labourers had worked for nearly a month to erect such a vast canopy using the most powerful tackle and machinery.[9]

All the buildings of the palace were covered with carpets, Kashmiri shawls and brocades. The roofs, walls and columns of the Diwan-e Aam were covered with velvet and silk from China and Turkestan.[10]

In front of the Diwan-e Khas, another shamiana was put up called *Saha Mandal* (the sphere of stars). It was so lofty that its pinnacle seemed to soar beyond the sky. These two tents took seven years to complete, and were made of Kashmiri Pashmina and Gujarati velvet. They were erected on columns made of gold and silver. Brocade and satin cloth stretched over these poles.

The Diwan-e Khas was decorated with Persian carpets and Banarasi brocades. The walls of every building were covered with embroidered brocade, satin and velvet, and the effect was spectacular.

In the middle of the Diwan-e Khas, the *Takht-e Murassa* (jewelled throne) or, as it later became famous, *Takht-e Taoos* (peacock throne) was set.

The celebrations continued for ten days and in the darbar the emperor rewarded many of the princes, nobles and those who had worked hard to complete this noble edifice. This included Makramat Khan, who had supervised the construction, the poets who had gathered and written couplets and chronograms in praise of the occasion, the artisans of 'wondrous talent and magical skills' who had embellished the private apartments.[11]

Reti – when the River Yamuna flowed between the Red Fort and Salimgarh From ASI Archives (Felice Beato, 1858)

Reti/Riverside

In 1663, Bernier[12] writes, the Qila presented a wondrous view of the river. There was a wide strip of sand between the river and the Qila, where elephant fights were held. The troops of *mansabdar*s, rajas and *jagirdar*s stood there for inspection by the emperor.

The wall on the riverside was 60-feet high, but had been built so beautifully that it blended in with the rest of the wall that was 12-feet high.

There was a high, sandy precipice between the wall of the Qila and the river where the water could not reach. The viewer who saw it from the opposite bank of the river would be awestruck by its lofty red sandstone walls, *darwaza*, towers and deep moats.

High Walls, Deep Moats

The walls seemed to be talking to the skies, for, as Bashiruddin Ahmad Dehlvi describes it in *Waqiaat-e-Darul Hukumat Dehli*, they were 110-feet high, out of which 75-feet was above ground and 45-feet in the foundation.

The deep moats used to inspire fear, as they were 75-feet wide and 30-feet deep and filled with crocodiles.

There were two small gates on the riverside: the Khizri Darwaza, under the Musamman Burj and opening on to the river, and the other in the north near the

Walls of the Fort

Salimgarh Fort. While the former opens on to the garden that has been built on the erstwhile reti, the latter is now inaccessible.

There were also two wicket gates – one in the southeast near Asad Burj, which is called the Water Gate, and one in the northeast between the Shah Burj and North Gate. Both have now been closed.

There were further battlements and parapets on the walls for defensive positions, with twenty-one small pavilions. Out of these, seven were round and the rest were octagonal. Bernier says that the Qila walls were higher than the city walls.

There used to be verdant orchards and gardens near the Fort, with the most beautiful flowers and trees of various kinds, but by 1919 nothing remained.

In 1919, Bashiruddin Ahmad Dehlvi wrote that a few years before, all the trees had been cut, and the area from the Qila to Fatehpuri Masjid became bereft of shade. Chandni Chowk too was stripped of all its trees and flowers. The trees on both sides of the road provided solace to the inhabitants in the severe Delhi heat with its summer wind (the loo) had been cut, and he wondered why the government of the day plundered and ravaged the bazar of Chandni Chowk, which was like the bedecked bride of Shahjahanabad.

He added that though the road was widened and trees replanted, it would take an age for the trees to grow enough to benefit the people with their shade.

Till the 1857 Uprising, some semblance of the area's former beauty was present, but after that the entire area was destroyed and rebuilt.

Today it's a nightmare of traffic, and carts/rickshaws with goods and shoppers, without trees, shade or stream running through it.

There used to be a huge square with a large tank, in front of the Lahori Darwaza, known as Lal Diggi. Here the nobles whose turn it was to mount guard inside the fort encamped for twenty-four hours of their duty. That Lal Diggi was also demolished after 1857.

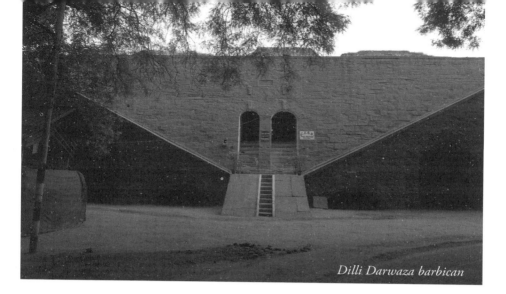

Dilli Darwaza barbican

Lahori Darwaza

The Lahori Darwaza, so named as it faced the road that led to Lahore, was and is the most frequently used gate of the Qila. So important was it that the British named it Victoria Gate when the Qila was under their control from 1857 to 1947.

The actual entrance is 41-feet high and 24-feet wide, and is flanked by two half-octagon turrets crowned by open pavilions. There is a row of seven small cupolas, each with a marble dome and flanked by slender minarets on either side. The Indian Tricolour flies high in the middle.

It's a grand monument, which never fails to strike awe in the heart of its visitors.

It has three storeys, and the commanders and soldiers who guarded the Qila lived in the upper rooms, while the guards were housed in the lower ones. Under the British, the Qiledar and other European officers lived here. It was the scene of the heinous murders of Captain Douglas, Simon Fraser the Commissioner, and Reverend Jennings and his daughter, on 11 May 1857, when the sepoys from Meerut broke into the Qila.

After 1857 and till Independence, the quarters at Lahori Darwaza were used by the British army and then by the Indian army. Now these rooms are lying vacant.

Originally this gate faced the Chandni Chowk bazar and there was a clear view from here to Fatehpuri Masjid. Since the entire Qila was built in perfect symmetry, a feature that is characteristic of Shahjahani architecture, there was a clear view from the Fatehpuri Masjid till the Diwan-e Aam via the Lahori Gate and Naqqarkhana. This meant that the nobles had to dismount at Fatehpuri Masjid and then walk to the darbar, for they could not ride their horses or elephants in front of a palace, which was in full view of the emperor.

This proved to be very inconvenient, and Emperor Aurangzeb had that changed. He got a barbican (*ghoonghat* or veil) built in front of it so that the nobles could dismount inside the Lahori gate itself. A barbican is a fortified outpost or gateway, such as an outer defence to a city or castle, or any tower situated over a gate or bridge, which was used for defensive purposes.

This barbican, from which the Prime Minister of India addresses the nation on 15 August, Independence Day, every year, is 40-feet high and 24-feet wide.

It is recorded that Shah Jahan wrote to his son from Agra Fort where he was under house arrest and said to him of these barbicans, 'You have made the Fort a bride and set a veil before her face.'

There was a moat in front of the Darwaza too with a wooden plank. During the reign of Emperor Akbar Shah II, a masonry bridge was built here with an inscription identical to the one in front of Dilli Darwaza.

Dilli Darwaza

This was called Dilli Darwaza because it faced Old Delhi, which then was what is present-day Mehrauli. Today, ironically, Shahjahanabad is called Old Delhi! Another name for this Darwaza was Akbarabad Darwaza, as the road led to Agra. It was renamed Alexandra Gate by the British. The emperor used this gate of Red Fort to go to the Jama Masjid for prayer. This gate is similar in design to the Lahori Darwaza. It is in the southwest corner of the Red Fort.

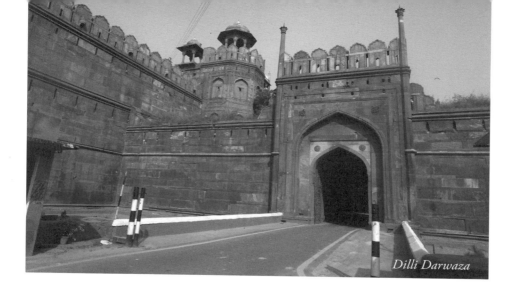
Dilli Darwaza

Here too, Emperor Aurangzeb had a barbican built and got the battlements removed and the tops of the walls covered with earth for purposes of defence.

Two huge stone elephants guard the gateway. These are not the original elephants that had been built by Emperor Shah Jahan's architects, but replacements built on orders of Lord Curzon in 1903. The original elephants were smashed to pieces apparently on orders of Emperor Aurangzeb as he felt that depiction of animate objects was forbidden in Islam. Nothing was heard of these elephants until 1863 when, according to Maulvi Zafar Hasan, some 125 fragments of the original statues were found buried in the Red Fort. Three years later, the elephant statues were reconstructed and set up in the Begum Bagh (Queen's Park – Town Hall Park today). There was a plaque placed near the elephants, which read that Shah Jahan had established these majestic and lofty elephants in front of his southern gateway in AD 1649.

Later a statue of the then Empress of India Queen Victoria was installed between Municipal Hall and the Ghanta Ghar towards Chandni Chowk, it was decided to return these elephants to Dilli Darwaza.

However, since the old statues, which had been patched together, were in a badly mutilated state, Lord Curzon ordered new statues to be made. Indian workmen, under the supervision and design of Mr R.W. Mackenzie, an artist with experience of Indian art, made these.

Today the Dilli Darwaza is used only by those people with a pass, or by officials of the Archaeological Survey of India (ASI).

After entering this darwaza, one can still see a long wide road beyond it. In the seventeenth century, a stream of the Nahr-e Bahisht flew in the middle and went off towards the open stables, and passing through the middle of the Jilaukhana, proceeded towards the south of the fort and fell into the moat of the Fort. No traces of it remain.

Chatta Chowk

After entering the Lahori Darwaza, which is the entrance from where tourists enter, one is immediately catapulted into a tourist bazar with various kinds of souvenirs being sold.

It is a 220-feet-long and 13-feet-wide, covered bazar, which was called *Bazar-e Musaqqaf* (covered market) in the reign of Shah Jahan.

Chatta Chowk

There is an octagonal chowk in the centre that is 30 feet in circumference with an open roof from where light streams in. There are small shops on both sides, which entice the tourist to buy various artefacts imitating Mughal style.

Muhammad Waris writes in *Padshahnama*:

From the Gate towards the capital city to the front of the *Jilaukhâna-i diwânkhana-i khâs wa âm* is a covered bazar (*musaqqaf bazâr*) which holds within itself (*watiqa*) a wide octagonal *chahârsuq* an example of which is not to be found anywhere. Neither has anyone heard about such a market anywhere in the whole of the heaven-like country of Hindustan. Although such markets do exist in countries like Iran yet they come nowhere near this in their embellishments and design.[13]

Nothing like that existed in India though it is fairly common in Central Asia and it is said that a painting of the Grand Bazar in Isfahan inspired the emperor.

I have seen the covered market from the sixteenth century in Isfahan, Iran, and an even older one in Damascus, Syria. The Chatta Chowk resembles them greatly, the only difference being that the market in Isfahan and Damascus are still in use as they were originally built while our Chatta Chowk is now only a souvenir market.

The height of its arched ceiling and the painting of waves and beautiful designs on it by the original architect used to make it appear to be the roof of the sky. It used to have thirty-two shops in Mughal era.

The Karkhanas/Workshops

Today when we come out of the Chatta Chowk we see an empty space on either side and till the *Naqqarkhana* (drum house). There are some barracks and a canteen. Under the Mughals this area was used for housing the various workshops that manufactured or repaired the goods used inside the Qila.

To the left of the visitor the lane led into a broad street, from which branched off other lanes and cross-lanes, towards the northern wall of the fort; the whole of the ground here was covered with buildings which were used as imperial workshops, and which Bernier describes in one of his letters to Monsieur de la Mothe Le Vayer:

> Large halls are seen in many places, called Kar Khanas or workshops for the artisans. In one hall, embroiderers are busily employed, superintended by a master. In another, you see the goldsmiths; in a third, painters; in a fourth, varnishers in lacquer; in a fifth, joiners, turners, tailors, and shoemakers; in a sixth, manufacturers of silk brocade and those fine muslins of which are made turbans, girdles with golden flowers, and drawers worn by females, so delicately fine as frequently to wear out in one night...[14]

Naqqarkhana

After leaving the Chatta Darwaza, one comes out into an area that under the Mughals was once the highly decorated and ornamented Jilaukhana Chowk. It was 200-yard long and 140-yard wide, with a beautiful tank in the middle.

Only royal princes could go on horseback/elephant back inside this gate, while the rest had to go on foot.

It was this tank that saw the horrendous murder of European women and children on 16 May 1857 by the rebel sepoys and courtiers. After that, the British levelled it.

To the south and north of the tank was a lovely bazar with a canal flowing in the middle. The bazar had attractive arcades, corridors and apartments on both sides, which were the apartments for use of the senior nobles and mansabdars, who were on duty or had to present themselves in court. There were apartments to the south and west of this chowk where the *arkaan-e daulat* or ministers of state and courtiers carried on affairs of state.

The courtyard itself was divided into two small squares by a road that ran from north to south. To the south, the road extended to the Dilli Darwaza, and to the north into the garden so well known as the Mahtab Bagh, and thence to the northern wall of the fort.

Bernier describes the portion of the road that extended from the court of the Naqqarkhana to the Dilli Darwaza where there was a bazar:

> The other principal gate of the fortress also conducts to a long and tolerably wide street, which has a divan on both sides bordered by shops instead of arcades. Properly speaking, this street is a bazaar, rendered very convenient in the summer and the rainy season by the long and capacious arched roof with which it is covered. Air and light are introduced by several large and round apertures in the roof.

Tree under which Europeans were murdered
From ASI Archives (Felice Beato, 1858)

This uncovered market has completely disappeared and it's hard to imagine it was ever there. Colonial-era buildings replaced this bazar called Meena Bazar.[15] It was in one of these houses that Emperor Bahadur Shah was kept as a prisoner after his capture by Major Hodson on 20 September 1857.

The imperial kitchen lay to its north, and the area from here to the northern wall of the fort was occupied by the imperial stables.

The buildings on either side were destroyed by the British after the Mutiny, though fortunately the Naqqarkhana itself survived.

Go back in time and imagine the Mughal era, when the sound of the *naubat* (drum), which played day and night, made people forget all sorrows and instilled a sense of happiness and contentment. It intoxicated not just the people but also jinns, animals, birds and even the inanimate objects.

The naubat players would sit on top of the Naqqarkhana in the five-arched gallery there. These windows used to be open then, but once the British army started living in it, they were covered.

The naubat would be played five times a day, and on Sundays it would be played the whole day as it was considered a blessed day. The birthday of the emperor would also be celebrated with the naubat playing the whole day. A special *taal* (beat/rhythm) was made to play here, known as the *Lal Qila Gat*.

The art of *naqqarshahi* (playing the drums) is such that it inspired the loyal and the brave, while it scares the enemies, who would turn pale with fear.

Under the British, the army lived in this Naqqarkhana initially. Then in 1909, the British opened a museum here, and that is still functioning.

This building is made of red sandstone, which has been recently plastered white as it was under the Mughals. It has two apartments and two floors on either side. There are steps leading up to it from small doors on the sides.

There is a huge doorway in the middle. As one enters it, one can see a beautifully carved, red sandstone portion embedded in the wall. To me it is very similar to the carvings on the tomb of Sultan Iltutmish, and I am pretty certain that it was brought from there, as recycling was very common then.

Some portions of the wall have been put in glass cases, which still have a few of the original paintings behind it.

There are four very attractive *burjis* (towers) on its four corners, which add to its beauty.

No one except princes of the royal blood and the emperor himself could ride beyond this point. Everyone else had to dismount and walk from this point. Mr Frances James Hawkins was dismissed from service as the British Resident (he served from 18 September 1829 to November 1830) because he rode his horse beyond this point.

During the months of the Uprising in 1857, the sepoys refused to follow the protocol and rode up all the way to the Diwan-e Aam and Diwan-e Khas, much to the distress of the emperor and his ministers.

Diwan-e Aam

The tourist who enters the Naqqarkhana finds himself in front of the majestic Diwan-e Aam. Nowadays there is a garden here with grass, but in Mughal times this was the assembly ground for nobles waiting to attend the court, and there were many sections according to status.

In its heyday, the Diwan-e Aam measured 1,550 feet in length and 300 feet in width. There were a series of apartments and arcaded galleries around it. All these were interconnected and were used by the nobles and courtiers who were on duty or call. They would be beautifully decorated on occasions of Eid and other festivals, and courtiers would vie with one another to decorate their own portion of the arcade. The columns would be wrapped in brocade, with velvet and satin curtains hanging in the arches. Exquisite Persian carpets would be spread on the floor and these rooms would look like a bedecked bride.

These arcades were demolished after the Uprising of 1857 by the British. Now all that remains is the hall.

Bernier describes it as: 'Opposite to the grand gate, which supports the nagar-kanay, as you cross the court, is a large and magnificent hall, decorated

Diwan-e Aam

with several rows of pillars, which, as well as the ceiling, are all painted and overlaid with gold.'

Today it is stripped of all plaster and paint and is the colour of its red sandstone.

After the 1857 Uprising, not only were all these apartments in the Diwan-e Aam and arcades demolished and levelled to the ground by the British, but the apartments of the heir apparent, which were to its left, were also demolished. No one remembers them. In 2015, I found some excavation in progress towards the left of the Naqqarkhana and saw the remnants of these galleries. Many hukkah bases were discovered here, obviously from the times when the nobles must be enjoying their peace pipes in gentler times.

The Diwan-e Aam now is a standalone structure, and I'm sure many visitors unaware of its original shape must be wondering what the fuss is all about! Why was this Qila called one of the grandest of its times?

This Diwan-e Aam that we see now was the centrepiece of the fort. Now it stands in isolation – mute testimony to the twists and turns of fate. It was here that the emperor would hold darbar during Public Audience Day.

It is a nine-arched hallway totalling twenty-seven arches built in the engrailed style, which became famous as Shahjahani arches. It is divided into three aisles with columns, which support the beautiful arches in every compartment. Though this hall is made of red sandstone, it had been plastered white to resemble marble, and the walls have stucco and gilded ornamentation on them. The columns would be wrapped in brocade and Chinese silks. Velvet curtains brought from Europe would cover the arches. One could sink into the carpets which were the finest that money could buy and had been procured from Iran and Kashmir. The hallways had beautiful shamianas in front of them to provide shade. The rings with which they were tied can still be seen.

The Diwan-e Aam was built on a platform and is 160 yards long and 104 yards wide. There is a red sandstone enclosure around it that was the height of a man, and used to be decorated with golden *kalsi*s (finials). These *kalsis* have now disappeared.

To the north of the Diwan-e Aam was a gateway leading to the twin courtyards in front of the Diwan-e Khas, which was destroyed in 1857 by the British. In the middle of the western wall of the first courtyard was a gate that was the entrance to the Diwan-e Khas. A red cloth awning was stretched in front of it, which gave it the name of Lal Pardah.

An ante-court built outside the Diwan-e Aam, the Gulal Bari, was reserved for minor officials, while the general throng attending the darbar stood outside the Gulal Bari. This structure is no longer present.

Maulvi Zafar Hasan notes, '[T]he lawns in front of the Diwan-e Aam are intended to represent the original courtyard, and the shrubberies at the sides and ends, the former colonnades.'

By the reign of Emperor Akbar Shah II, the Diwan-e Aam had been ravaged and was in a bad shape.

Nasheman Zill-e Ilahi

In the centre of the back wall of the Diwan-e Aam is a 21-feet wall with 318 panels that depict the famous Orpheus legend. An apartment behind this wall, overlooking the Rang Mahal, housed the flight of stairs by which the emperor came to the Diwan-e Aam. The back wall has a door through which the emperor entered the Diwan-e Aam to grace the throne.

Nasheman Zil-e Ilaahi

A canopied throne was set in front of the panel, on an 8-feet-high and 7-feet-diameter, circular platform. Ebba Koch calls this a Solomonic throne.[16] Solomon is a revered prophet in Islam and his throne a motif of justice and prosperity.

This area was called the *Nasheman Sultani* (seat of the emperor), and the throne was called *Takht-e Shahi* (royal throne) *or Aurang-e Zill-e Ilahi* (throne of the shadow of God on earth). Its beauty in the time of Shah Jahan would have inspired awe in the hearts of even angels. Even today, confined within a glass enclosure, it hints at its former glory. It is a mute witness to the glory of emperors and the reality that everything in this world is transitory.

The throne is made of pure marble and is 4 square yards wide, with four cypress-shaped columns that support a curved dome.

Near the base of the throne is a marble seat, which was for those nobles who presented themselves before the emperor. The *wazir* or prime minister would present his petitions or make representations from this location to the *Huzur-e Wala* or emperor.

Today what we see are stark red walls of sandstone and perhaps that is why the name Red Fort has become so popular, but it was not always so. The walls and columns were gilded and the floors covered with rich carpets.

On Public Audience Days the *Badshah Salamat* would come and give *darshan* (audience) to his *raiyyat* (subjects), and that is why it was called Diwan-e Aam – '*aam*' being Hindustani for 'common' – where everyone could come and meet him.

A Mughal Darbar

Let's go back to the seventeenth century.

Zill-e Ilahi, the Shadow of God on Earth, himself has emerged from the door at the back of the throne with his heir, sons and retinue of *khwajasaras* (eunuchs). He has decided to illuminate the assembly with his presence. To the sound of 'Attention! Present your salutations with respect. *Mahabali Badshah Salamat!*',[17] the emperor comes and sits with his legs tucked under him in the *vajr asana* on this throne. Some of the khwajasaras who are his personal attendants stand nearby and fan him with the *morchal* or whisk made of feathers.

A line of very senior nobles stand in front of the throne with folded hands and lowered eyes; to the emperor who towers above them in his lofty seat they appear insignificant.

Beyond them, inside a silver enclosure, stand some more nobles – the *mansabdar* – according to their rank, with the highest ranks in the front row. Like the senior nobles they too have folded hands and lowered gazes. Second-tier nobles stand behind the mansabdars, and sundry other nobles stand behind them.

If some noble or courtier has to present a petition, he gives it in advance to the *arz begi*, the officer whose job it is to present the petitions to the emperor. The arz begi announces the names of the petitioners from the corner of the throne dais, and the concerned person comes forward and stands on the dais below the throne. He speaks only after kissing the legs of the throne and offering salutations to the emperor.

His petition is then read out. If the emperor approves it, another official in charge of the royal ink stand presents the gold and silver inkstand and quills, and the royal signature is affixed to the petition.

The Mughals maintain an excellent army, and on the day of the darbar once the petitions and court issues have been addressed, the emperor inspects his horses, elephants and forces.

Horses are arraigned in gold and velvet jewellery and cloth, and bend their heads in respect and show their paces to the Badshah. Then the elephants, similarly caparisoned, are led forward. These elephants have been rubbed with a paste to darken their skin and make it shine. On their head till the base of their trunk two red lines have been drawn with *sindoor* or vermillion. They are decorated with jewellery especially designed for them. Two silver bells hang on either side at the ends of silver chains. Yak-tail hair are strung in their ears and give the appearance of long, curly whiskers.

Two smaller elephants suitably ornamented walk on either side of the main elephants as their attendants. Even the elephants have their own servants, apart from their mahouts, ready to obey his every wish and command.

The elephants tread slowly and majestically as if quite aware of their own importance. When they reach the throne, the mahout signals to the animal and the elephant bends one foot, raises his trunk and trumpets loudly in obeisance to the emperor.

Then other animals are brought in, all wearing beautiful jewellery – deer, rhinoceroses, blue bulls, Bengali buffaloes that can fight tigers, cheetahs, Uzbeki hunting dogs, and in the end the birds used for hunting such as falcons, eagles, hawks, pheasants, quails, cranes, followed by rabbits, etc. The dogs have golden collars with bells.

Some troops also march past the emperor. The cavalrymen on decorated horses in their full uniforms go past the throne showing off their skills. They display their swordplay and spearing skills by cutting a goat in two with a single blow of their sword.

Horses are put through their paces. Noblemen show off their athletic skills.

The emperor personally inspects all his troops in detail and rewards or suspends them…

Emperor Farrukhsiyar (reigned 1713–1719) was the last emperor to hold such a court.

Orpheus Panel

Orpheus was a Greek prophet, a legendary musician and poet who could charm all living things and even stones. In this panel he is shown playing the lute, while a lion, a leopard, a deer, a dog and a hare sit at his feet, listening in complete rapture. The occurrence of this panel as a backdrop to the Mughal throne is deliberate according to Koch.[18] She saw it as approximating the legendary throne of Solomon, the prophet king and ideal ruler on whom birds and beasts sat in peaceful attendance.

Solomon's age represented a golden age of justice and peace, and was used by the Mughals as imperial propaganda. Shah Jahan positioned himself as the Solomon of his age. The message was clear that just as both wild animals and their prey sit together in peace and harmony in the panel, in his reign too the powerful and weak could live with each other in peace.

Its 318 panels, said to be the work of European jeweller Austin de Bordeaux, with various exquisite carvings of birds and beasts made in inlay work are placed in a special marble recess that measures 7 yards x 2.5 yards. Its artistry is confounding for the human mind.

Beresford, in his book, *The Delhi Guide*,[19] describes it before the 1857 Uprising and says it was an 8-feet panel with precious stones also embedded in it. In September 1857, after the fall of Delhi, many treasures from the Red Fort were looted. This panel was one of them. It was appropriated by Captain John Jones and sold by him to the British government for 500 pounds. They placed it in the South Kensington Museum.

Gordon Sanderson says in his book *Delhi Fort*:

> [T]his tablet was removed after the capture of the Palace in 1857 and placed in the South Kensington Museum, while eleven others of the inlaid panels were also removed. They were restored to their original position some years ago, at the instance of Lord Curzon. It was fortunate that old drawings of the mosaic existed, from which it was possible to restore the decoration to its original form, and for this purpose an Italian 'mosaicista' was especially brought to India, and the work completed in 1909.[20]

Sir John Marshall reports in the Archaeological Survey Annual Report 1902–03 that it was hoped that the plaque would be restored in time for the Delhi Darbar (Lord Curzon's Darbar of 1903), but it arrived too late to be in time for that. He also adds that the panels 'have now been replaced behind the throne, and many other panels have also been cleaned of the lac with which they were covered, and their mutilated surfaces re-polished. There still remain some of the gaps where panels are partly or wholly missing.' These were supposed to be filled up as per the original design, after procuring the precise stones from Europe, and the work was to be done either in Europe or artists were to be brought from Italy. It was completed in 1909.

Since a glass covering seals off the throne, one has to strain their eyes to see the panel.

Shah Mahal or Diwan-e Khas

From the Diwan-e Aam we now head for Diwan-e Khas through what was a 110 feet by 180 feet courtyard once again called *Jilaukhana* or Abode of Splendour, which had been described by Bishop Heber[21] as being very beautiful.

Shah Mahal/Diwan-e Khas

Under Shah Jahan it was named it Shah Mahal, but since this was the hall of private audience for special courtiers and guests of state, it became famous as Diwan-e Khas.

The Diwan-e Khas was at its zenith the most beautiful building of Hindustan, but now lies neglected.

I invite you to now imagine it in its heyday, when it was indeed heaven on earth.

This beautiful rectangular pavilion has no parallel on the face of this earth. It is made of marble from top to bottom. The marble is so pure that the whiteness of dawn would seem darker than it. It measures 90 feet x 67 feet, with engrailed arches and a flat ceiling. The lower parts of the piers are inlaid with floral designs, while the upper portions are gilded and painted. The four corners of its roof are surrounded by pillared *chhatris* (cupolas) that had golden pinnacles.

The present wooden ceiling of the hall was painted in 1911. Through its middle flows the 4-yard-wide Nahr-e Bahisht, which is covered with marble slabs.

In the middle of this edifice is another room of 18 x 10 yards, built by erecting twelve square columns around a platform in the centre. It is on this platform that the Takht-e Murassa, more popular as the Takht-e Taoos

(Peacock Throne), is kept. When the emperor graced the darbar with his presence, he sat on this Throne.

Around this a row of elevated columns has been used to make a hall.

The walls, columns, arches and floor of this hall are made of marble. It is inlaid with cornelian, corals and other precious stones right down till the dado, in which flowers and foliage have been carved.

These were looted probably after 1857.

If only it could speak, it would describe the scene here in 1716, when the Scottish surgeon William Hamilton, who cured Emperor Farrukhsiyar on the eve of his marriage, was rewarded with the permission of his employers to establish a factory and to maintain a territory of thirty-eight villages on the banks of the Hooghly river. It was this that began the East India Company's fortunes in India, and ultimately led to the end of the Mughal Empire.

It was here that Nader Shah, the Persian invader, received the submission of Emperor Mohammad Shah and took the Kohinoor diamond in 1739. He also took away the Peacock Throne, and the later Mughal rulers used a pale replica of it.

In 1759, the Marathas captured Delhi. In 1761, they were defeated by Ahmed Shah Abdali in the third battle of Panipat, but once again captured Delhi in 1771 and restored Emperor Shah Alam to power. In 1788, a Maratha garrison was stationed in the Qila-e Mualla and the Marathas were de facto rulers of north India.

In the eighteenth century, when the Marathas were in control of Delhi, they took out all the silver and gold from the ceiling and sent it to be melted and made into coins. At that time, the gold and silver was valued at ₹28 lakh.

In 1803, they were defeated by Lord Lake in the Battle of Patparganj.

It was in this same Diwan-e Khas that Emperor Shah Alam II thanked Lord Lake for delivering him from the house of Scindhia. The Mughal Emperor thus became a pensioner of the British instead of the Marathas.

In 1788, Ghulam Qadir, the Rohila, captured Mughal Emperor Shah Alam II (r. 1759–1806), who had been a Maratha pensioner, and imprisoned him in the adjoining Salimgarh Fort. Ghulam Qadir ordered the emperor to be brought into the Diwan-e Khas and asked him to give up the secret of his treasure house. The unfortunate emperor had no treasure to give up and had already told his captor that many times. The emperor dared his tormentor to do his worst. Thereupon, the Rohila threw him on the floor of the same court where courtiers would quake under the royal gaze, and blinded him. The Marathas defeated and killed Ghulam Qadir and once again established their sway over the emperor.

It was here that Shah Alam II thanked Lord Lake for delivering him from the Marathas in 1803 after the latter defeated the Marathas in Patparganj.

On 14 September 1803, the British forces under Lord Lake entered Delhi.

Two days later, General Lake had an interview with the poor old blind king in the Diwan-e Khas and received high-sounding titles. Delhi came under John Company, as East India Company was then known.

By the time Emperor Akbar Shah II (r. 1806–37) came to power, the Diwan-e Khas was being used as a storeroom for unwanted items (broken palanquins, empty boxes, etc.) and no darbars were held there any more.

The British Resident Sir Charles Eliot (1823–25) told Bishop Heber that the Timurid rulers were careless of their own legacy and neither cared for nor undertook any repairs of the glorious Qila built by their forefathers. They had even stopped getting it swept or dusted. The Nasheman Zill-e Ilahi was covered in so much pigeon droppings that even the jewels could not be seen.

These two buildings are mute witnesses to the twists and turns of fate.

It was in this building, the Diwan-e Khas that Emperor Mohammad Shah surrendered to Nader Shah and the symbol of Mughal power, the Peacock Throne, was surrendered to the Persian king.

When the sepoys came from Meerut in 1857, they took out a silver throne from one of the recesses of Diwan-e Khas, and on 12 May 1857 crowned Bahadur Shah II as the emperor of Hindustan once again. He held daily darbars here during that period, which were attended by the important residents of Delhi and officers of the 'mutinied troops'.

It was here that one of the sepoys addressed him as, *'Arre Badshah! Arre buddhe!'* (O Emperor! O, old man!).[22]

During this period, after the 1857 Uprising, the Diwan-e Khas was often full of armed soldiers milling about, much to the horror of Emperor Bahadur Shah Zafar – hitherto, only royalty or nobles and courtiers had entered the Diwan-e Khas, and that too without weapons.

On 14 September 1857, the British army breached the Kashmiri Darwaza and entered the walled city of Shahjahanabad. On 17 September, the emperor fled the fort, and on 20 September he surrendered to Major Hodson and re-entered the fort as a prisoner.

Having taken control of the Fort, the British soldiers drank to the health of the British sovereign in the Diwan-e Khas. They established headquarters in it, and on the morning of 21 September, a royal salute was fired to celebrate the victory.

On 27 September 1857, the British held a Thanksgiving service in the Diwan-e Khas for the fall of Delhi into their hands.

In January 1858, the emperor was put on trial in the same hall where his ancestors had decided the fate of countless others. In a trial that lasted for forty days, he was convicted of having waged war against the British, abetting rebellion, proclaiming himself the reigning sovereign of India and causing or being the accessory to the death of many Europeans. He was sentenced to exile for life and sent to Rangoon.

The Diwan-e Khas is visited by hundreds of visitors every day, but few among them know the triumphs and tragedies it has seen.

The British occupied the Fort after the 1857 Uprising and changed its contours with their additions. They used the Diwan-e Aam and Diwan-e Khas as ballrooms.

The teak wood ceiling of the Diwan-e Khas was repaired once by the British.

It has now started sagging once again, and though it is a Herculean task given that it is difficult to procure Burma teak (which was the original material used), the ASI has embarked on it. They are cleaning the yellowed marble too as part of the efforts to restore the Diwan-e Khas to a reflection of its former beauty.

Agar Firdaus Bar Ru-ye Zamin Ast

Above the inner corner arches of the Diwan-e Khas on the north and south is inscribed the oft-quoted golden couplet:

> *Agar firdaus bar ru-ye zamin ast*
> *Hamin ast-o hamin ast-o hamin ast*
>
> *If there is heaven on earth*
> *It is this, it is this, it is this*

A reference in *Taj Mahal: The Illumined Tomb* by Begley and Desai says that when Shah Jahan made his first state entry into the newly completed fort, and as a sign of royal approval, the following couplet was ordered to be inscribed on the interior of the Hall of Private Audience.[23] It was after all conceived as a heaven on earth with its paradisiacal char-bagh garden scheme and the Nahr-e Bahisht flowing through the palace and fort buildings.

There are many versions as to who is the poet, the most popular choice being Amir Khusrau. However, Prof. Sunil Sharma,

'Agar Firdaus' verse in Shah Mahal or Diwan-e Khas

37

an authority on Hazrat Amir Khusrau, said no diwan or masnawi of Hazrat Amir Khusrau includes it. Since the conclusive proof regarding authorship of a verse is its presence in his collected works – was it his or not?

This led me to research the verse, including spending a good few hours searching the Black Pavilion in Shalimar Bagh in Srinagar, Kashmir as there is a common perception that the original verse was inscribed in the Black Pavilion built during the early part of Emperor Jahangir's reign (1569–1627) on the top terrace of Shalimar Bagh. Emperor Jahangir was a connoisseur of beauty so it was entirely possible that he should have it inscribed. However, I hunted high and low and could not find it – either physically present on the Black or any other pavilion of the Shalimar gardens, or any reference to it in any book on the gardens.

Where I did find it was in Bashiruddin Ahmad Dehlvi's *Waqiaat-e-Darul Hukumat Dehli*[24] in which he says this is Sa'adullah Khan's famous inscription and it was inscribed on marble slabs below the cornice of this hall by the famous calligrapher of the time, named Rashid.

This made me read about Sa'adullah Khan. According to Begley and Desai, Allami Sa'adullah Khan, prime minister to Emperor Shah Jahan, was in charge of checking the manuscript of Abdul Hamid Lahori's *Padshahnama*, a dazzling performance of literary standards. So, Sa'adullah Khan was indeed a proficient poet and writer himself.

Since Sa'adullah Khan has written beautiful verses on the arches of the khwabgah, and is possibly the author of the rubai in the Musamman Burj, I felt inclined to believe Bashiruddin Ahmad Dehlvi that the writer of this verse is indeed Sa'adullah Khan. After all he was only the second person after Allami Abul Fazl to be given the title of Allami (very learned man).

For me this was an exciting chase and one, which I wanted to resolve. This led me to Prof. S.H. Qasemi, a Persian scholar and the one who translated *Sair-ul Manazil* [possibly the first description of monuments of Delhi written in first half of nineteenth century] from Persian to Urdu. His mastery over Persian and monuments of Delhi is undisputed. He claimed to have seen the verse once in the diwan of the poet Mirza Muhammad Tahir 'Aashna' (AD 1628–71), entitled Inayat Khan, son of Zafar Khan, the governor of Kashmir. Mirza Muhammad Tahir 'Aashna' was a historian who wrote the Shahjahannama (Mulakkhas-e Shah Jahan). This was an abridgement (*mulakkhas*) of the three volumes of Abdul Hamid Lahori's *Padshahnama*, which was commisioned by Emperor Shah Jahan.

He was the son of Zafar Khan, who held the post of governor of Kashmir, twice under Emperor Shah Jahan. Zafar Khan was also a poet who wrote under the nom de plume of Ahsan. He was a patron of poets and painters and constructed a beautiful garden called Bagh Zafarabad in Kashmir.[25]

Mirza Muhammad Tahir's mother was the daughter of Buzurg Khanum, daughter of Malika Banu who was the elder sister of Mumtaz Mahal Begum. Mirza Muhammad Tahir was not only Emperor Shah Jahan's nephew but also a very close friend and his librarian. He once also served as Deputy Governor of Kashmir in the absence of his father.[26]

Prof. S.H. Qasemi further said that this diwan was present in the National Museum, New Delhi. He referred me to Prof. Jameel-ur Rahman, Persian Dept, Zakir Husain Delhi College, University of Delhi. Prof. Rahman obviously said that we must go and look it up in the museum before coming to any conclusion. He had edited the *Mulakhkhas-e Shahjahan-Nameh* (abridged: *Shahjahan-nameh*) compiled by Mirza Muhammad Tahir Khan Aashna entitled Inayat Khan[27] and was very well acquainted with his work. Even Prof. Rahman was quite clear on the fact that it was not in Hazrat Amir Khusrau's Diwan.

I was enjoying this research into something that is such an important part of our cultural heritage. There is a reference that poets had gathered and had written couplets and chronograms in praise of the occasion of the inaugural ceremony of the Qila on 18 April 1648.[28] So, it was entirely possible that the verse inscribed on the walls of Diwan-e Khas could be from one of those poets especially one who was a close friend.

But before we could set off for the museum we had to find out the accession number of the manuscript. Here the Director General and Mr Khatibur Rahman, Assistant Curator (Arabic Manuscripts), National Museum, New Delhi, were of immense help.

Once again, Prof. Rahman came to my help and accompanied me to the National Museum. He went through each and every page of the fragile manuscript (accession number 62.999) titled *Diwan-e Aashna*, paying special attention to the verses on Kashmir but he drew a blank. Looking at my disappointed face he said, that I shouldn't worry as this was just a first look and such manuscripts needed detailed study. He went back to the section named *Masnawi-ye Saqi Nama*, while I kept looking on with expectation. Suddenly, he put his finger on a line and softly said, Here it is!' On page 88 of the diwan in a long nazm (poem) were the lines we were looking for:

> *Gar firdaus bar ru-e zamin ast*
> *Hamin ast-o hamin ast-o hamin ast*

And at that moment if there was a heaven on earth for me it was that small office in the National Museum where we were viewing this precious manuscript.

In our excitement we only saw that line written there. We realized later that the preceding line says:

> *Since Khusrau composed meaningful verses,*
> *You'd say he wrote this [verse] for here [this garden],*[29]
> *If there is a paradise on earth...*

Aashna quotes these lines that he attributes to Hazrat Amir Khusrau in his masnawi on the Qila e Mubarak (Shahjahanabad) and its gardens.

Prof. Jameel-ur Rahman went through all the official biographies of Emperor Shah Jahan and he finally found it in the *Shahjahannama* of Mohammad Salih Kamboh (d. AD 1675), Emperor Shah Jahan's official biographer. In the third volume where he is waxing eloquent on the Qila-e Mubarak he talks of its beauty, gardens, the smiling buds, the fragrance and goes on to say its beauty is such that it makes the wise and learned minds go insane; he declares that its beauty matches that of paradise, or rather its even more heavenly than the gardens of the seven heavens. A mere gaze and the eyes of the insightful can visualize the meaning of Hazrat Amir Khusrau's couplet, a more inquisitive glance can rob all sanity from the already intoxicated head. From the moon to the fish [metaphorically it means each and everything, whether in the sea or sky] and from dust particles to the sun [here it means that everything no matter how great or insignificant in stature] swear by this meaning:[30]

Agar firdaus bar ru-ye zamin ast
Hamin ast-o hamin ast-o hamin ast
If there is Paradise on earth
It is this, it is this, it is this

Though we should never under estimate him, in whose hue the entire city of Delhi is dyed: Delhi's beloved poet saint Hazrat Amir Khusrau, even in the seventeenth century, many verses were attributed to him since he was a great classical poet. Also, since he had praised Delhi in his works, it would have been the natural thing to do. Why is it not in his diwan and in what context were the lines written is still a question in the mind of scholars of Hazrat Amir Khusrau. One thing is certain that it was not written for Kashmir as Hazrat Amir Khusrau never visited it. Did he then write it for Delhi?

Khas Darbar

Let us go back in time and imagine the scene when Emperor Shah Jahan was holding court in his Shah Mahal, sitting on a throne that seems too unbelievable to be true now.

The courtiers in charge of announcing the emperor's presence have received the indication that the emperor is about to illuminate the Diwan-e Khas with his blessed presence. Any minute now, he will emerge from the Tasbihkhana and head towards the Shah Mahal with his royal retinue following in his wake.

The curtain opens and the courtier calls out to the nobles and princes around to stand still and pay their respects.

The emperor makes his way towards the Takht-e Taoos. He reaches it, turns and sits on it, facing the gathering.

The court is ready to begin.

First a description of all the princes, rulers, nobles and emissaries who are present in the court:

There are silver enclosures at a little distance from the throne. These enclosures are of exquisite workmanship and meant to seat or stand the princes and nobles. Inside the enclosures, on the right and left flanks, stand the emperor's personal bodyguards and princes of the blood. Behind them the raja and maharaja, and the emissaries of various countries, stand according to their rank.

Once the emperor enters everyone has to stand with their eyes lowered to the ground and ears straining to hear their emperor's commands.

Every arch of the Diwan-e Khas has two *khas bardar* or royal bodyguards standing with guns encased in velvet cases on their shoulders and silver whisks in their hands, standing at attention, immobile.

In the outer arches, other courtiers, jagirdars and mansabdars wait for their orders.

Three imposing Abyssinian slaves stand in each of the outer row of arches dressed in *zar-baft* or golden brocade uniforms, silently in pursuance of their guard duty. They carry iron *gurz* or maces on their shoulders, and silver *bairaq* or standards in their hands.

Outside this stand the in charges of the various karkhanas or workshops. The clerks and scribes, with inkpots and quill stands in their hands and their satchels in front of them, stand to attention, waiting to be called if needed.

In the rest of the arches stand soldiers with naked swords, ready to strike down anyone who dares make an uninvited move.

Outside the Diwan-e Khas, at a distance of 30 yards, is another silver enclosure where the royal bodyguards in their brocade uniforms stand with golden and silver standards in their hands. On the right are the Turks, on the left the Afghans and in the centre the Rajputs – all tall and imposing at attention.

From here till the gateway are cavalrymen on either side of the path, with soldiers standing at complete attention behind them. Any courtier who comes has to first identify himself to them and then go forward.

There is such an atmosphere of awe and intimidation that whoever comes is quaking with fear, in case they put a wrong foot forward.

There are three stations for the courtiers to present their *kornish* (salutations by bending from the waist downwards and raising their hand to their forehead in salute) after entering the darbar.

When the *naqib* or royal herald calls out their names and asks them to present their salutations to the Jahanpanah Badshah Salamat, with their hearts in their mouths they present the *kornish ka adab* from the first enclosure.

The first order of the day is presenting of honours to the princes. The 'royal gaze' goes over the princes and they are given *khilat* or robes of honour and their *mansab*s or ranks are increased as their actions merit. The gaze is still there but it is of gawking tourists peering from below the terrace trying to soak in the beauty of this pavilion.

Lal Pardah

On special occasions, a red broadcloth shamiana would be erected screening the door, measuring 44 feet x 35 feet, called the Lal Pardah.

At the time of the darbar, the nobles present their respects and salutations from near this Lal Pardah.

Towards the north of the Diwan-e Khas was the way to the Bagh-e Hayat Baksh and towards the south was the *Deorhi Mahlat Shahi* (passageway leading to the royal harem).

Takht-e Murassa/Takht-e Taoos/Peacock Throne

Chu tareekhash zabaan purseed az dil
Ba guft aurang Shahenshah-e Adil

When the tongue sought its date from the heart
It said 'The throne of the just emperor'.[31]

The words 'the throne of the just emperor' were the chronogram taken out for the year of building of the throne. It yielded the date AH 1044 which corresponds to AD 1634.

The Takht-e Taoos was a unique throne, fit for an emperor. The throne alone cost double the amount spent on the construction of the Taj Mahal because of the extraordinary gems and gold used in it. The gems that had been captured from conquered territories and paid as homage to the Mughal emperor were used to decorate it. It was covered from top to bottom with intricate gemstone work.

It stood on twelve bejewelled pillars that supported a jewel-studded and enamelled, canopied roof. From top to bottom there was *kundan* (traditional Indian gemstone work) work on it.

Where Takht-e Taoos would have been kept

Two golden peacock statues studded with precious stones and holding a string of priceless pearls in their beaks stood on top of the canopy. It is they that gave it the popular name Peacock Throne, as its original name was Takht-e Murassa or the Jewelled Throne.

It has been described by Abdul Hamid Lahori in *Badshah Nama*. He writes that the emperor felt that the rare gems of an empire were not meant to be stored in the treasury and the greatest service they could do was to adorn the royal throne so that people could see them and it would add to the majesty of the emperor. Thus, jewels worth ₹86 lakh were handed over to Bebadal Khan, the superintendent of the goldsmith's department, along with 1 lakh *tola*s of pure gold (1 tola = 10 g) worth ₹14 lakh. It took seven years to complete it. The famous 186-carat Kohinoor diamond adorned the throne.[32]

It was 6-feet high and 4-feet wide, with four legs about 2-feet high. A golden stool was kept for ascending it. The emperor would sit in the middle, with exquisite bolsters around him. The nobles and courtiers would be standing on a separate platform at its foot. The aura created by the emperor on this throne, in his rich robes, and the nobles and courtiers in their festive clothes, must have been enough to dazzle any spectator and strike awe in his heart. Alas! It is lost to us for ever.

When Nader Shah invaded Delhi in AD 1739, he also took the Peacock Throne with him. It was lost in Persia during a tribal raid on Nader Shah's camp, in which he lost his life. The throne was broken into pieces and sold, and no one knows where the pieces are now. All the thrones now bearing its names are imagined replicas.

I recently saw the Irani version of the peacock throne in the Central Bank in Tehran, Iran. It was built in 1836 by the Qajar kings, and is a grand golden throne covered with jewels. It is, however, completely different from the Mughal peacock throne as shown in the miniature from Shah Jahan's reign. Such was the lure of the Mughal peacock throne that many ornate, jewelled thrones were given that name.

Jashn-e Mahtabi/Feast of the Night

The anniversary of the emperor's coronation was celebrated with pomp and show. Royal guests would come from all over the empire and be hosted in the Qila. Lavishly prepared food trays called *tora* would be distributed to the houses of nobles in the city and there would be an air of gaiety all around for forty days.

Just before the actual anniversary day, there would be a *ratjaga* or all-night celebration by the people in the fort. The ladies in the harem would be dressed up in their fineries to celebrate the occasion.

The entire Diwan-e Aam would glow like a house of light. There would be white brocades and white carpets spread on the floor. The walls would be covered in beautiful white satin, curtains of silver brocade and silver cloth would be hanging on the arches.

Every possible illumination and decoration would light up the building and make it look like a piece of the moon itself.[33]

The *Mahtab Bagh* (Moonlit Garden), which was laid out near the Diwan-e Aam, had white flowering bushes, plants and trees planted in it. The effect of the candles and lamps that illuminated the Diwan-e Aam on this garden would make even the grass and trees glimmer like silver in the dark.

The courtiers would be all dressed in white, wearing only silver jewellery with pearls. There would be a river of moonlight flickering and swirling in the dark.

Hammam-e Athhar

Zahe safai imarat ke dar tamashayash
Ba-deeda baaz na gardad nigaah az deewar

The beauty of the building is such that one can't stop gazing at it.[34]

A hammam is an essential part of all Mughal architecture. These were not only used for bathing, but also for meetings, relaxing and solitude by the emperors.

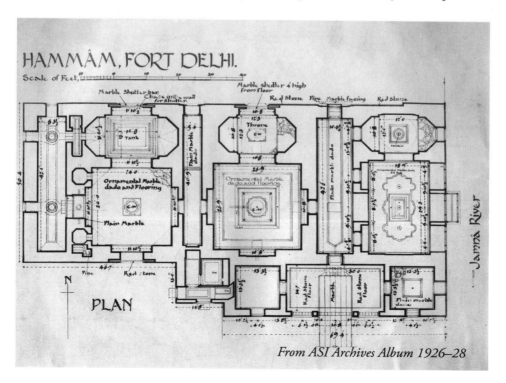

From ASI Archives Album 1926–28

Secret and important meetings were held here too. Sir Thomas Roe had met Shah Jahan in the hammam in the Agra Fort.

During winters, these were the warmest places in the palace, and in summers the coolest.

In the Lal Qila, not only is the hammam very beautiful, it is also in a somewhat better condition than the rest of the Qila and is kept locked to preserve it.

It is to the south of the Diwan-e Khas and is incomparable in relation to other Mughal hammams I have visited.

Muhammad Waris in *Padshahnama* calls it *Hammam-i Athhar*, and as I am describing the fort as built by Shah Jahan, I have retained that phrase rather than just hammam. The word *atthar* means pure, and refers to the purification process of a body in a hammam — something that modern spas offer as a holistic experience today.

Between the Diwan-e Khas and the hammam was an area called *Aqab-e Hammam* (behind the royal bath) where the royal princes had their apartments. The British demolished this area.

A three-arched marble hall with two rooms on either side led to the hammam, and was called the *Hammam ki Deorhi* or the Hammam's entrance.

The Hammam itself is divided into three parts, all made of marble with inlay of precious stones. Now only some of the inlay work designs remain. The streams of Nahr-e Bahisht wove through it.

I had visited Hammam in earlier years when it wasn't locked, but for purposes of this book we took special permissions and revisited it. We entered through a dingy doorway and not the royal deorhi, and our eyes took a while to adjust to the dark. I started imagining, and I ask you too to imagine it in its heyday: Fountains spouting water, streams lazily weaving through the floor, the aromatic scents and oils spreading a languorous smell and seducing the senses...

Jahanpanah salamat! Hoshiyar!' ('Long live the refuge of the world! Attention!') shout the macebearers, announcing the emperor's arrival.

The emperor enters through the royal deorhi, which is in front of the Diwan-e Khas.

His retinue enters in his wake. Only the very trusted and reliable nobles and attendants are allowed to accompany him here. This is not just a room to have a bath, but a room where he can let down his guard and enjoy confidential discussions.

His closest attendants disrobe him and present the finest oriental wines and refreshments to him in the *Jaam-e Kun* (changing room). As per the weather, he goes to the *Sard Khana* or *Garam Khana*. Incense is burning, candles are glowing, and it is a piece of heaven on earth.

There are dull mirrors placed in chosen spots to reflect light but not daze the viewer.

Jaam-e Kun

The first room was called *Jaam-e Kun* as it was the place used to disrobe and to wear bathing robes, relax and partake of refreshments after a bath. It was the first room that the emperor entered.

Jaam-e Kun
From ASI Archives Album 1931–32

It is like a large room and is made of marble till the dado, with inlay work decorations. It had three hauz with fountains in it. One fountain only spouted rose scented water.

The Jaam-e Kun was on the riverside. To the east, there were exquisitely carved screens decorated with mirror work in which the flowers, greenery and river were reflected very clearly, and the viewer didn't want to remove his gaze from it.

There are two fountains in it. The most interesting feature of this part of the hammam is a very shallow, rectangular, marble basin with roses carved in it. Each rose was a fountain from which rose water was sprayed.

Sard Khana

Sir Sayyid Ahmad Khan when describing this room says that even *chashm-e falak* or the inhabitants of the sky would not have seen anything like it.

Its main attraction lay in a unique marble *shah nasheen* or royal seat placed in the middle of the room. This alcove has a singularly spectacular floor design of floral inlay work.

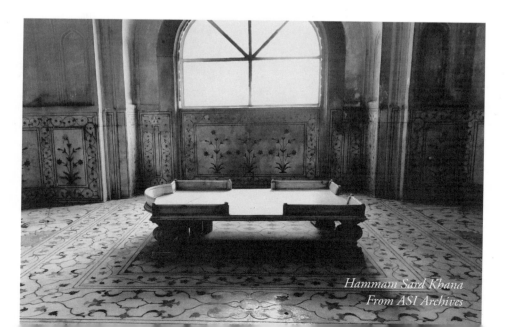

Hammam Sard Khana
From ASI Archives

It is still standing, having withstood the travails of time, while those who sat on it are now dust. There is no emperor to sit on the royal seat and admire the beauty of the inlay. Once in a while, some curious visitor like me comes and sighs at the Qila that was.

Beyond that is a quadrangle made completely of marble, with mosaic of various coloured stones from the floor to the window level, and has all kinds of floral designs. The inlay design on the floor is so beautiful that a thousand Persian carpets would look dull in front of its design.

In the middle of this room is a square pool with inlay work work, which had golden fountains on its four corners. They have been designed in such a way that the jets from all four fountains combined to fall together in the centre of the pool. One of the streams of Nahr-e Bahisht flowed near the wall.

This was the most beautiful room of all. The special feature of this room was that the temperature of the room and of the water in the stream and the fountains could be kept cool in the summers.

During winters, if the emperor wished, then the room could be heated from the floor to the ceiling. Cold or hot water would flow from this rivulet, as per need.

Garam Khana

This is the third room of the hammam. It was used in winters for having hot water baths. The western wall had all the necessary provisions needed to heat the water. It required quite a lot of wood for heating, and as Sir Sayyid says, '125 mann ka luqma …' – in other words, even 125 maunds of wood were but a morsel for heating it.

In the north overlooking the Bagh-e Hayat Baksh was a pool for a hot water bath made completely of marble. Once upon a time, it was inlaid with precious stones and had golden jets for spraying water in all the four corners.

Hammam Garam Khana's floor

The windows in this as well as in all the other rooms were decorated with stained glass through which brightly coloured light must have poured in like rainbows. Today they are dull and dismal.

The floor, platform, pools and the walls were all beautifully carved and decorated with mosaic and inlay work until the dado. The floral inlays were studded with precious and semi-precious stones and with such skill that they gave the effect of a garden. This is one room which still retains some semblance of its former beauty.

Behind the hammam was a well, built on Emperor Bahadur Shah Zafar's orders, with a date inscribed on it: AH 1257/AD 1841. The Mughals were very fond of chronograms which were verses yielding the year of construction through the numerical value of its letters. The chronogram for this is:

Zafar tamer shud iin chaah-e shireen
Ke aabash sherbet-e kand nabat ast
Azi'n khushtar nabashad
Saal wa tareekh huwaida
Chashma-e aab-e hayat ast

AH 1257

Zafar constructed this sweet well
It is sweet as sugar
The date and year of this sweet well is evident
(from) the spring of water of life

AH 1257/AD 1841

Moti Masjid

Emperor Shah Jahan had made no provisions for a private royal mosque inside the fort. Initially he went to the Akbarabadi and Fatehpuri mosques to pray, and later he gave orders for the Jama Masjid to be built. Emperor Aurangzeb Alamgir felt the need for a mosque nearer to his bedchambers, so that he could pray at all hours, especially in the wee hours of the morning. He had this mosque built in AD 1659 just after his ascension to the throne – at a cost of ₹1,60,000.

Moti Masjid was the private mosque of the emperor and the queens of the Qila. There was a path for them to come from the Zenana Mahal and

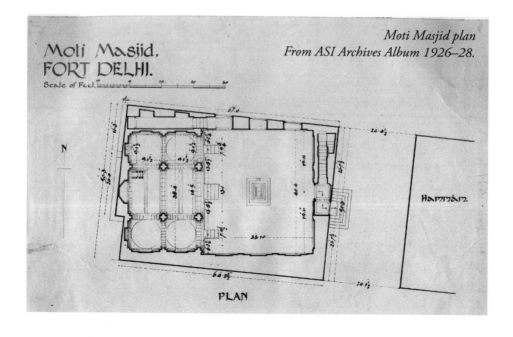

Moti Masjid plan
From ASI Archives Album 1926–28.

Moti Masjid, FORT DELHI.
Scale of Feet

N

Hammam.

PLAN

Moti Masjid

enter through a door set in the northern wall of the mosque and perform their namaz along with the emperor.

Built completely of marble, it is still very beautiful, though out of bounds for tourists. I had visited it some years ago, and remember thinking what it must have been when it was newly constructed. On my recent visit for research connected with this book, I was once again left spellbound.

The mosque is raised on a plinth of 3½ feet, with steps to climb up. There are three exquisite engrailed marble arches in the façade: the side arches are quite low, while the central one is higher. There are two aisles created by the arches inside. The central portion of each compartment created by these arches is pristine, with no decoration, while the rest are beautifully carved with delicate floral designs in marble. It is one of the prettiest and most delicate marble structures in the entire fort.

In the wall at the back is a beautiful marble *mehrab* (niche) indicating the *Qibla* wall or direction for namaz. The marble pulpit is elegant and exquisite with its delicately carved legs.

Black marble has been used to mark the prayer mats. The flooring, parapets and walls are all built of marble with marble floral carvings on them.

There are parapets with inlay work on top of the entrance arches, with tiny minarets on either side of the arches. The central eave is arched over the engrailed arch below it and flat on the side arches.

In the middle of the courtyard is a small water tank for ablution, measuring 10 feet x 8 feet. It is too shallow and does not have the depth, size[35] or alternatively flowing water as prescribed by sharia for *wuzu*, or ablution for namaz. Since this qualified as still water, which is *haraam* or unsuited for wuzu, a very clever arrangement had been made whereby water from Bhado'n flowed into the tank and overflowed from it, thus making it pure for wuzu.

There is a small room to the northern side of the mosque, which was for the purposes of prayers and meditation. This room also contained a small, shallow, but very beautiful hauz. It was decorated with glass mosaic.[36]

The mosque is 40-feet long and 30-feet wide. It is 25-feet high, till the roof, and about 12-feet more from the roof to the top of the central finial.

The mosque has three tall, bulbous domes that can be seen soaring above the box walls of the mosque. Sir Sayyid describes them as being golden (gilded) in the 1847 *Asar-us Sanadid* edition, because of which it was called Sunehri Masjid too. A painting by Ghulam Ali in the 1840s also shows golden domes.

During the Uprising of 1857, a cannonball fell on the domes of Moti Masjid and destroyed them.[37] The British later replaced the gilded domes with marble ones when they repaired it. It has also been said that they failed to keep the proportion of the masjid in mind when replacing it and the new domes seem inordinately large in proportion to the rest of the building.[38]

Another reason to keep Shah Jahan, with his obsession for symmetry, twisting and turning in his grave!

Another interesting fact is that since the mehrab of the masjid had to face Mecca (Qibla), it was not in line and broke the symmetry with the hammam and other buildings in the same line. So, a box was built which housed the masjid, adjusting its direction towards Mecca within it, and continued the symmetry. This can be seen in the plan drawing in the ASI archive.

The entrance is a small marble gateway with brass-plated doors, with elegant decoration on them. These are now darkened with age and the worse for disuse. The outer wall is 20-feet tall, which is red sandstone (painted white now) and marble from the inside.

At regular intervals there are marble columns built in the wall on the interior, which can be seen soaring outside with delicate cupolas (which were once upon a time golden on top as seen from a painting by Mazhar Ali Khan).

There is a chronogram written by Aqil Khan:

Annal Masajida Lillah Fala Tadu ma'Allahi Ahada

And (He revealed) that the masjids are for Allah, so do not invoke with Allah anyone. [Quran 72:18]
(Yielding AH 1036 as the year of its construction.)

Hira Mahal

When you walk past the Hammam towards the Shah Burj, you come across a solitary pavilion standing all by itself looking quite out of place. Anyone who has read that Qila Shahjahani was one of the most magnificent edifices of its times wonders what was in it to merit such praise?

Let me take you through the tour that the visitors of those days would have taken and see what was and is.

Towards the north of the Hammam is a small courtyard in which flows the 4-yard wide Nahr-e Bahisht or river of heaven. Here it takes a winding course and continues its sparkling journey with twists and turns into the Diwan-e Khas and Rang Mahal. The twenty-four golden and silver fountain jets installed in this nahr, which used to flow constantly, further dazzled the visitor.

The beauty of this Nahr defies description and soothes the heart. Who was in greater need of solace and solitude than the last Mughal Emperor, Abu Zafar Sirajuddin Mohammed Bahadur Shah II, simply known as Zafar, the pen name he had adopted?

Soon after his accession to the throne, he ordered the construction of a marble *baradari* (twelve-arched pavilion) in the middle of this courtyard. It measured 22.3 feet on the north and south, and 19.4 feet on the east and west sides.

At the four corners of its roof were four small *chaukhundi*s (cupolas) with golden domes. Perhaps one could see the poet emperor seated there and penning some of his famous verses in this delicate and aesthetically made pavilion.

The emperor's son and heir, Mirza Fath-ul Mulk Bahadur known as Mirza Fakhru, was also a poet, and perhaps he also wrote there for it was famous as *Mirza Fakhru Wali Ahad ki Baradari* (the pavilion of Mirza Fakhru, the heir apparent).[39] Mirza Fakhru was the crown prince who died in 1856.

Near this was a magazine built by the British after they occupied it, and a storeroom for keeping unused weapons. (It's no longer there.)

Today the fountains are now long gone and buried.

As Sir Sayyid Ahmad Khan wrote, 'The fountains drink their own tears and are silent.'

Moti Mahal

If one kept walking, one would have come across a lovely red sandstone building. The columns were marble till the dado and plastered white above that and generously decorated with floral designs. Parts of it were gilded with designs in gold.

It stood right in front of the waterfall in the Hayat Baksh garden.

A painting from a AD 1830 folio of Mohammad Salih Kamboh *Amal-i Salih* (*History of Shah Jahan*) one can make out the opulent beauty of this palace. Kambo completed his account of Emperor Shah Jahan's reign in AD 1659–60 and would have seen the Fort at its best. The painting is probably based on his description.

In the painting the river is flowing behind it and the white marble tank is kept in front of it. The char-bagh design of the Bagh-e Hayat Baksh can be seen. There is a fountain in the middle of the pool which must be the tank in which Zafar Mahal has been built. There are ducks and men swimming in the water. On two sides of it are luxuriant trees, bushes and flower-beds, with the Nahr-e Bahist flowing behind it. I saw this painting in the book *Delhi: Red Fort to Raisina*[40] and my heart stopped at the beauty of this painting and the wanton loss of it.

Apart from the Persian descriptions in court chronicles of Emperor Shah Jahan's era we find a detailed description of this in Sir Sayyid Ahmad Khan's *Asar-us Sanadid*, where he describes the two royal seats or shah nasheen, which were placed here. This was part of the original Qila Shahjahani and so you can imagine its grandeur and finish. The emperor would sit here to enjoy the Bagh-e Hayat Baksh on one side and the River Yamuna flowing on the other.

The first part of the Mahal was 15 yards x 8 yards, with a pond in the middle that was 4 yards x 3 yards. Behind each shah nasheen was a section 8 yards x 5 yards, with lofty five-arched rectangular halls overlooking the river on the east. Towards the west, they overlook the Hayat Baksh gardens. Each hall is 30 yards x 60 yards in size.

There was a monolithic marble basin (4 yards square and 1.5 yard deep) in which the water cascaded via a chute, in this part of the Nahr-e Bahisht. It was made from a stone mined from Makrana on Emperor Shah Jahan's orders. It was transported carefully and installed here. It has disappeared into the dust of time and I could find no reference to its current whereabouts in any book.

There also used to be a small basement under this palace where the emperor would rest. It's bricked up now.

The Moti Mahal didn't fare any better. Hearn[41] says that the Moti Mahal was demolished after the Mutiny because it prevented the free passage of air to the barracks. In fact, he expresses surprise as to why the unimportant Hira Mahal was left standing.

Military barracks for the officers/soldiers of the magazine was made here according to Bashiruddin Ahmad Dehlvi. In 1913, however, Ahmad adds, the barracks was removed.

The mansions and arcades to the north and south of the gardens belonging to princes were destroyed.

Shah Burj

The Shah Burj or royal tower was exclusively for the use of the emperor and his trusted confidantes. He would hold privy councils here with the his wazir (prime minister) and most trusted ministers. Barring them and a few fortunate royal princes, no one else was allowed in this which is on the corner of the platform that starts from the back wall of the Hammam. In AD 1784, Shah Alam's heir apparent, Jawan Bakht, had escaped from this burj by making a rope of turbans. He'd had enough of his father's tyranny, and ran away to take shelter under the British!

Shah Burj is again out of bounds for tourists and one can only see it from below. It overlooks the river and used to be three-storeyed once upon a time. Now only two storeys are left as the domed pavilion was destroyed in 1857 and no longer exists. It is very close to Salimgarh, which was in the firing sights of the British from the ridge.

This burj had suffered damage prior to 1857 also, as the Rohillas under Ghulam Qadir 'stripped many of the rooms of their marble ornaments and pavements and have even picked out the stones from the borders of many of the floorings.'[42] They also spent three days digging up the floors for treasure, which they had supposed the Emperor Shah Alam had hidden in this palace. This was

Shah Burj

also an apartment used exclusively by the emperor for resting, reading and, as it was out of the seraglio region, for meeting with his courtiers and ministers. It housed a royal library.

What is now a yellowing white marble was once upon a time beautifully decorated with mosaic and inlay work till the dado. The rest of it had been plastered white, over which floral designs were painted in gold. Vetiver screens would cover its openings in summer, ensuring that it stayed cool in the hot months.

Sanderson writes that 'for many years after the Mutiny the building served as an officer's residence but in 1902 conservation work was taken up and the marble cascade being reconstructed and modern additions removed.

The Shah Burj itself was damaged in a 1904 earthquake and almost completely rebuilt. It is not in a good state of preservation, and though the niche and fountain bed are still intact, it is heart breaking to compare them to paintings by Mazhar Ali Khan in the reminiscences of *Imperial Delhi* or

Dehlie Book. The *Dehlie Book* was a collection of paintings by Mazhar Ali Khan commissioned by Sir Thomas Metcalfe in 1844.

What we see is an apology of the original burj.

The first level had a marble basin measuring 3.5 x 2.5 yards, beautifully decorated with inlay work and floral embossing. Both are inlaid with *aqiq* (cornelian), *marjaan* (coral) and other priceless precious stones. Today it lies bare and forsaken like the rest: just a piece of history curious onlookers gaze at. This was the place that Muhammad Waris described as, 'This is such a place that it (appears to be) fragrant with the heavenly perfumes and embroidered with myriads of floral carvings which draw envy year after year.'

The second storey is also octagonal, with a diameter of 8 yards, surrounded by a gallery supported by twenty-four pillars.

The third storey was the domed pavilion of eight pillars. The dome was made of marble with a golden *kalasa* (finial). This was destroyed along with the dome in the 1857 Uprising.

The Faiz Nahr entered the palace from this burj by an innovative device called *shuturgulu* (camel's neck), which lifted the water from the ground to the level of the burj.

The entire water system of the Nahr-e Bahisht was controlled from here, and Sir Sayyid Ahmad Khan writes in *Asar-us Sanadid*, 'From this point onwards, a canal runs through the entire fort, and in fact the water system for the entire fort is controlled from here … Each pipe bears a label of the tank or canal it flows into.'

Nahr-e Bahisht/Stream of Heaven

A water stream called stream of heaven flowed into the entire palace complex. This was in keeping with the paradisiacal theme of the Fort: it was *firdaus* (heaven) on earth as inscribed on the Diwan-e Khas walls. This stream as described above originated in the Shah Burj and flowed through all the palaces going through pools with silver fountains in the channels. It went out into the

Bagh-e Hayat Baksh, flowed into the Sawan and Bhado'n pavilions and went through the Mahtab Bagh and other areas of the fort.

Tea Room

This is just behind the Shah Burj and was built in the last days of the Mughal Empire. It was probably the haveli of one of the royal princes, as they had their residences in this area. It was altered considerably by the British and became the tea room of the British soldiers.

Today it is a colonial-style building which is called the Tea Room. It is a large, double-storeyed hall. While the engrailed arches talk of a Mughal past, the fireplace talks of a British past. One can imagine the British officers enjoying their cup of tea here with a blazing fire to keep them warm on a cold winter evening.

Sawan and Bhado'n

Sawan and Bhado'n are two unique buildings that recreated the effect of monsoons in the month of Bhado'n and Sawan. They now stand mutely testifying to the wheels of time. No water flows into or out of them. All the holes and fountains are choked. They are identical pavilions facing each other in the Bagh-e Hayat Baksh. Today the northern pavilion is Sawan and the southern one is called Bhado'n. But is it possible that they had different names in the Shah Jahan era? Muhammad Waris talks of *Bagh-i Ruh Parwar* and *Ruh Afza* (the pavilions 'Sawan' and 'Bhadon'?) in *Padshahnama*. These are much more in keeping with the grandiose scheme of things in the Shahjahani times. Sawan Bhado'n sound more later-Mughal-era names.

Contemporary historian Mohammad Salih in *Amal-e Salih* likens them to the magical throne of the Queen of Sheba (a story given in the Bible and the Quran) or of King Solomon. He writes that they were decorated with paintings and pictures like the enamelled throne of the Queen of Sheba.[43]

They measure 48.4 feet x 35.3 feet and are made completely of marble. Sixteen beautiful columns are built on a plinth to create an attractive square hall which had a pool in the centre.

On the four corners of the roof were four golden cupolas. A stream of the Nahr-e Bahisht flowed into the pool and dropped like a cascade into the marble tank below. From here it flowed into a red sandstone channel with silver fountains in them. This water channel flowed into the Hauz-e Hayat Baksh.

The front part of the plinth of the pavilions from where the water cascaded had small arched niches. These held flower bouquets in the day and lit camphor candles at night. One can imagine the sensuous pleasures enjoyed by a walk in the gardens when the water cascaded near and around these candles and flowers.

There is no camphor or bouquets or even water to flow any more, but Sawan and Bhado'n are still standing, cast in white that is yellowing with age, as if mourning the passing of a glorious era.

Bagh-e Hayat Baksh/The Life-Giving Garden

Let me take you on a round of a garden of which no traces remain. My intention is to acquaint the reader with the wanton destruction that Mughal

Location of Mahtab Bagh

monuments, especially in Shahjahanabad, suffered at the hands of the British after the 1857 Uprising.

I give you the words of Sir Sayyid Ahmad Khan who wrote the first edition of *Asar-us Sanadid* in 1847 and so saw the Qila when its light was flickering but still burning:[44]

This garden is a sign of God's Divine Grace and rejuvenates the heart of the onlooker and makes him ecstatic and cheerful.

The gardens of Heaven come up in front of the eyes. The height of the trees can make men envious of its stature (*rashk-e qaamat-e yaar*). Every flower can make a fair maiden blush (*ghairat-e gul-e rukhsar*) and its tendrils put to shame the beloved's curls.

Even the finest poet would find it difficult to describe its beauty.

In the middle of this Bagh is a large tank and all around it flow canals of red sandstone, measuring 6 gaz wide. Each channel has thirty silver fountains, which kept flowing.

This garden with its fragrant flowers and trees is the reason for the ever-present freshness here. It is 250 x 125 gaz in size.

The ambience produced by the greenery of the plants and trees and the fragrance of the flowers, the soft flowing breeze can't be captured in words.

Sad hazaran gul-e shaguftah dar oo
Sabzah bedar wa aab-e khuftah dar oo

A hundred thousand flowers bloom in this garden
The greenery is fresh and sweet sound of the water is soothing.

In 1902, the remnants of this bagh were found buried deep in debris: that is, those portions that had not become part of the roads the British had built for their convenience inside the Mughal Qila.

Its nahr, waterfalls, water channels, flowerbeds and footpaths for roaming in the garden were all destroyed. The Hayat Bagh, the Life-Giving Garden, had now become *Mamaat Bagh*, Garden of Death, laments Bashiruddin Ahmad.

Whatever we see today are the portions that were preserved and repaired by Lord Curzon. He replanted lawns and trees in the portion not occupied by the ugly barracks.

When one walks on or around the grass lawns today, do remember that grass lawns with flowerbeds on the sides is a British concept. The Mughals believed in flowers, planted the gardens with it and had made footpaths for people to walk in them. The concept of lawns with organized flowerbeds was a British introduction.

Muhammad Waris wrote of the bagh:

...[I]t was full of multiples of varieties of Heavenly flowers (*gul-i riyâhîn*). In its middle is a tank like the *hauz-i kauthar* (the heavenly tank mentioned in the Quran). It is 8 gaz and on its purity, the worldly tanks would hide in humility! Its ornamentation and dazzle dims even the brightness of the sun. In the middle of this tank are forty-nine fountains from which the water spurts out as if from water-laden clouds in the sky!

On the margins of this tank are another 112 fountains. The four lanes of the garden (*chahâr khiyâbân-i bâgh*) are 20 gaz broad. The floors of these walkways are made of red stone and in their middle is the 6 gaz wide water channel. In each of these four water channels are three rows of fountains, which are embellished with gold and silver plating, and thus appear very enchanting.[45]

Hauz-e Bagh-e Hayat Baksh

Dil ishq ka hamesha hareef nabard tha
Ab jis jagah ke daagh hai yaa'n pahle dard tha

The rivals always trouble the lover's heart
Only a scar remains where once there was an ache[46]

In the middle of the Life-Giving Garden is a large hauz that measures 158.3 feet x 153 feet. Once upon a time it had forty-nine silver fountains, which were always flowing. Apart from these, there were 112 silver fountains all around the tank, which were inclined towards the hauz. No traces of these fountains remain – all one can see are blocks of stone with holes in them.

Zafar Mahal/Jal Mahal

In 1842, Emperor Bahadur Shah Zafar got a mahal made inside the Hauz-e Bagh-e Hayat Baksh, which was completely of red sandstone.

نقشه ظفرمحل مع حوض هیایاع

*Hauz-e Bagh Hayat Baksh from Asar-us-Sanadid
(National Archives of India)*

It is planned in such a way that there is an open space in the middle with alcoves and enclosures all around it for sitting. On one side is a bridge for entering and exit.

Under the British, their officers used this as a swimming pool.

Today it is a dry tank with a sorry-looking building in the middle. The bridge to it has broken. I can imagine Zafar composing his ghazals here, with Tanras Khan, the great khyaal singer, singing nearby.

Mahtab Bagh

Once again I ask my readers to imagine the Qila as it would have been in the seventeenth and eighteenth centuries when it was built.

Next to Hayat Bagh, the architects had designed a moonlit garden with white flowering bushes, trees and plants. It was for enjoyment in the heavenly evenings and nights when the scent from the flowers overpowered the senses, the camphor lamps and candles from the Sawan and Bhado'n pavilions made one languorous and dreamy.

The Badshah walked here with his begums, the princes and princesses perhaps dreamt of crowns and palaces.

In the centre of this garden flowed the Nahr-e Bahisht. Emperor Bahadur Shah Zafar had replicated the *jharna* in Mehrauli in the west of this garden in red sandstone.

This garden contained a dargah of Qadam Sharif (imprint of the footprint of the Prophet [PBUH]), but of which no traces remain. When Emperor Bahadur Shah Zafar left the Qila on 17 September after the fall of Delhi, he took all the relics of the Prophet that he had and handed them over to the Sajjadanasheen of the Hazrat Nizamuddin Dargah. Maybe the imprint was also part of it.

Return to the stark and ugly reality of the solid barracks standing there today where these heavenly gardens once lay.

Excavation has been started in this area, and I have seen the many spouts where fountains would have been, and the water channels through which the water would have flowed.

Sir Sayyid Ahmad Khan mentions that a little beyond the Mahtab Bagh were two buildings used as kitchens and which are famous as Chhota Khasa and Bada Khasa.

Today that entire area is a grassy expanse and all modern buildings that had come up have been demolished and the area is being cleared.

Baoli/Step well

To the west of Hayat Bagh is this historic *baoli*. It is quite spectacular in its architecture and depth. The octagonal well is 21.4 feet in diameter and is 46.10 feet deep. From it forms a small hauz in the northern wall, which is 20 square feet in area, and 27.5 feet deep. The Hauz was designed in such a way that the water level always remained the same.

Steps lead down to it from the west and northern side. It is a picture perfect baoli, with great angles for photographing. This hauz was used for swimming. There are steps on the north and west sides, with rooms on either side of the west side. These rooms were used to house the senior prisoners, such as Gen. Shahnawaz Khan and Gen. Dhillon of Indian National Army, in 1945.

Now even this has been closed to the public.

Chobi Masjid/Wooden Mosque and Dargah

Till 1857, there was a dargah inside the Red Fort, where relics of the Prophet were kept. *Bazm-e Aakhir* and *Dilli ka Aakhri Deedar*, written in the nineteenth and twentieth centuries, respectively, describe the daily routine of the badshah, including a daily visit to the dargah. When Emperor Bahadur Shah Zafar escaped after the Uprising of 1857, he took the relics and handed them over to the hereditary caretakers of the dargah of Hazrat Nizamuddin Auliya, where they are kept safely till date and displayed every year on the Prophet's birthday.

Step well

There is also mention of a *chobi* (wooden) masjid. Emperor Ahmad Shah built it in AD 1750. Emperor Bahadur Shah Zafar had it repaired in 1850. Chobi Masjid's location is given as beyond Mahtab Bagh, near the kitchens. It is probable that the dargah may have been there too.

Bashiruddin Ahmad Dehlvi mentions that to the north of Chatta Chowk, Emperor Bahadur Shah Zafar had built a mosque that measured 42.6 feet x 24 feet. It was just a simple dome-less structure with a five-arched façade and no courtyard. The British used it as a godown for supply and transport.

Barracks

Though these barracks came up after 1857 and were built by the British to house their troops, no mention of the Qila can be complete without them. They loom large over the fort. These are huge, utilitarian, and thus unattractive, three-storeyed buildings. Today they are being converted into museums housing relics from the Indian National Army and the Mughal era.

The Private Apartments of the Emperor and the Seraglio

These are to the south of the Diwan-e Khas and were the areas where the emperor had his private apartments and which also housed the ladies apartments. No male, except the emperor, was allowed to enter in this area. It was guarded by female soldiers and eunuchs, known as khwajasaras.

Tasbihkhana, Khwabgah and Badi Baithak

To the south of Diwan-e Khas is a set of three apartments made completely of marble through which the Nahr-e Bahisht flows. These were the emperor's private apartments.

The Diwan-e Khas and Tasbihkhana are separated by a 46-feet-wide marble platform. The Tasbihkhana faces the Diwan-e Khas and is one in a row of three rooms, the other two being the Khwabgah and Badi Baithak.

The emperor used the Tasbihkhana, which was on the outer side, for meetings with special nobles. In the middle of this hall is engraved a weighing scale in marble, with *Mizaan-e Adl* (Scales of Justice) written on it. It had a lot of golden work on it. The architect must surely have built it as a reminder to the emperor that he has to serve justice to all for he too

Tasbhihkhana
From ASI Archives Album 1931–32

will be weighed in the same scales of justice on Doomsday. The emperor held a daily darbar here to give quick redressal to grievances. Sometimes he would sit here twice a day to dispense justice. The Mizaan-e Adl could not ensure that the Mughal emperor got justice at the hands of the British imperialists, and he was banished from his own kingdom and people.

The screen of this exquisite room had gaping holes and is currently being repaired by the ASI as per the original design.

The way to the Khwabgah, called *Khasi Deorhi* or special/private passageway, is located inside this Tasbihkhana. Beyond that is a hall open on one side and half the size of the khwabgah, which is known as the Badi Baithak or Large Sitting Room.

On the arches of the khwabgah is an inscription written in gold water by Sa'adullah Khan that describes the entire history of the Qila's construction. Despite the dirt and veneer of neglect that has gathered all over the Qila, this inscription is still shining and clear. When I stood in front of it, I was awestruck by its beauty. Though I couldn't read it there, I did come back and read its English translation. This area is out of bounds for normal tourists and I was only allowed for purposes of research for this book.

Inscription on the arch of the Khwabgah:

> God is pure! How beautiful are these painted mansions and charming residences. They are a part of high heaven. I may say the high-souled holy angels are desirous of looking at them. If the residents of different parts and directions of the world would come to walk round them, as (they walk) round the old house (Ka'ba) it would be allowable; or if the beholders of the two worlds should run to kiss their highly glorious threshold as (they kiss) the black stone (of the Ka'ba), it would be proper. The commencement of the great Fort which is higher than the Palace of the Heavens is the envy of the wall of Alexander, and of his pleasant edifice, and of the Hayat Baksh (life-bestowing) Gardens, which is to these buildings as the soul is to the body, and the lamp to an assembly; and of the pure canal, the limpid water of which is to the person possessing sight as a mirror showing the world, and to the wise, the unveiler of the secret world; and of the water-cascades, each of which you may say is the whiteness of the dawn, or a tablet containing secrets of the Table and Pen (of Fate).

Inscription on the northern arch of the Khwabgah:

> …and of the fountains, each of which is a hand of light inclined to shake hands with the inhabitants of heavens, or is a string of bright pearls made to descend to reward the inhabitants of the earth; and of the tank, full to the brim of the water of life and in its purity the envy of light and the spring of the sun announced on the 12th Zil-hajjah in the 12th year of the holy ascension, corresponding to AH 1048, the tidings of happiness to men. The completion of it, at the expense of fifty lakh of rupees, by the power of the auspicious feet of the sovereign of the earth, the lord of the

world, the originator of these heavenly buildings, Shihabuddin Mohammad, the second lord of felicity, Shah Jahan the King, the champion of the faith, opened on 24th Rabi Awwal in the 21st blessed year of the ascension, corresponding AH 1058, the door of grace to the world.[47]

One of the rooms of the khwabgah is kept locked, and its inlay work and gilding is almost intact. It gave me a heady feeling just to stand in the middle of so much beauty. Not an inch of marble is without decoration and one can just imagine what the Qila must have looked like in its glory days.

This room was called the Mughal room and kept furnished by the British to give a feel of the Qila. This room has two doors made of beautifully carved copper cladding, with elephant riders as the doorknobs. These are spectacular, though a little worse for wear.

Musamman Burj

The word *musamman* means 'eight-sided', hence this domed octagonal hall attached to the eastern wall of the Khwabgah is named Musamman Burj. Three sides of the octagon are towards the khwabgah, and five overlook the river. Four of these used to be covered with elegant marble screens, while the fifth had the *jharoka* (balcony) attached to it.

Bernier never saw the Musamman Burj himself but describes it as heard from the khwajasara: 'The eunuchs speak with extravagant praise of a small tower, facing the river, which is covered with plates of gold in the same manner as the towers of Agra; and its azure apartments are decorated with gold and azure, exquisite paintings and magnificent mirrors.'

The copper plates that covered Musamman Burj and gave it the name of Burj Tila, or Golden Pavilion, were removed after 1857 Uprising. It is now covered with lime plaster.

However, what remains in pristine condition is this rubai or quartrain which reads:

Aye band ba-paay o qufl bar dil hushdaar
Way dokhta chashm, paaye dar gil hushdaar
Azm-e safar-e maghrib o roo dar mashriq
Aye raah ro-e pusht ba manzil hushdaar

O you, whose feet are tied and heart is caged, beware!
O you, with sewn eyes and feet stuck in mud, beware!
You intend to travel towards the west but you are heading towards the east.
O you, who is turning his back on his destination, beware!

Sir Sayyid Ahmad Khan or Maulvi Zafar Hasan have not mentioned it, so I sent it to Prof. Sunil Sharma, and he said that this rubai did display mastery over Persian verse. As all other inscriptions in this area are attributed to Sa'adullah Khan, would it be safe to attribute this to him also?

Emperor Shah Jahan gave Jharoka darshan from this pavilion.

Jharoka

This is the famous balcony from where the later emperor gave *jharoka darshan* (balcony of viewing). It is a small balcony with a vaulted roof. Jharoka darshan was a custom started by Emperor Jalaluddin Mohammad Akbar where he appeared before his adoring public. The early morning puja of his Hindu subjects would be completed only after this. The others would just stand underneath in the early mornings to catch a glimpse of their beloved emperor.

Sir Sayyid writes that, 'The *Bandagan-e Khaas Akbari* (Hindu servants of Emperor Akbar, the people of his realm) would not talk to anyone until they had seen the emperor's face.'

This served a dual purpose as the subjects could see the face of their emperor and the 'harrowed and oppressed of the population may freely represent their wants and desires.'[48]

This helped the administrators of justice to grasp the substance of a case and later lay it before His Majesty in the Diwan-e Aam or Diwan-e Khas so that justice could be dispensed.

Agra Fort also had a similar jharoka. Emperor Aurangzeb stopped this custom during his reign, but it was restarted by his successors.

The jharoka in Qila-e Mubarak was added by Emperor Akbar Shah II, and it seems from contemporary accounts that this custom was revived to some extent in Delhi under the later Mughals.

It was from here that the emperor also watched the elephant fights in the reti.

Under this very balcony the soldiers who had come from Meerut after rebelling against their British masters had gathered on 11 May 1857 and entreated Emperor Bahadur Shah Zafar to let them fight the British under his banner and leadership, thus changing the course of history for ever.

In 1911, when the Delhi Darbar was held to celebrate the coronation of King George V, he and his consort, Queen Mary, came and gave darshan to their Indian subjects from the same jharoka.

Today the jharoka is out of bounds for general tourists.

Khizri Darwaza

A few steps led to the river from Musamman Burj. Nowadays there is a grassy patch where the reti used to be and a road where the river flowed. Only royalty used this Darwaza. It is this door that was used by Emperor Shah Jahan to enter the Qila in 1648 and the same darwaza by which Emperor Bahadur Shah Zafar left the fort on 17 September 1857.

It is the same darwaza that Captain Douglas had wanted opened on 11 May 1857 so that he could talk directly to the rebel sepoys who had come from

Meerut and gathered under it. He wanted to reason with them and tell them to go back to their regiments and wait for their grievances to be addressed. The emperor, fearing for his life, had refused to let him go down.

The lower level of Musamman Burj, known as Tahtani Manzil, is actually an entrance or deorhi to this darwaza, with windows.

Rang Mahal/Imtiaz Mahal

Today when you enter the Red Fort you can see a large marble pavilion behind the Diwan-e Aam. Tourists are not allowed to enter inside but can only see the state of disrepair from outside. The ceiling has gaping holes and it has fared badly over the years. The floor which, according to contemporary historian Mohammad Salih (in *Amal-e Salih*), was covered with various types of floral cotton carpets and beautiful, bright, colourful Kashmiri carpets is now bare and yellowed with age.

The flower fountain is in good shape, but there are no fountains, jewels or inlay work and floral designs.

Khizri Darwaza
From ASI Archives Album 1931–32.

Rang Mahal/Imtiaz Mahal antechamber with glass work

When the Qila was under the British army, the Imtiaz Mahal was used as the officers' mess, and the damage is there for all to see.

It's just a testimony to the vagaries of time.

This was the largest of the palaces in the Fort complex. It was 153.6 feet in length, from north to south, and 69.3 feet in width, from east to west.

When it was built, it used to have a huge courtyard with canals, fountains and gardens inside it. Under the later Mughals, ugly houses had been built in the charming courtyard, ruining the look of the palace, rues Sir Sayyid Ahmad Khan. A lithograph in *Asar-us-Sanadid* shows these changes with the house of Mirza Babur looming behind the Diwan-e Aam spoiling its symmetry. Another house labelled as the house of the Wali Ahad or heir apparent can be seen built in the Zenana Mahal itself.

The British later removed these houses after they occupied it.

Today we see red sandstone everywhere and feel that the title Red Fort is justified, but when the Qila-e Mubarak was built, all the buildings were plastered, polished and gilded. The Imtiaz Mahal, which is marble till the dado, had been whitened with plaster on its upper walls till the ceiling (which were of red sandstone) and the whole surface was covered with gold decorations.

Earlier the courtyard had a pond that was 48–50 square yards in size, containing five fountains, as well as a stream flowing through, which had twenty-five fountains. There was also a garden, 107 x 115 yards in size, around

Rang Mahal Fountain

which a red sandstone screen had been built with 2,000 golden finials in it. Three of its sides had charming mansions and arcades, in a width of 70 yards. Towards the west of the buildings, overhanging the river and the *Pai'n Bagh* (a miniature garden) was the Imtiaz Mahal, whose praise, according to Sir Sayyid Ahmad, is beyond the capacity of a mere mortal.

It was built on a plinth with two elegant basements below it. The terrace has an intricate three-aisle hall with a five-arched façade, which is 57 x 36 yards in size.

In front of the middle arch of this palace was a garden, and in it a big marble basin. This was made from a single piece of marble raised above the ground on legs.

This is the garden that lies between Imtiaz Mahal and the rear of the Diwan-e Aam.

After the Revolt of 1857, this basin was removed by the British and taken to the Queen's gardens. I suppose we should be grateful that it was not smashed or broken into pieces.

It was brought back when the Fort was being decorated and spruced up for the Delhi Darbar in 1911, and is a mute reminder of the destruction and plunder of this beautiful palace and fort.

The garden had fallen into disuse and was excavated for the darbar. A study of Ghulam Ali's paintings from the 1840s shows this garden.

The basin is very close to the palace and not in the position it used to be in. Also missing are the stone kiosks in front of the palace, which were covered with vetiver screens to cool the palace in summer months.

I took permission to go near it as it is out of bounds for tourists. I had just read *Asar-us Sanadid* and was very excited. I can't tell you how heartbroken I was when I climbed the platform.

This monolithic marble basin, which defied description, now looks like a second-hand bathtub that one could buy in any *kabadi* shop, with a broken spout in the middle.

Sir Sayyid Ahmad Khan gives us a beautiful description in *Asar-us Sanadid* of the interior of the mahal with another matchless marble basin that was the crowning glory of Nahr-e Bahisht. He said that the beauty of the pool was such that it baffled the mind. His description of the pool in the centre is lyrical. He calls it a flower in full bloom:

> Its petals are so beautiful that every jasmine from all the gardens can be sacrificed over its beauty and inside it the inlay work of flowers and foliage in various coloured stones has been executed so exquisitely, that it is beyond description. It's like a picture gallery in front of an ardent audience.

He goes on to say that the flowers and foliage created by the inlay work sway in the wind as if in a garden and transport the viewer into heaven. His description is invaluable for it describes a cup that was attached to the fountain, which no longer exists:

> Inside this pool there is a marble *kaasa* (cup), which is actually a beautiful flower on whose beauty many a thousand flowers can be sacrificed. On every curve and arched cusp, flowers and leaves of coloured stones spring from creeping plants, and the creeping plants in turn emerge from flowers and leaves. In that bowl is a

hole and a hidden underground stream that bubbles out of this bowl. The water overflows from the brim of this bowl, and the swaying of the flowers and plants seems like a magical moment.

Today that kaasa is nowhere to be seen, but even in its depleted state this flower is exquisite.

The Nahr-e Bahisht passes through the middle of this palace and goes out towards the south. From here a stream flowed outside towards the façade and its niches and pool can be seen.

Every stream has been decorated with the same carving, inlay work and mosaic that were used for ornamenting the pond.

The columns which support the arches in the Imtiaz Mahal are made of marble. This palace was apparently used as a mess by the British and is in a state of criminal neglect, with sagging holes in the ceilings and yellowed marble. The marble of this very room was described by Sir Sayyid as 'fairer than the complexion of a thousand beloveds, and the redness of the stones used is more attractive than the ruby-red lips of innumerable beauties.'

Its ceiling was also once silver, but in the reign of Emperor Farrukhsiyar it was replaced with copper. In reign of Emperor Moinuddin Mohammad Akbar Shah II, this copper ceiling was also removed and was replaced by wood, but even that is now in ruins. The silver and copper were minted into coins.

Bernier had not seen the seraglio, but describes it based on hearsay:

You must be content therefore with such a general description as I have received from some of the eunuchs. They inform me that the seraglio contains beautiful apartments, separated, and more or less spacious and splendid, according to the rank and income of the females. Nearly every chamber has its reservoir of running water at the door; on every side are gardens, delightful alleys, shady retreats, streams, jets d'eau, grottoes, deep excavations that afford shelter from the sun of day, lofty divans and terraces on which to sleep coolly at night. Within the walls of this enchanting place, in fine, no oppressive or inconvenient heat is felt.[49]

After the British quelled the 1857 Uprising and occupied the Qila, it was wantonly destroyed. The precious stones were literally wrested out. There is one panel of what must have been a inlay work flower design, which gave me the impression of a man tortured till his eyes had been gouged out of his sockets. All that remains in that panel is a smudge of red and pitted scars.

On either side of it were antechambers with mirror work on the walls and ceilings. These are badly damaged and don't present a very pretty picture. On a recent visit to Iran, I saw some of the Safavid and Qajar palaces in Tehran and Isfahan. The mirror walls and ceilings are intact and give the visitor a sense of being in a magical world. All the while I was there, I could only think of what the Mughal palaces must have looked like before their wanton destruction. Emperor Shah Jahan rivalled the Safavid Empire in almost every way…

Darya Mahal

According to Hearn, a small pavilion known as Darya Mahal was situated between the Rang Mahal and Choti Baithak. He writes that projected on to the river, thus giving it the name Darya Mahal. It had two openings towards the river.

It was a very well decorated and ornamented palace for use of the ladies of the harem. It had an eave on which a beautiful bird was painted on the inside.

There are no signs of this palace any more. Sir Sayyid does not describe this palace in *Asar-us Sanadid*.

Chhoti Baithak/Khurd Jahan/Chhoti Duniya

This building was near Imtiaz Mahal and was famous as *Chhoti Baithak*.

It originally had flowering plants, shrubs and trees, fountains, waterfalls, a baradari, benches for sitting and bowers – perhaps it was meant to create a small piece of heaven on earth and thus the name Chhoti Duniya. This palace was kept very cool with sprinklers, and in summers was far cooler than the rest of the palace. It provided a scented green haven in Delhi's summers.

It was elegant and attractive like the rest of the palaces, but Mirza Jahangir Bahadur had made modern additions to it, which had spoilt the Shahjahani look.

This was the last palace facing the river but it is no longer extant, having been demolished after 1857 when the British took control of the Qila.

Mumtaz Mahal/Zenana Mahal Shahi/Chota Rang Mahal

This 88 feet x 81.10 feet palace was one of the more important palaces of the Qila. Till recently it was the ASI museum and housed relics of the past. These have now shifted to the museum in the barracks.

After the 1857 Uprising this was used as a prison. Later it was made the Sergeant's mess house. The golden chhatris on the four corners of the roof were removed.

In 1911, the Zenana Mahal was renovated, and is no longer what it originally was.

This palace, with its intricate workmanship, was meant for the chief ladies of the harem. I can only imagine Jahan Ara Begum illuminating this space with her presence. It has a five-arched hall inside, which is 33 yards long, and behind it is another hall that is 16 x 8 yards wide. This building is made of marble till the dado, above which there were beautiful decorations in stucco and painting on white plaster. There are some signs of the mirror inlay and gilding on the walls.

The Nahr-e Bahisht ran through this palace too and there was a marble pool in it. It is no longer visible.

There used to be a 67-square-yard garden in the courtyard, with this 25-yard octagonal pond in the middle of it, within which there were, once upon a time, twenty-five fountains.

This building is now standalone and there are lawns in place of the garden.

Asad Burj

This is the southern burj of the fort and similar to Shah Burj.

This tower was destroyed in the chaos that ensued in the aftermath of the bombardment between Ochterlony and Harnath Chela, but was restored to its original state during the reign of Emperor Akbar Shah II.

Today it can be seen only from the road, and tourists are not allowed in this area. It is under the CISF and as we had taken permission, we were allowed to see it under their escort. It has a 'haunted by the past' look.

Asad Burj

Near the Asad Burj was a rose garden, which was used for the purposes of making *attar*. Today it is just a grassy mound. Royal princes Mirza Jahanger son of Emperor Akbar Shah and Mirza Nili (1762–1825) son of Emperor Sha Alam II had their mansions here.

Badar Roo Darwaza/Water Gate

This is on the south-west corner of the Qila and has a barbican, probably added by Emperor Aurangzeb. It can be accessed via Asad Burj, but this area is out of bounds for tourists.

The princes and nobles used this gate if they came via the river route.

Entrance to Badar-Roo Darwaza

Salimgarh: The Bridge of Boats which connected the two sides of the River Yamuna near Salimgarh. From ASI Archives (Felice Beato, 1858).

Salimgarh

According to *Tarikh-e Daudi* written by Abdullah in AH 983, when Salim Shah, the son of Sher Shah, heard in AD 1546 that Humayun was planning to return with a force to recapture Delhi, he returned from Lahore to Delhi and built Salimgarh Fort in the middle of Jumna near Din Panah, on an island.

The fort is in the shape of a semi-circle, and once upon a time had nineteen bastions of different sizes. It was built at a cost of ₹4 lakh. However, even after almost five years of construction, only its walls were ready when the king died and it was left incomplete.

Emperor Jahangir had got a bridge built here in AD 1622 to enter Salimgarh. This was removed by the British to make way for the new Railway bridge. The present bridge was made later. The inscription from Jahangir's era is kept in the Red Fort museum.

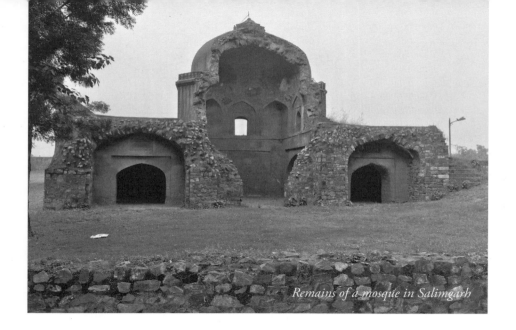

Remains of a mosque in Salimgarh

The fort was then was given to Farid Khan, an important noble in the reign of Emperor Akbar and Emperor Jahangir, as part of his estate, and he built many buildings inside it.

Jahangir had a bridge built in AD 1622, and this was incorporated in the Qila as a way between the two. It had been named Nurgarh after Emperor Nuruddin Mohammad Jahangir. Its inscriptions are kept in the ASI museum. The British demolished this bridge to make the railway bridge. Only a shelled mosque with its shattered domes remains from the medieval era.

All these were in ruinous condition by the time Emperor Bahadur Shah Zafar ascended the throne, and in 1857, the Indian soldiers used it as a battery. There are many magazines and batteries built later by the British, which are still visible.

The fort was used as a prison and we know that Emperor Aurangzeb had imprisoned his daughter Princess Zeb-un-Nisa here. According to a late eighteenth-century plan in the Maharaja Sawai Man Singh II Museum, City Palace, Jaipur, Kapad Dvara Collection, there is a building called Salatin ki Haveli which was a prison where surplus Mughal princes were kept.[50] I have seen this map and can tell you it is quite fascinating.

Later, the fort was again used as a prison to house the INA soldiers and those cells are still standing. A museum dedicated to the INA has been built there.

A bridge has since been made to cross over the railway line to go to Salimgarh.

A Peep into the Past

The Qila started on its downward slide under Emperor Mohammad Shah and the attack and plunder by Nader Shah. A glorious memorial to Mughal power was allowed to sink into decay.

Dilapidated huts and royal palaces stood together and disfigured the beauty of the palace.

The most objectionable act, according to Bashiruddin Ahmad Dehlvi, who calls it *tufaan-e be-tameezi* (storm of impropriety), was that the lofty, soaring palaces built by Shah Jahan to decorate his seat of power were compromised by ugly additions.

Open spaces that had been left near them so that their beauty would not be spoilt and they would not be deprived of breathing space were filled up with ugly, ungainly and unconnected buildings. The moon was eclipsed!

The walls in which one could see one's own reflection were sullied with dirt and neglect. The scratches and marks on the wall made it look forsaken.

The precious stones inlaid in the columns and walls were gouged out, the gilding was scratched off. They were layers of dust on the places of royal assembly where one's gaze would be blinded with its brightness and beauty. The royal thrones were dusty and no darbar was held.

The galleries and roofs of corridors were in a ruinous state with no one to use or repair them.

Those who had read tales of its splendour from travellers and came from far and wide to see it would go away dejected and disappointed.

Khwaabgah antechamber
From ASI Archives Album 1931–32

The Mughal Room

This room in the Royal Khwabgah near the Mizaan-e Adl was decorated by the British and named the Mughal Room. It was furnished with the items found by the British in the Qila itself. Bashiruddin Ahmad Dehlvi describes it saying that the original decoration in this room is still almost intact but now it is devoid of furniture.

He goes on to write that it was furnished with carpets, cushions, bolsters, Shah Jahan's hookah, spitoon and his sword. It seemed as if it is still in use.

It is clear that the emperor would sit on a wooden settee richly covered with velvet and other such fabrics. There would be a hookah, trays of sweets, fruits, and his weapons, such as the sword and dagger, were kept nearby. A small swordstick would be used for leaning and sitting.

This has been replicated so that Europeans can see for themselves the lifestyle of the grand Mughals. However, since much of the Qila was looted and destroyed in the aftermath of the 1857 Revolt, there is hardly anything of worth left in it, and to Bashiruddin Ahmad Dehlvi it was like any ordinary nobleman's house, not the palace of the grand Mughal.

It is now kept locked to preserve as much of it as possible, and the intricate designs on the walls are still intact and the gold decoration still dazzles.

II

SHAHJAHANABAD

*Jo hum pe guzri so guzri
magar shab-e hÿraan
Hamaare ashk teri aaqibat
sanwaar chale*

Whatever befell us, let it be
but o night of separation
At least our tears beautified
your fate.

—Faiz

Zeenat-ul Masajid

Wall and Gateways

Shahjahanabad was a walled city, a name by which it is known even today. The wall that ran around the city was built first with mud and then rubble plaster. It was approximately 9-km long, with thirteen gateways, or darwaza, and fourteen *khirki*s or wicket gates, through which one could enter the walled city. The wall, as can be seen in some of the places where it survives, had battlements. There were twenty-seven bastions.

The gateways were:

1. Dilli Darwaza
2. Rajghat Darwaza
3. Khizri Darwaza
4. Nigambodh Darwaza
5. Kelaghat Darwaza
6. Lal Darwaza
7. Kashmiri Darwaza
8. Badar Roo Darwaza
9. Kabuli Darwaza
10. Pathhar Ghati Darwaza
11. Lahori Darwaza

Delhi Darwaza

12. Ajmeri Darwaza

13. Turkman Darwaza

The wicket gates were:

1. Zeenat-ul-Masjid ki khirki

2. Nawab Ahmad Baksh Khan ki khirki

3. Nawab Ghaziuddin Khan ki khirki

4. Musamman Burj ki khirki

5. Salimgarh ki khirki

6. Nasirganj ki khirki

7. Nai (new) khirki

8. Shahganj ki khirki

9. Ajmeri Darwaze ki khirki

10. Sayyad Bholi (Bu Ali) ki khirki

11. Buland Bagh ki khirki

12. Farrashkhane ki khirki

The northern wall of the wall had Kashmiri Darwaza, which saw much action in 1857 and has been cordoned off today as a historical monument.

The western wall had Kabuli Darwaza, Lahori Darwaza, Ajmeri Darwaza and Farrashkhane ki khirki. From among these, only Ajmeri Darwaza exists near the New Delhi railway station.

The southern wall had Turkman Darwaza and Dilli Darwaza, both of which are standing strong.

The Rajghat Darwaza, Khairati Darwaza, Calcutta Darwaza and Nigambodh Darwaza were river-facing, and none remain, though Rajghat is famous as the Samadhi or memorial of Mahatma Gandhi, and Nigambodh Ghat is known for its cremation ground and crematorium.

None of the wicket gates remain. Those were all broken down when the British rearranged the city after 1857.

Nigambodh Ghat

According to legend, there are two famous remnants and reminders of Indraprastha. These are Nigambodh Ghat and Neeli Chhatri.

Nigambodh Ghat

Nigambodh Ghat was opposite Salimgarh Fort, and today has shifted with the river Yamuna along the Ring Road. It gets its name from *nigam*, which means the Vedas (Hindu religious texts), and *bodh*, which means knowledge or enlightenment. As per Hindu mythology, at the beginning of the Dwapar Yug (5,000 years ago), Lord Brahma, who had forgotten all the Vedas, came and had a bath in the River Yamuna, which rekindled his memory and the knowledge of the Vedas returned to him. Thus, this *ghat*[51] was named Nigambodh. This is the oldest burning ghat or cremation ground in Delhi, and now an electric crematorium has been built here as well.

This is also said to have been the site of a temple known as Neeli Chhatri, built by Yudhisthira, the eldest of the five Pandava brothers.

The Calcutta Darwaza of Shahjahanabad used to be here and was broken by the British to make two culverts for the railways. There are many temples and pavilions built here for prayers and cremation. All major Hindu festivals are celebrated here on the ghat.

Neeli Chhatri

This was the place where Raja Yudhisthira performed the *ashvamedha* sacrifice and did the havan. Even today, there is a havan here that is kept going constantly, with continuous chanting by priests.

When I went there and made the *chadhaava* (offerings to the gods), the priest put a tilak on my forehead and blessed me. I automatically replied, 'Inshallah!' He looked at me, surprised, then nodded and said, 'Yes.'

Neeli Chhatri lies between the Nigambodh Ghat and the Bahadur Shah Gate of Salimgarh.

There are no remains of the temple that is said to have been made by the Pandavas – the building is new, with blue tiles. The Marathas are said to have made some additions to the Neeli Chhatri, but I found nothing medieval about the structure there.

Neeli Chatri

There is a silver-cased *shivling* here, which is said to be from the ancient temple and is revered greatly.

There was a small pavilion here built by Emperor Humayun, but that too has no trace left. He used to enjoy the view of the River Yamuna from it. Emperor Jahangir had visited it on his way to Kashmir and got an impromptu verse inscribed there:

> *Ajab pur faiz jaa-e kaamrani ast*
> *Nasheman gaah-e jannat aashiyani ast*

> What a graceful and happy place,
> The seat of 'Dweller in Paradise'

Hazrat Bhure Shah ki Qabr

This tomb is near the walls of the Qila between the Dilli Darwaza and Lahori Darwaza. It is quite popular, though not much is known about the saint himself except that he belonged to the Chisti silsilah.

Hazrat Bhure Shah ki Qabr

Sunehri Masjid (near the Qila)

Khwajasara Javed Khan built this beautiful mosque in AD 1747 on orders of Nawab Qudsia Begum.

Nawab Qudsia Begum, who started life as a dancer named Udham Bai married Emperor Mohammad Shah. She was very powerful in the initial years of Emperor Mohammad Shah's reign, but later fell from grace. When her son, Ahmad Shah, succeeded to the throne in AD 1748, Nawab Qudsia Begum's stars ascended once again – leading to her and Khwajasara Javed Khan becoming the centre of power.

Khwajasara was the title given to eunuchs, who were an integral part of medieval India. They guarded the harems and were also confidantes of the emperors and women of the harem. Javed Khan was a favourite of Nawab Qudsia Begum and was put in charge of the harem and given the title of Nawab Bahadur.

The mosque is surmounted by three domes, which were originally gilt with copper plates, from which it derived its name.

The mosque has a main prayer hall and two minarets. These minarets were also gilded, but were damaged and replaced by *sang-e bassi* (salmon-coloured sandstone) by Emperor Bahadur Shah Zafar in AD 1852. The golden finials have also disappeared.

Sunehri Masjid (near the Qila)

The mosque has three double-engrailed arches, and the central arch of the mosque bears an inscription about the builder of the mosque and the date of its construction.

It has a lovely darwaza for entering it, with small niches and arches on it. From a study of paintings in the British library, one can see that they were originally level with the road. But now it is in a depression and the road is much higher. There was originally a compound wall with bastions and arches attached to the darwaza, but these too are no longer present.

When I visited it, the afternoon congregation was in full swing and there was a lovely atmosphere there.

It's an excellent specimen of the later Mughal architecture.

Before the Uprising of 1857, it was in the middle of habitation, but the British levelled these houses when they tried to create an open space around the Qila in order to control the area better.

This mosque had a well and tank for ablution on the right side in a courtyard with a fountain, as described by Sir Sayyid, but no traces of it remain.

It played an integral part in the lives of the people of Shahjahanabad. Fourth-generation resident Ashok Mathur tells me that when he was in school (Happy Hours School, Daryaganj) in the 1980s, they would stop here on their way home to feed the parrots the scraps that they had saved from their tiffins.

Sadiah Aleem, a girl who grew up in Shahjahanabad, says, 'We called it *jinn waali masjid*, and as children we were told stories that people were slapped by jinns if they dozed off while listening to the Quran during *taraweeh* (supererogatory prayers during Ramzan).'

Amit Mitra, another resident, says, 'Sadiah is right! As precocious kids in the 1960s we used to be scared of the jinns in this place. They could even report you to schoolteachers for playing hooky! And chewing gum wasn't allowed inside! But there was also a belief that when exams are near, if you go and ask a *mannat*,[52] the jinns will ensure that you perform well ... But what if they eat you up? Mindey urf Mujeeb researched and found the solution: After entering the exam hall, write 'Ram' or 'Rahim' or even your own name on your right palm with your left fingers. We tried. We failed in the history paper. We lost faith in the technique. Mindey fell from grace.'

Mass Grave of the British Killed in 1857

Though I have visited the Red Fort innumerable times, I have never gone into the parking lot. I always get off before that, so it was a pleasant discovery that there was a memorial cross marking the mass grave of the British killed in 1857. Hilal Ahmed mentioned it on Twitter, and I immediately tagged Rameen Khan, fellow heritage enthusiast, to investigate, who found it near the bus parking.

Mass grave of the murdered British in 1857

Zahir Dehlvi mentions in *Dastan-e Ghadar* that the emperor had given orders for those British and

European men, women and children massacred in front of the Naqqarkhana on 16 May 1857 to be given a proper burial, but he doesn't mention the location. Given the location of the parking lot just outside the walls, perhaps they were buried here?

The majority of those killed in 1857 are buried in the Lothian or Nicholson Cemetery near Kashmiri Gate.

The cross mentions the date in Roman Numerals (MDCCCLXI), which corresponds to AD 1861, which is probably the year when the cross was erected as a memorial.

Khas Bazar

Khas Bazar was the area between the Jama Masjid and the Qila Darwaza. It now houses the pigeon markets and wholesale cloth markets. Between Khas Bazar and Urdu Bazar was Khanum ka Bazar, which was a market for arms and weapons.

Sheikh Kaleem-ullah Jahanbadi ka Mazaar

Sheikh Kaleem-ullah Jahanbadi ka Mazaar

Inside the erstwhile Khas Bazar is an important dargah from the Mughal era.

Hazrat Shah Kaleem-ullah Jahanabadi was the grandson of Ustad Ahmed Lahori, the architect of Taj Mahal, and lived in Emperor Shah Jahan's newly founded capital, Shahjahanabad, or simply, Jahanabad. Hence, he used the title Jahanabadi, where he commanded much respect as a Sufi.

His father's name was Sheikh Nurullah Muhanddis, and it is he who did the calligraphy of the inscriptions in Jama Masjid.

His life spanned the era of Emperor Aurangzeb to Emperor Muhammad Shah and coincided with Emperor Aurangzeb' campaigning career in the Deccan. He crossed the age of eighty, during the reign of Emperor Muhammad Shah, and died on 24th Rabi-ul Awwal 1142, or 17 October 1729.

Hazrat Shah Kaleem-ullah Jahanabadi established a madrassa that attracted a large number of students from far and wide who enjoyed free boarding and lodging. Emperor Aurangzeb later ordered the construction of a *khanqah* (hospice) for him.

Emperor Muhammad Muazzam Bahadur Shah became Jahanabadi's disciple in his fourth year of reign (AH 1123/AD 1711).

Shah Kaleem-ullah followed the Chisti convention of inclusiveness and had disciples of all faiths.

After the mutiny of 1857, the British pulled down the entire quarter wherein his khanqah stood, but his grave was spared. It had remained in a state of neglect and disrepair for some decades when Khwaja Ghulam Farid, spiritual guide of the ruler of Bahawalpur, contributed a large sum for its reconstruction.

This mazaar is now behind the Kabootar Bazar (bird market) of Purani Dilli. Once upon a time it could be seen from the Jama Masjid as it was just 300 steps away from it, but that is now impossible due to dense habitation and construction.

The masjid built around his grave platform is very popular with the shopkeepers and workers of the area, and is always full at prayer times.

* * *

Daryaganj

> *How hard to read, O Soul,*
> *The riddle of life here and life beyond!*
> *As hard as in the pearl to pierce a hole*
> *Without the needle-point of diamond.*
>
> —*Princess Zeb-un-Nisa*[53]

Faiz Bazar

This was between the Dilli Darwaza of the Qila and the Akbarabadi Mosque (Subhash Park). Bashiruddin Ahmad Dehlvi has compared it to paradise. He writes that there were houses and shops on both side of the Faiz Nahr that flowed through it, with a lovely hauz in the centre, and it was a very vibrant and lively place. It was planned along with the city of Shahjahanabad and was 1,650 yards long and 30 yards wide. It extended all the way to the Qila walls. With trees that provided shade and the cooling effect of the stream, it was a piece of paradise for the residents.

Nawab Akbarabadi Mahal, wife of Emperor Shah Jahan, built this bazar along with the Akbarabadi Masjid in AD 1650. The shops stocked goods from European and Central Asian countries. Today, it is still a vibrant and popular market known as Daryaganj.

The area that was now famous as the Sunday book bazar and was near the city's Dilli Darwaza, was part of this famous bazar.

Sunehri Masjid Roshan-ud Daula

In the erstwhile Faiz Bazar, there was another Sunehri Masjid in Qazi Wada near the Phool ki Mandi, built by Nawab Roshan-ud Daula Zafar Khan, in AD 1744. He built the other Sunehri Masjid too that stands in Chandni Chowk.

Nawab Roshan-ud Daula Zafar Khan, whose actual name was Khwaja Muzaffar, was descended from a Naqshbandi saint's family. His grandfather, Khwaja Mohammad Naseer, had come to India during the reign of Emperor Shah Jahan.

In the reign of Emperor Farrukhsiyar, Roshan-ud Daula was appointed to the post of *bakshi* (superintendent) and given the title of Roshan-ud Daula Zafar Khan and a mansab of 7,000.

All the domes of this mosque were golden (copper gilt), but the copper gilt plates were taken out from here and put on the Sunehri Mosque in Chandni Chowk at some point of time before 1854, as Sir Sayyid mentions it.

Sunehri Masjid Roshan-ud Daula

I had been unable to find it, but heritage enthusiast Rameen Khan discovered it, hidden in plain sight as he says. I am indeed grateful to him for discovering many of our forgotten monuments and documenting them.

It is on a first floor on the main Daryaganj road and approached from a side door. It's distinctive feature is that it is dome-less – the copper plates from the domes having gone to replace the ones in the other Sunehri Masjid built by Nawab Roshan-ud Daula Zafar Khan on Chandni Chowk near Gurudwara Sis Ganj.

It is comparatively smaller and was obviously built more as a family or private rather than public mosque, but it is very well-maintained. All the inscriptions are intact.

Akbarabadi Masjid

In AD 1650, Aziz-un-Nisa Begum, wife of Emperor Shah Jahan, was given the title of 'Akbarabadi Mahal' after the place of her birth, and thus the masjid also became famous by that name.

It was lovingly described by Sir Sayyid Ahmad Khan in the first edition of *Asar-us Sanadid* as being a 'beautiful and heart-pleasing masjid', one that 'refreshes the eyes and rejuvenates the spirit'. He went on to write, 'In front of it, even the Masjid of the Green Dome (in Medina) looks small.'

The mosque followed the prevailing style of the era and was built with three domes, seven arches in the façade and two lofty minarets. Sir Sayyid wrote, 'In front of that there is a square 12 x 12 yards hauz, which can make the springs of the sun and moon blush.' It stood in an area earlier known as Faiz Bazar.

After its destruction in 1857, when Sir Sayyid visited the place, he was in tears to see the rubble. He allegedly said, *Sahab, angrezon ne Akbarabadi Masjid ko shaheed kar diya hai*' ('Sir, the Englishmen have martyred the Akbarabadi Masjid'). The foundation and platform of the mosque were

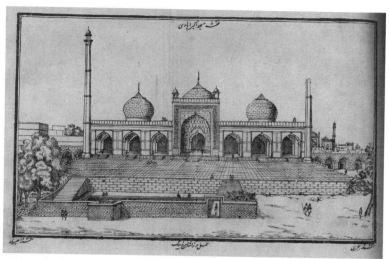

Akbarabadi Masjid from Asar-us-Sanadid (National Archives of India)

completely demolished when Edward Park was built in 1911. It is now known as Subhash Park.

In the aftermath of the Uprising of 1857 and the systematic persecution of the Muslim community, especially the elite who the British felt were mainly responsible for the 'revolt', Sir Sayyid set about thinking of ways to rehabilitate the community. One of them was to integrate them into Indian society via Western education, and thus was born the idea of the Muhammadan Anglo-Oriental College, which went on to become the Aligarh Muslim University.

Although the foundation of a *Jama Masjid* (congregational mosque) for the college's students was laid in 1877, its construction was delayed due to various reasons, being completed much after Sir Sayyid's death. It was declared open in February 1915.

Ali Nadeem Rezavi, a professor at AMU's history department, tells me that the inscriptions on the Akbarabadi Mosque, which included the *Surah Fajr*, were unique as they were done by Abdul Haq Amanat Khan, the same genius behind inscriptions on the Taj Mahal and Emperor Akbar's tomb in Sikandra.

To cite the AMU's gazette, these inscriptions were presented to Sir Sayyid for use in the Jama Masjid by Shahzada Sulaiman Jah Bahadur. The latter had bought them from a scrap dealer in Aligarh, who had the rubble of 1857 monuments brought for sale.

As Prof. Rezavi says, 'These Shahjahani calligraphic panels in black stone on white marble connect the AMU Jama Masjid with the Taj Mahal and Emperor Akbar's tomb in Sikandra. At all three places one can see the workmanship of the same master-calligrapher.'

The British demolished both the Faiz Bazar and the mosque after 1857.

In 2012, remains of a Mughal building were found in Subhash Park when the Delhi Metro Rail Corporation was digging to make way for the metro lines. Following Delhi High court orders that area has been cordoned off pending investigations into the matter.

Zeenat-ul Masajid

Princess Zeenat-un-Nisa (1643–1721), the second daughter of Emperor Aurangzeb and his wife Dilras Begum, had this mosque built. She was given the title of Padshah Begum (first lady of the empire) and was her father's companion in his old age along with his concubine, Udaipur Begum. Like her elder sister, Princess Zeb-un-Nisa, she chose to stay single as no suitable match had been found by/for her.

This was built in Daryaganj near the Khairati Ghat in AD 1707 when the Yamuna flowed here. It occupied a unique location as its two lofty minarets could be seen from the river and it was the only mosque that came close to Jama Masjid. However, now it's surrounded by buildings and has lost its uniqueness and much of its beauty too.

Zeenat-un-Nisa Begum's grave

Maulvi Zafar Hasan calls it Masjid Ghat because of its proximity to Khairati Ghat. It is possible the name got corrupted along with its connotations once the river shifted course.

As one enters the very shabby gateway, the first thing that meets the eye is the tailor shop inside the gateway. The tailor was missing when I visited, but wares of his trade were on display.

As soon as one comes up the dark staircase into the open, the majestic soaring domes and minarets of the mosque come into view, and it becomes very obvious why it was nicknamed Ghataa Masjid, as the black lines running in its dome really do resemble monsoon clouds from a distance, *ghataa* being the word for monsoon clouds. It is a functioning mosque, and there was a lone man praying in the courtyard when we went inside.

This mosque was badly treated after the British victory over Delhi in 1857, and was made into an artillery barracks for the army. For ages after that, it was a bakery, which despoiled the entire place. Many small rooms were built for residential purposes at that time and these are occupied even now by people working in or connected with the mosque, which greatly detracts from its beauty. The original design may have been different. The marble pulpit was removed. It was also used as a bakery for the troops.

Sir Sayyid's description that 'the ornamentation and carving on the mosque, the greenery all around, the waves of the river all contribute to a beautiful mood. Very few mosques have such a beautiful atmosphere and surroundings…' now seems meaningless.

It is built completely of red sandstone and has three marble domes with black stone stripes in it.

According to Sir Sayyid, 'The black stripes in the dome are meant to ward off the evil eye and the shining golden finials on the domes seem to compete with the brightness of the sun. The minarets soar so high, as if they're in conversation with the sky.'

This mosque has seven arches, with a large one in the centre and the rest smaller than that.

The mosque itself is 150 x 60 feet, and stands on a plinth of 4 feet from the courtyard. It has seven scalloped arched entrances in which are seven arched doorways facing the east. Over each doorway except the middle one are marble slabs – they are empty, but were probably meant for inscriptions.

Three huge bulbous domes with black bands surmount the top. They are topped with copper gilt pinnacles atop an inverted lotus. The domes are hollow. The front of the mosque is flanked by two tall minarets, each 100 feet high, supporting an octagonal pavilion of white marble. The inside of the mosque is two-aisle deep and there is a green flower painted on the dome. The arches inside are also scalloped and supported by red stone pillars.

There is a tank in the courtyard, which used to be fed by a well, but which is no longer functional.

The well which fed the tank, is in disuse and completely dry. The courtyard is 195 x 110 feet, with an oblong tank 43 x 33 feet in the centre.

There was a long courtyard behind the masjid adjoining its rear wall with three doors. When the British army vacated it, this courtyard was also broken.

According to Carr Stephen, at the back of the masjid there were four big burjis that have disappeared without any trace.

Zeenat-ul Masjid
From ASI Archives (Felice Beato, 1858)

There used to be a terrace near the city wall with thirteen rooms, and on the north and south of these rooms there were two arched entrances with seventeen steps in each leading up to the court of the masjid. I could only see this one entrance and I believe the other one has been closed down and next to it is now the Crescent School.

The Princess was buried in the north of the mosque in a tomb built by her in her own lifetime but demolished by the British after the Uprising in 1857. The only description we get of it is from Sir Sayyid's book where he writes, 'There used to be a small pavilion for keeping offerings and below it there are two *muhajjar*. Inside an enclosure of *sang-e bassi* [salmon-coloured stone] is another one of marble. The flooring and headstone are also of marble.'

The marble headstone bears a Quranic verse and the epitaph:

For a friend in my grave, God's forgiveness is alone sufficient
The canopy of my grave is the shadow of the cloud of God's mercy
In the hope of a righteous end.
Fathmah Zeenat-un-Nisa Begum
Daughter of Badshah Mohiuddin Mohammad Alamgeer Ghazi
May God illuminate his works
AH 1122

The tomb has been rebuilt on the southern end of the mosque in a corner, as a memorial to the princess who built this mosque, with the rest of the space being taken up by a Jamat-e Ulema office.

On our return, we met Jameel Bhai, the tailor, who was very bitter at the state of affairs regarding the mosque. There were offices and homes in the courtyard and precincts of the mosque, which very visibly upset him as he felt that the princess had been relegated to a corner. In fact, we would have returned without reciting a *fatiha* over her grave as it was tucked away behind trees had he not told us where to look for it.

III

JAMA MASJID AND ITS ENVIRONS

Subah huyi gajar baja murgh-e seher ka gul huwa
Karne lage chaman chaman murgh-e chaman navagiri
Masjid-o-khanqah se shor utha salat ka
Daer mein jaake barhaman karne lage 'Hari, Hari!'

As the day broke the alarm sounded and the rooster crowed
In every garden the birds chirped away their lovely songs
From the mosque and the monastery, sounds of the benedictions emerged
And the Brahmins went to the temple to invoke the Lord 'Hari, Hari!'

——Zahir Dehlvi

Jama Masjid
From ASI Archives

Masjid-e Jahannuma/Jama Masjid

Once Emperor Shah Jahan began living in the Qila and the settlers in Shahjahanabad grew in number, he felt the need for a congregational mosque bigger than the existing ones.

This was the *Badshahi* or the imperial mosque, built on the orders of the emperor himself. Thus, the emperor had to care for many sentiments, primarily that the mosque had to be built on a higher plinth than that of the emperor's residence and its pulpit had to be set higher than his throne. How could the Nasheman Zill-e Ilahi or the seat of the Shadow of God on earth be higher than that of the imam, who was calling the faithful to prayer!

The location chosen, thus, was a hillock called Pahari Bhojala, at a distance of 1,000 yards (0.91 km) from the Qila. The mosque was planned in such a way that it would cover the hillock in its entirety. To this day, the area of Shahjahanabad is hilly, and if one walks down the narrow alleys of the walled city, one can see huge rocks from the medieval time supporting old mansions.

On 6 October 1650, the emperor himself laid the foundation stone of the Jama Masjid, and it was built under the supervision of Sa'adullah Khan, the prime minister, and Fazil Khan, the *Khan-e Saman* or the head of the imperial household establishments. According to Carr Stephens, the mosque is a specimen of the Byzantine Arabic style.

When the foundation stone was to be laid, Emperor Shah Jahan said that it could only be laid by someone whose namaz had never been delayed and

who was present behind the imam at every prayer as soon as he said *'Allahu Akbar'* and who stood up for *tahajjud* or optional night prayers.

When he laid down these conditions, everyone bent their heads and stayed quiet in embarrassment. The emperor, on seeing this, said, *'Alhamdillah,* I fulfil all these conditions, but had not wanted to make them public. Unfortunately I have no choice but to declare it today.' After that, he laid the foundation of the mosque with his blessed hands.[54]

Six thousand workers built the Jama Masjid in six years at the cost of ₹10 lakh. The cost did not include the price of the stones that were presented by various rajas and nawabs, according to Bashiruddin Ahmad Dehlvi in *Waqiaat-e-Darul Hukumat Dehli.*

The mosque, set on a plinth of 30 feet, is 261-foot long and 90-foot wide. Its three marble domes with black stripes are a landmark, a symbol of Shahjahanabad if you will, and visible from miles around.

Thus, it was appropriately named Masjid-e Jahannuma – a mosque that commands a view of the world.

Jama Masjid has always been a symbol of faith for the Muslims of the country. It was also a focal point for the community living in Delhi. Although it is not the largest mosque in India (that distinction goes to Taj-ul Masjid in Bhopal), it is certainly one of the most majestic.

It has three huge darwazas on the east, south and north, with more than thirty steps each that lead into the mosque. The west side is, of course, the Qibla wall or the wall that is in the direction of Mecca, which the faithful must face while offering prayers.

The mosque is built of red sandstone from top to bottom, with marble used up to the dados. The red stone is interspersed with stripes of marble and inlaid with black stone. Every wall is artistically decorated with calligraphic inscriptions above the eleven arches in the Tughra script, on marble tablets written in black slate.

The inscription on the central arch is simply '*Yaa Hadi*' (one of the ninety-nine beautiful names of Allah; it means 'O Guide'), while the other inscriptions give details of the construction, besides praising the emperor.

A beautiful hauz in the centre of the huge courtyard was built for wuzu, the ablution before namaz. A small beige sandstone kiosk stands there, which was built by Mirza Salim, son of Emperor Akbar Shah II, as a *mukabbir*, a place from where someone would repeat the words 'Allahu Akbar', so that those who could not see the imam knew when to bend, bow or stand. The white marble mukabbir was built in front the central arch of the mosque in 1829.

Sundial in Jama Masjid

On three sides of the courtyard are beautiful corridors and galleries where I have often offered prayers. On all four corners of the mosque are four pavilions with attractive baradaris. During the holy month of Ramzan, the announcement to break the fast is made from one of these pavilions.

There is also a sundial in the southeast to indicate time, but it lies in a decrepit state today. Mirza Salim built this too in AD 1829. During one of my visits, I saw clothes being hung out to dry on it. A map of the world suffers an even worse fate as people sit on it to get a better view of the mosque.

The First Namaz in the Jama Masjid

Eid-ul Fitr was approaching and the masjid was nearing completion. The *mir-e imarat* (superintendent of the building) received the royal message that the Badshah wanted to recite the Eid prayers in Jama Masjid. There were tonnes of debris and building material still lying all over the place, and it seemed impossible that the masjid would be readied in time.

So, royal orders were issued: People can take whatever they needed from the materials lying around. All too soon, it had been all cleaned up!

Namaz in Jama Masjid
Photo courtesy Jayshree Shukla

On the day of Eid, a drum roll was heard in the Qila, and the emperor set off for the mosque in a royal procession, accompanied by rows of cavalrymen, led by mace bearers. The princes, dressed in finery, followed. The emperor was at the end of the procession on his beautifully caparisoned elephant. They would all enter the mosque in the same order.

The mosque was full of people and prayers were to be recited. The emperor appointed an imam (the present imam of the Bukhari family belongs to the lineage of that family), *muezzin*s and chamberlains. As described by Bashiruddin Ahmad Dehlvi.

The mosque became, and continues to be, an integral part of a Muslim's life in Delhi. Under the Mughals, the 10th of the Islamic month of Moharram, the day of the martyrdom of Imam Hussain, would be solemnly observed in the mosque as well as the Qila. Imam Hussain, the grandson of the Prophet Mohammad, was martyred in the battle of Karbala in Iraq. The battle was fought between the small, determined band of followers of Imam Hussain, the Prophet's grandson, and the mighty army of Yazeed, the ruler of Syria. Yezeed flouted almost every norm that had been preached and followed by Hussain's grandfather, the Prophet of Islam, Mohammad (PBUH).

Yazeed wanted Hussain to accept him as his spiritual leader and pledge allegiance to him. But Imam Hussain said, 'The likes of me will never pledge allegiance to the likes of Yazeed.' Even though Hussain left Medina for Kufa in Iraq to avoid confrontation, a confrontation was forced upon him by Yezid. On 10th of the Islamic month of Muharram, Hussain was martyred with every able male member of his family, including a six-month-old son, Ali Asghar. This martyrdom is observed worldwide every year by followers of Hussain on the 10th of Muharram.

Even today, processions of *taziya*s (replicas of the shrine of Imam Hussain) pass in front of the mosque. The eastern darwaza (present-day gate no. 2), which was exclusively kept for the emperor and his retinue, has thirty-five steps. In the evenings, pigeons and other birds would be sold here. This area was called Gudri ka Bazar. Even today, clothes and other household articles are sold near this darwaza. These shops are always crowded with shoppers.

The Jama Masjid area is also famous for its food stalls and restaurants. The famous eating joint 'Karim's' is in a lane opposite the southern darwaza. In fact, the Matia Mahal lane has many stalls and restaurants selling the typically Delhi *nahari* and *biryani*.

Dargah Aasar Sharif

There are some very old relics of the Prophet and Islam kept in this dargah, but access to them is restricted. It is said that they were passed on via Timur, who got them from the Byzantine Emperor Bayazid I.

It is said that a Quran Sharif written by Hazrat Ali and a Quran written by Imam Hussain is among its treasures.

According to Bashiruddin Ahmad Dehlvi, under the Mughals, there would be *nazar* and *niyaz* of Chief of Martyrs Imam Hussain, on the 10th of Moharram.

Dargah Asar Sharif

Masjid after 1857
From ASI Archives (Felice Beato, 1858)

When this mosque was built, Emperor Shah Jahan wanted to appoint a suitably pious and noble imam for the grand mosque. In those days, the name of Syed Abdul Ghafoor Shah was very famous in Bukhara. The emperor invited Shah Bukhara to Delhi with great respect in AH 1065, and in AH 1066 (AD 1655) appointed him as the *Syed-ul Masjid* or imam of Jama Masjid, Shahjahanabad. The imam would also officiate at the coronation ceremonies of the Mughal emperors. The Mughals also awarded him *jagir*s for his upkeep. This post has now become hereditary.

Jama Masjid after 1857

The mosque was a focal point for gatherings during the siege of Delhi in the 1857 Uprising. It was on the walls of Jama Masjid that posters were put up by the forces (British and local British sympathizers) that were trying to create communal differences among India's people. These were immediately taken down on the orders of Mughal Emperor Bahadur Shah Zafar. These posters called upon Muslims to wage a *jihad* or holy war against the Hindus, for as per the Sharia the Christians were their friends as *ahl-e kitab*, or people of the book (followers of divinely revealed books). The advertisement also said that no pig fat was used in the cartridge, implying that cow's fat had been used.

Heena Yunus Ansari has written her dissertation for M.Phil on *Dehli Urdu Akhbar*. She writes that Maulvi Muhammad Baqir countered these posters in his newspaper, the *Dehli Urdu Akhbar*, in which he said that Hindus and Muslims were *ahl-e watan* (compatriots) and had been living together for a thousand years.[55] Regarding the issue of cow's fat used in the cartridges she quotes the newspaper, 'The British officers say that the rifles were filled with the fat of cows and not of pigs. If that is so it will hurt the Hindus and if today Hindus are suffering, tomorrow it will be our turn.'

Since the mosque had been such a symbol of togetherness and rebellion against British power in 1857, after the Uprising, the British occupied it and stopped people from offering prayers within its premises. Its gateways were guarded by British Indian troops to prevent entry. It was used as a mess, and horses were tied along its corridors, with alcohol being freely consumed by the troops inside.

As Sadia Aziz writes in her paper, 'Mosque, Memory and State: A Case Study of Jama Masjid (India) and the Colonial State c. 1857', the Muslim population was specifically targeted as the British perceived the Uprising of 1857 as a 'Muslim conspiracy' against them.[56]

Consequently, numerous mosques in the city of Delhi were demolished, leaving no trace of their existence. Various options were discussed in higher official circles as far as the fate of the Jama Masjid was concerned. Plans ranging from its demolition to converting it into a church or a more 'secular' college floated in the bureaucracy. But finally, the plan to convert it into a barracks was passed. It was used to house the British Indian soldiers who had participated in the Siege of Delhi and were unable to maintain the sanctity of the mosque as a place of worship.

After five years, on 28 November 1862, following innumerable petitions by Muslims, the government returned the mosque to the Muslims. A committee was formed for its administration, with ten Muslims on it. The British put down many conditions, including that they could enter with their dogs and would not take off their shoes.

This was a cause of much anguish among the Muslims. It was later decided that no dogs would be allowed inside the premises, and the British would take off their hats but not their shoes, as was the custom in churches.

After many years and further petitions, new rules were framed, ensuring that no one could enter the edifice wearing footwear (if at all, they would have to wear covers over them), no dogs would be allowed inside, and intoxicants such as liquor – prohibited in Islam – would not be carried into the premises.

A mosque whose grand gateways were once the lifeblood of the city – with *dastango*s (oral storytellers) reciting stories on its steps and sellers showcasing their unique wares – have now deteriorated to host the hawking of cheap material and beggars.

The Emir of Afghanistan, Habibullah Khan, had presented a silver chandelier (costing ₹50,000 then) to the mosque when he visited Delhi in 1907. This used to hang in the central hall of the Jama Masjid. According to Bashiruddin Ahmad Dehlvi, despite security, it was stolen and no one could trace it later. According to Sadia Aziz,[57] who accessed the police report for her thesis, it was stolen in 1910 and was never recovered, though rumours to that effect were spread. All that was recovered was a green cloth in which it was supposed to have been wrapped.

Today a beautiful chandelier hangs in the main hall, perhaps a gift from some other grandee.

Jama Masjid's interiors are still grand, and every day the mosque sees thousands of visitors who gather to pray or just admire its beauty. Though it's still as majestic, every time I go there, I wish it could be restored to its former glory.

Hare Bhare Shah aur Sufi Sarmad ka Mazaar

Hare Bhare Shah aur Sufi Sarmad ka Mazaar

> Who can determine
> The cost of dying in love?
> Every such martyrdom
> Is an obligation on me.
> For it is I who should have died
> Not he.

> —Sarmad[58]

To the right of the eastern gateway of Jama Masjid is an often-missed dargah. This belongs to a man who long ago came to buy goods in India but instead got 'sold' in the bazar of love.

That was Muhammad Sa'id Sarmad Kashani. He was born as an Armenian Jew in the Iranian city of Kashan in Isfahan province around 1590. He later converted to Islam, the details of which are hazy, and adopted this name. He came to Thatta in Sindh in 1634 to trade Iranian goods for famed Indian rubies, emeralds and spices. Instead, a divine glance from a young boy named Abhai Chand changed his destiny.

In Sufism, *ishq-e majazi* (pure love for God's creation) is often the way to *ishq-e haqeeqi* (love for the divine). This is exactly what happened in Sarmad's case. He said:

I am sold in the market of love
 I know not my buyer, nor my price
 —Translated by Maulana Abul Kalam Azad[59]

Initially, Abhai Chand's parents were against their son meeting Sarmad. The earliest written account of the relationship between Sarmad and Chand is in the 1660 work *Dabistan*, written by Mubad Shah and translated by David Shea.[60] Shah writes about the meeting:

Abandoning all other things, like a *sanyasi*, naked as he came from his mother, he sat down before the door of his beloved. The father of the object of his love, after having found by investigation the purity of the attachment manifested for his son, admitted Sarmad into his house, and Abhai Chand became Sarmad's student, studying Jewish religion and the Hebrew and Persian languages well enough to translate sections of the Hebrew Bible into Persian.

Sarmad then gave up all worldly attachments. He stopped wearing clothes and roamed around naked in a state of divine intoxication. He was not in control of his senses – a state known as *mazjub*. He went to Lahore from Thatta and appeared in Delhi some years later. He became the spiritual teacher of Prince Dara Shukoh, the favourite son of Mughal Emperor Shah Jahan. Prince Dara Shukoh, himself a mystic, found a worthy preceptor in Sarmad and admitted him in his circle of saints and Sufis.

The *Rubaiyat-e Sarmad* (Quatrains of Sarmad) is a source of knowledge and delight. Several people translated it, but one of the most famous translations is by Maulana Azad, who compared himself to Sarmad for his freedom of thought and expression. Azad later wrote an essay on the great Persian mystic. Historians have traced in this essay the growth of Azad's own religious thought and political life.

When Prince Dara Shukoh lost the war of succession, he was executed by his brother, Emperor Aurangzeb, who had become the next Mughal emperor. Sarmad's disapproval of Emperor Aurangzeb and constant praise of Prince Dara Shukoh was a thorn in the emperor's flesh. Emperor Aurangzeb asked his *qazi* (Islamic judge), Mullah Abdul Qavi, to find charges against Sarmad. His nudity became the charge, but it was not serious enough to warrant severe punishment. Other ulema were then called and charges of blasphemy were framed against him, one of them being that Sarmad did not go beyond the first few words of the Islamic creed (kalima). He only said, *'La-ilaha'* ('there is no God'), and did not complete it by adding *'illa'llah'* ('except Allah').

When he was asked to complete it, Sarmad is said to have replied, 'Presently, I am drowned in negation; I have not yet reached the (spiritual) station of affirmation. If I read the full kalima in this state, I will be telling a lie.' Sarmad refused to retract his words and was taken to the Jama Masjid to be executed. A crowd gathered to watch the execution. According to legend, his decapitated head started reciting the full kalima (*La-ilaha illa'llah* – there is no god but Allah), showing that in death he achieved his affirmation of faith.[61]

He was buried there in a simple grave next to his spiritual master, Syed Abul Qasim Hare Bhare Shah. Not much is known about Hare Bhare Shah, but it is commonly believed that he was the pir of Sufi Sarmad and had come from Subzwar to Delhi in AD 1654–55. Today, the portion with Sarmad's grave is painted a bright red as testimony to the fact that he was a martyr of love, and Hare Bhare Shah's side is painted green. A neem tree divides the two shrines. The contrast between the two colours is probably a mute testimony to their lives too. One lived a full and prosperous life as the name Hare Bhare suggests, while the other's life was cut short.

The headstone of Sarmad's grave has a Persian inscription, which reads:

God is great
When Shah Sarmad in the reign of Alamgir set out on a journey
to paradise
Poor Akbar said the date, 'this is the grave of Sarmad, the martyr'.[62]

One is left to meditate, supplicate or just investigate in peace.

As you enter the mazaar, you find a small well to the right of the graves, with the leather *dol* (waterwheel with a leather bucket) still intact, waiting for water to be drawn.

The entrance to the mazaar is either through the main gate where the two boards are displayed opposite the mazaar, or via a slippery passage which leads inside from a chai shop on the right side (if you are facing it with your back to the Jama Masjid).

Chah Rahat/Rahat ka Kuan/Well with the Persian Wheel

Chah Rahat

The River Yamuna, which is now quite far from Shahjahanabad or Old Delhi, used to flow approximately where MG Road runs now, so it could not have been used for supplying water to the Jama Masjid. Water was supplied to its ablution pool by a well situated at a short distance from the mosque. Water was pumped from the well into a Persian wheel. The wall still bears an inscription describing its purpose. There is an old wooden doorway behind which the well is locked. I entered the place where the wheel is situated. The old iron machinery is visible in the room next to the well, which has been converted into a small workshop by some residents. The entrance to the well from inside is dirty, dark and clogged with filth and waste. I did try to go in, but the rats, darkness and rubbish made me think it was prudent not to venture further.

The area is called Chaah Rahat or Well of the Persian Wheel even today, though the *chaah* (well) itself is choked and locked.

Paiwalo'n ka Bazar

This is now a rundown, congested area, but was once the area where beautiful bedsteads were sold. It was a thriving market for trousseau shopping with its intricate, carved beds, canopies, settees and various other items associated with bedroom furniture.

Iskon Temple

I read about the Radha-Krishna Temple with a beautiful black statue of Shri Krishna in Chippiwala in Maulvi Zafar Hasan's book. It used to be known as the Jhajjarwala Temple as the Brahmins of Jhajjar built it.

Despite many trips, I could only find one old temple in Vakil Pura. But this didn't have any black statue. After much interrogation with the local residents, I discovered that the new ISKCON temple was actually the medieval Radha-Krishna Temple that has Radha's statue in white marble and Krishna's in black marble.

The founder of ISKCON, Swami Prabhupada, used to live in a room on the first floor of this temple. It is from here that he went to the USA and later founded ISKCON, the International Society for Krishna Consciousness. It is now under their management and is a very beautiful sacred space, with

many devotees sitting in prayer, telling rosaries. The idols are very attractively decorated. I had reached early when their *shringar* (decking up the idols as if dressing the gods themselves) was being done, and the moment it was complete, lights came on, the curtains opened and the devotees prostrated themselves. It was a very spiritual moment.

The Radha-Krishna Temple in Vakil Pura with its brightly painted façade and door is equally attractive. It has a black marble Shani Dev image, and a white marble image of Radha-Krishna.

Shahjahani Masjid near Pataudi House

When Emperor Shah Jahan first came to Delhi and stayed in Kalan Mahal, he had a mosque built for his soldiers. This mosque thus has the distinction of being the first Shahjahani mosque in Shahjahanabad.

It's in a busy lane but once we entered it was serene and peaceful. It is a very attractive masjid with three engrailed arches and is in good shape. It is also well-maintained. Earlier a madrassa in the name of Mirza Bulaqi used to function here.

Shahjahani Masjid near Pataudi House

After the Uprising of 1857, the Nawab of Pataudi bought some land around it and built his kothi here so this mosque became famous as Pataudi Masjid.

The Pataudi Kothi was bought by Rai Bahadur Sultan Singh, a rich businessman of the nineteenth century,[63] and presently there is a maze of flats and apartments in that area. A school runs on the premises of the Kothi.

IV

MATIA MAHAL AND ITS ENVIRONS

Deeda-e giryaan hamaara nahr hai
Dil kharaaba jaise Dilli shehr hai

My tearful eyes are no less than a lake
And this ruined heart reminds me of Delhi.

—Mir Taqi Mir

Syed Rafa-e Saheb ki Masjid

Matia Mahal

This is the area opposite gate no. 1 of Jama Masjid. This name is derived from a mahal of the same name that existed when Shahjahanabad was being built, but is no more.

Behind the lanes that house the famous Karim's restaurant is a gateway, or *phatak*, whose deorhi (porch) now gives way to innumerable small houses, built probably in the last century after the Partition. This is said to be the location of Matia Mahal. There are some glimpses of red sandstone slabs in the gateway, but whether they date back to Emperor Shah Jahan's reign or were restorations in the later Mughal era is unclear, as they now lie hidden under cement.

It is said that it was built as a temporary residence for Emperor Shah Jahan who would come to inspect the construction of the Qila. It was later given to Nawab Azizabadi Begum, the wife of one of the Mughal princes. There are no signs of the original mahal, which has been built over, but the name remains.

It was a locality with huge havelis of Mughal nobles. After the Uprising of 1857, when the nobles of Shahjahanabad fled from British wrath, these havelis were sold off by the British. Whatever little remained of them was destroyed during the Partition riots of 1947 with the migration of Muslims and an influx of refugees. There exists a gateway behind which are many flats and apartments, but to my untrained eye it did not seem to be from the seventeenth century.

Matia Mahal

Today, the beginning of this area is full of food joints, including Karim's.

Syed Rafa-e Sahib ki Masjid

This mosque is on the right side of the road, which leads from Matia Mahal to Chitli Qabr. It is a medieval mosque, which has been completely renovated and has a brand new, tiled look. Syed Rafa-e Sahib didn't build it, but since he lived in it and repaired it in the later Mughal era, it got named after him. He died in 1817–18.

Sir Sayyid Ahmad Khan describes Syed Rafa-e Sahib as a very pious and devout man. A specialty of the gatherings in this mosque used to be a special assembly where the attendees, who were his disciples (women weren't allowed), would go into a state of ecstasy and forgetfulness (of the world). They would recite the kalima and stab each other with knives. No one was hurt, and in case they were, Syed Sahib would apply his spit to the wound and the injured would be immediately healed.

Today this is a busy masjid and there is a famous kabab-seller, Babu Bhai, who sells seekh kabab and tikka in a small alcove in the middle of the masjid walls. During the Ramzan, he serves an unprecedented number of customers, and I have often stood in line with them.

The stall next to his sells fried fish. Mohammad Farid, the owner, says that he is the second generation to sit in the shop. He tells me that there has been a lot of change from the time his father used to sit there. When I asked him to explain, he said, 'In those days there was a lot of *mohabbat* (love and affection), while today hatred has increased.' He went on to analyse it and said that it is because earlier, people were at peace with themselves, whereas today everyone is busy chasing money. 'Today there is money, but no peace of mind. Earlier, if one man earned he could feed a family of ten, and today, even with all ten members earning, it's never enough.'

Despite all this, Farid said he wouldn't exchange his country for any other. He strongly feels that there is no other country in the world with this kind of love and affection amongst various communities and people.

Chitli Qabr

This area is famous as Chitli Qabr because it houses the grave of a saint, Syed Roshan Sahib Shaheed, who was buried here in the fourteenth century. It is called Chitli because it had a mosaic design of different-coloured tiles – the word *chitli* means spotted or speckled.

The door of the mazaar itself is kept closed, but one can push it open and go inside. There's a small grave that is covered with a green cloth and has some flowers on it. The flower vendor who sits outside looks after it. Today this area is famous for its eateries, especially Pahalwan ki Biryani.

The bazar divides into two branches here, with one going towards Dilli Darwaza and the other towards Turkman Darwaza.

Suiwala'n

This area was originally called *Suzangaran* (*suzangar*s are needle-makers).

Syed Roshan Shah's dargah

Abu Sufiyan, who is a fifth-generation Shahjahanabadi, lives here with his family and tells me that it was an area where skilled embroiderers lived. They were experts in the crafts of *zardozi* and other embroidery prevalent in the Mughal era.

Abu Sufiyan has been a great help to me while I was researching for this book, and over the past few years, I have spent a lot of time with him exploring the lanes of Shahjahanabad.

He tells me that when he was growing up he never liked the place, and when he got admission to an engineering college in Chandigarh, he grabbed the opportunity to escape. It was only when he went there that he started missing home. One day, his mother called him and, in a typical Shahjahanabad *'Begumati zabaan'*, started scolding him. This was an idiomatic language spoken by the ladies who drew parallels in life from day-to-day domestic things. A typical sentence that was used by his grandmother whenever he would be on the roof around dusk would be, *'Kambakht, mare, neeche utar aa! Donon waqt mil rahe hain, balaayen utar rahi hain!'* ('O you unfortunate one, come down. Dusk is approaching and all kinds of evil spirits would be descending right now!'). That day he recorded her and started a Facebook page called 'Purani Dilli Walon ki Baaten'. He posted conversations using a feminine pseudonym.

That became very popular, and Sadia Syed joined him too. She posts under the pseudonym Winki Phuppo.

Shahjahanabad was home to two dialects. One was *Begumati Zabaan*, used by the ladies, and the other was *Karkhandhari Zabaan*, used in the streets. While Begumati Zabaan is a very idiomatic dialect with words and phrases picked up from daily domestic life, the latter was actually a way of pronunciation where words became softened, such as *unne* instead of *unhone* (that person), *kar riya hai* instead of *kar raha hai* (he/she's doing it).

Today, Sufiyan is not only back in Delhi but also says that he can't imagine leaving the city ever. He has quit his job in an MNC, and is devoted to his beloved city.

He is committed to reviving the memory of the walled city through curated tours. He says he started this to counter the negative approach that many tour operators adopted towards Old Delhi, making it sound like a den of pickpockets and thieves, a city of potholes, with only its food to recommend itself to outsiders.

Currently he is working on creating virtual tours and preserving them digitally through virtual reality/augmented reality. He wants to recreate the days of glory of that city so that an outsider can get into the skin of the city and love it for what it used to be.

His Facebook page is extremely popular, and he is using it to not only perpetuate the languages and heritage of Purani Dilli, but also to bring about some reforms. He has used humour to correct social evils such as the ill-treatment of daughters-in-law, and discrimination against girls.

As he says, this is not only a city of monuments and food, but also a living city with flesh-and-blood people, and he can see a palpable change in the attitude of outsiders.

Tiraha Behram Khan

This was so called because it was the confluence of three roads. One of them came from Dai ki Masjid, one went up to Jama Masjid, and the third went to Faiz Bazar (Dilli Darwaza).

Tiraha Behram Khan

The flower market or *Phoolon ki Mandi* was located here. Today some flower-sellers stand under the huge tree that demarcates the *tiraha* (three roads).

Further, I am describing the important landmarks on the two roads that lead to Dilli Darwaza and Turkman Darwaza.

Bangash ka Kamra

The road that goes from Chitli Qabr to Dilli Darwaza is still known by this name, and has shops selling readymade garments, etc.

This got its name from a beautiful and lofty apartment built by Nawab Faizullah Khan Bangash.[64] Now there's no trace of it.

Dai ki Masjid

The famous Dai ki Masjid is on the road that leads from Tiraha Behram Khan towards Dilli Darwaza. It was built in 1653. It is now famous as the masjid near the Pipal tree. A small doorway leads to a fairly big courtyard and a single-aisle mosque. An inscription on the façade of the masjid reads:

> Thanks be to God that this mosque, through its glory, became a place of adoration to the saintly persons.
>
> Wisdom said the year of its foundation, 'Another Kaba has been populated'.
>
> The year 1064 (AH).

When I went in, a group of young boys were learning Urdu, and I had an interesting time interacting with them and their teachers. One boy sang a *naat*, or poem in praise of the Prophet, for me.

I climbed up to the top to see its single dome, which has been painted a bright green. The shape of the dome is very interesting as it is not bulbous like the other domes in the area.

Dai ki Masjid

Prachin Jain Mandir

Prachin Jain Mandir

As we walk towards Dilli Darwaza in Daryaganj, we come to the Prachin Jain Mandir. This is an extremely popular mandir and belongs to the Shri Digambar Jain sect. I have always seen it crowded with devotees. Lala Ishwaridas, a treasurer in the reign of Emperor Akbar Shah II, built it. Maulvi Zafar Hasan writes that the date on the oldest image in the temple is 1830, so it must have been built around that time.

There are images of all twenty-four *Tirthankar*s within its walls. As one enters the main hall, there are three images. The black image is of Tirthankar Neminatha, and the others are of Tirthankar Adinatha and Saptrishi.

A room to the right of the main hall has a gorgeous painted ceiling. The interiors of the temple are profusely painted in gold and the outside walls and arches of the rooms have creeper and flower designs in pastel colours.

The roof is very interesting as it houses a series of domes. These domes with their inverted lotuses and finials are of the same design as found in the mosques all over the city.

Pahari Imli Mohalla

Kya zamaana thha wo jo guzra Mir
Humdigar log chaah karte thhe

Ah! How wonderful were those days bygone!
People were in love, each with the other.

—Mir Taqi Mir

As one walks down from Jama Masjid to the Chitli Qabar area, the road turns to the left, and this area is called Pahari Imli – after a tamarind tree that grew on this hillock, though it's no longer there. Like most trees, it fell to urbanization and one can only be nostalgic for the days when trees grew in the houses' courtyards and were a focal point for the family. There are no palatial houses, no courtyards and no trees any more: only memories remain.

Fortunately, a group of dedicated men and women have had different ideas, for some time. This group of crusaders from Shahjahanabad – today's Old Delhi – call themselves the Delhi Youth Welfare Association (DYWA),[65] and owe their coming together to the riots that happened in the old city thirty years ago (1989), when strict curfew was imposed and a large chunk of the population had to do without food, medicines and even milk for babies for three days.

When the curfew was relaxed on the fourth day, Muhammed Naeem, a resident of Old Delhi, and a few friends set out to find provisions for those who needed them most. DYWA was born, and Naeem became the president of the NGO. For years, the men met in two tiny rooms in Pahari Imli, a little way

Shah Waliullah Library

off from Jama Masjid. Unfortunately, builders have cut down the tree, levelled the hill and made flats there.

Anyway, Naeem and friends, who would spend their time playing cards and carrom before the riots, now decided to put their time and resources to better use. In the beginning, they gave stipends to a few widows to learn some skills. They arranged for free medical aid so they could see a doctor. But soon enough, the DYWA was expanding its activities to education and career planning. They realized that Old Delhi had fallen way behind the rest of the city ever since Partition, and especially in the field of education.

In March 1994, Naeem and his friends opened a library – the most unique and beautiful space in the entire city. Another founder member, Sikandar Mirza Changezi, brought some books from his own collection. Naeem, an ex-cricketer, donated books on sports. Very soon, people started donating entire collections from their homes. The young men started scouring bookshops in and around the old city. The Hazrat Shah Waliullah Library was born.

Today the library has as many as 25,000 books in Arabic, Persian, Hindi, Urdu and English. In the space of one tiny room are original works of Ghalib, Emperor Bahadur Shah Zafar, Zauq, Momin, Sir Sayyid Ahmad Khan, an Urdu translation of the Bhagwad Gita, a 700-year-old Arabic book on logic and medieval Sufi treatises, along with more contemporary books. Since all their books don't fit in there, they have kept some books in someone's house. As Naeem says, 'We have so much, by God's grace – now all we want is space.'

The library makes the evenings of this crowded area, with no parks, clubs or places to hang out, very pleasant. Friends gather here to read, play carrom and board games, or simply to share their joys or just unburden their problems to a sympathetic ear.

Education remains their priority. The NGO distributes around 500 sets of textbooks to students every year, of which 70 per cent belong to Shahjahanabad and 30 per cent to students who live across the Yamuna. The education of fifteen meritorious students is fully funded by them.

By day, Naeem and friends work to earn an honest living; by evening, they are found in the Shah Wali-ullah library, helping students fill up scholarship forms under various government schemes, schools and colleges. Last year, 150 children got scholarships as a result of their efforts.

Pahari Imli Mosque

There is a small mosque in Pahari Imli, and, like many of the late Mughal mosques in the area, has been renovated. This one has a brightly painted door with floral designs, and stands at the corner of the road.

Haveli of Mir Panjakash

The haveli of Mir Panjakash, the famous calligrapher who was also the *ustad* or master of Emperor Bahadur Shah Zafar, is the only mansion on this steep slope. His name was Syed Mohammad Amir, and according to Sir Sayyid Ahmad Khan, 'he had no comparison in *khat-e nastaliq* and can be said to have revived this style. Each letter that he inscribes is a testimony to his skill.' He was also an accomplished arm-wrestler, hence the title Mir Panjakash.

His haveli is quite extensive, stretching all the way up on the hillock. Today it has been divided into small workshops, an MCD (Municipal Corporation of Delhi) school and some private residences. Mir Panjakash was executed by the British, immediately after the fall of Delhi in September 1857, and is buried inside his house. Though it's impossible to get inside, as

Grave of Mir Panjakash

the workshop owners and workers don't like strange visitors, especially ones inquiring after old days, Sufiyan and I managed to go inside, once when the tenant was present, with his permission. In a room lying towards the northern part of the haveli is a grave painted bright green. The room itself is dark, but Sufiyan and I shone our mobile torches on it and were able to photograph it, the words on the tomb were faded, but we managed to read them. The translation reads:

> This is the grave of one preoccupied with oppressions of the soul,
> Syed Muhammad Amir Rizvi, Master of the Age,
> May God forgive him.

Ek Burji Masjid

Just a little way after the haveli on the slope is a mosque and a dargah. The mosque is famous as Ek Burji Masjid, or one-domed mosque. This name is derived from the dargah of Shah Mohammad Ali Waiz, in whose compound the masjid is located.

Ek Burji Masjid

Dargah of Shah Mohammad Ali Waiz

Shah Mohammad Ali Waiz (d. 1718) was the ustad of Emperor Alamgir II. He came from Gujarat and lived in the Jama Masjid, where he taught and preached.

There are two other graves here – one belonging to his brother Asadullah and another probably of a disciple or a family member.

Sikander Mirza Changezi

Sikander Changezi Sahib is a direct descendant of Chengiz Khan (twenty-fourth in the line of descent) and lives just beyond this dargah in his ancestral haveli. He has a genealogical tree that traces his family's roots from Chengiz Khan to his father.

He was born in 1956 and has seen the city change. His story is very important and interesting. His ancestors were in Mughal service, and when Emperor Shah Jahan shifted the capital from Agra to Shahjahanabad, they came with him.

As someone whose family has been in Delhi for over three-and-a-half centuries, his love for it is unequalled. He recites a verse to me, which he says his father who would quote often:

Dekho nigah-e naaz se yeh Dilli ke nazaare
Yeh tehzeeb ki jannat hai Jamuna ke kinaare

Look carefully with an indulgent eye at the sights of Delhi
This is a paradise of civilization on the banks of River Yamuna.

His great great grandfather, Mirza Shah Beg Changezi, was the Deputy Collector of Hissar (Haryana) in 1857, when he heeded the call of Emperor Bahadur Shah Zafar I. He handed over the charge of the *kacheri* (courthouse) and all its treasures to the Indian sepoys fighting the East India Company. He was hanged, and his considerable property was confiscated by the British government for his role in the Uprising of 1857. The papers relating to the case against him are kept in the National Archives of India, New Delhi.

I was fortunate enough to meet Sikander Changezi's father, Mirza Naseem Changezi (1910–2018), during the course of my research for this book, and hear his story of how he helped Shaheed Bhagat Singh when he was on the run and hiding in Old Delhi.

Mirza Naseem Beg Changezi had joined the Congress in 1925. In 1928, Bhagat Singh and Rajguru fatally shot an English officer, John Saunders, in Lahore. They had mistaken him for James Scott, who had ordered a lathi charge against Lala Lajpat Rai, which resulted in Lala Lajpat Rai's death. After this incident, Bhagat Singh was on the run for many months, assuming pseudonyms. In the course of this time, he came to Delhi. Mirza Sikander Beg Changezi tells me that Jugal Kishore Khanna and Asif Ali, who were helping Bhagat Singh in hiding, asked the nineteen-year-old Mirza Naseem Changezi to help a man coming from Punjab and to house and feed him. According to him that man was Bhagat Singh, and Changezi hid him in his friend Mr Daya Ram's haveli in Koocha Dakni Beg. Naseem Changezi helped him for the duration he was hiding in Delhi and fortunately was never caught. Bhagat Singh was caught for throwing a bomb in the Central Legislative Assembly in Delhi in April 1929 and sentenced to death and hanged in 1931. Though this story finds no mention in official records, Prof Chaman Lal (honorary Advisor Bhagat Singh Archives and Research Centre) says that though there is an element of exaggeration and the entire narration may not be correct, there could be a bit of truth in Naseem Changezi meeting Bhagat Singh. Prof. Lal met and interrogated Naseem Changezi on this episode a few years ago.

Sikander Mirza Changezi recounts an interesting anecdote, which I had heard from his father too: Bhagat Singh would come and sit at a *pyau* (water stall) in Daryaganj Sabzi Mandi, wearing a *janeo*, and offer water to all passers-by in the evening. Obviously, the most visible place is the best to hide in!

At the time of Partition, Mirza Afrasaib Beg Changezi, Sikander Changezi's grandfather, was asked to migrate to Pakistan. Sikander Sahib tells me that his grandfather retorted that his ancestors had given their lives in India's war of Independence and he could never leave it. However, if they still insisted, they would have to meet a few of his conditions: Did the Jamuna (colloquial name for River Yamuna) flow in Karachi? Only if Karachi had the Taj Mahal, Qutub Minar, Jama Masjid and Lal Qila would he be willing to go there. Otherwise he was happy in the land of his birth where his ancestors were buried.

Sikander Mirza Changezi has many interesting stories about the city. He recalls the River Yamuna flowing behind the Red Fort and tells me about his childhood trips to eat *kakdi* (Armenian cucumber), a summer delicacy. He reminisces about the *falsa, bael, khus* and other fruit sherbets of his childhood and says now only aerated drinks are served. There used to be a famous kulfi-wala called Mohammad Kulfiwala who had a stall near the gate no. 2 of Jama Masjid, and they would sit on the steps and enjoy his kulfi.

He remembers the time when *tonga*s (horse-driven carriages) plied the roads of Shahjahanabad, and the whole family would go to Bara Hindu Rao on the Ridge, where his maternal grandmother lived. In monsoons, the entire family would shift to Mehrauli for a few weeks and enjoy the rains and mangoes there. Swings would be put up in the Andheria Bagh near the Hauz-e Shamsi (the hauz still exists, but the bagh does not), and they would enjoy fried savouries and sing songs of monsoons.

In summers, he would go with his friends to the baoli of Hazrat Nizamuddin Auliya to learn swimming and diving.

On Sundays, there would be various kinds of *tamasha*s (spectacles) in the Urdu Park in Meena Bazar, beyond gate no. 2 of Jama Masjid. These included cockfights, quail and pheasant fights, ram fights, and *pehelwan*s (bodybuilders) would show their prowess in wrestling bouts. Concerns about animal safety have thankfully put an end to the former, and since mechanical and motor spare parts shops have taken over the Meena Bazar, there are no wrestling matches held there any more.

Like his father, grandfather and great grandfather, Changezi Sahib studied in the Anglo-Arabic School and Delhi College, one of the oldest north Indian educational institutions.

The Shahjahanabad he grew up in had the families living in their havelis who, like his, had rejected the two-nation theory. Today, except for a handful of families, most have shifted out, and the walled city is a maze of godowns and warehouses. He attributes the sad state of civic amenities to the fact that while the population has grown hundredfold, the amenities have remained the same and the walled city is unable to cope.

'I wish I could go back in time to the era when *saqqas* (water-carriers) came twice a day to fill the *ghadas* and *surahis* (*earthen pots for keeping water cool*) and brought news with them of the neighbourhood. Today we wake up to running water and Twitter news, and I don't think we are happier for it.'

V

TURKMAN DARWAZA
AND ITS ENVIRONS

Time has transfigured
them into
Untruth. The stone fidelity
They hardly meant has come
to be
Their final blazon, and to
prove
Our almost-instinct almost
true:
What will survive of us is love.

—Philip Larkin

Towards Turkman Darwaza
Photo courtesy Jayshree Shukla

Shah Ghulam Ali ki Khanqah

On the way to Turkman Gate from Chitli Qabr lies a very important khanqah. It is famous as Shah Ghulam Ali ki Khanqah. It houses the shrines of four very important saints of the Naqshbandi silsila. These are as below.

Shah Ghulam Ali ki Khanqah

1. Hazrat Shamsuddin Habibullah Mirza Mazhar Jan-e Jana'n (AD 1700 – AD 1781)

Mazhar Jan-e Jana'n, as he is popularly known even today, was a very famous Islamic scholar and spiritual master. Mazhar was his pen name for writing Persian poetry.

2. Hazrat Shah Ghulam Ali Abdullah Dehlavi (AD 1743 – AD 1824)

One of Mazhar Jan-e Jana'n's most famous successors or *khalifa*, he was also a very respected Islamic scholar. He bought some more portions so as to enlarge this Khanqah. He constructed a mosque on the north western side of the premises, which was known as 'Masjid Hazrat Shah Ghulam Ali'. He stayed here for the next forty-five years, until his death, and was laid to rest beside his spiritual master, Mirza Mazhar Jan-e Jana'n. During this period, a large number of devotees from all over the world thronged the khanqah to receive blessings and spiritual enlightenment from him. Consequently, this place gained popularity as 'Khanqah Shah Ghulam Ali'.

3. Hazrat Zaki-ul-Qadr Shah Abu Sa'eed Farooqi Mujaddedi (AD 1782/ AH 1196 – AD 1835/AH 1250)

Shah Abu Sa'eed was appointed khalifa (successor), and given charge of the khanqah by his spiritual mentor, Shah Ghulam Ali, before the latter's demise. Shah Abu Sa'eed was also a renowned Islamic scholar and served the Naqshbandi Mujaddedi order for around ten years from this khanqah. Before proceeding for Hajj, Shah Abu Sa'eed handed over the charge of the khanqah to his son and successor, Shah Ahmed Sa'eed. He died on his return journey to Delhi from Mecca in Tonk (Rajasthan). He was laid to rest nearby his spiritual master, Shah Ghulam Ali.

4. Hazrat Shah Ahmed Sa'eed Farooqi Mujaddedi (AD 1802/AD 1217 – AD 1860/AD 1277)

He succeeded his father Shah Ghulam Ali and served the khanqah for twenty-four years. He stayed in the khanqah with his family and two brothers, Hazrat Shah Abdul Ghani Muhaddis Mujaddedi and Shah Abdul Mughni Mujaddedi.

During the revolution of 1857, Shah Ahmed Sa'eed and his family, along with his brothers, was forced to leave India; hence they migrated to Medina in Saudi Arabia. Before leaving, he handed over the khanqah to his khalifa, Haji Dost Mohammad Qandhaari.

Dargah of Hazrat Shah Turkman Shamsul Arifeen Bayabani, famous as Shah Turkman

When one comes to Turkman Darwaza, there's a small dargah adjacent to the Chandni Mahal Police Chowki. It is known as the dargah of Shah Turkman Bayabani, and people flock to it thinking it is the shrine of the famous thirteenth century saint. Bashiruddin Ahmad Dehlvi writes that in 1919, there were some unknown graves near the Turkman Darwaza and the Police Chowki. After 1947, many changes took place in the walled city and this was one of them. The actual shrine of Hazrat Shamsul Arifeen Bayabani, famous as Shah Turkman, is behind the Turkman Darwaza, in an area called Mohalla Qabristan. The saint is also known as Dada Pir.

Shah Turkman was one of the saints who accompanied the army of Sultan Qutbuddin Aibak. His name was Shams-ul Arifeen, and he became famous as Bayabani since he had given up material comforts and lived in seclusion in the forests, away from the cities, though his devotees always surrounded him. He was seventy-eight years old when Hazrat Qutbuddin

Dargah of Hazrat Shah Turkman Shamsul Arifeen Bayabani

Bakhtiyar Kaki became popular in Delhi. He died on 19 February 1240, during the reign of Muizuddin Bahram Shah, Sultan Raziya's successor. It is he who got the mazaar built.

The River Yamuna flowed near the area where he is buried. Though it has been renovated with green tiles, his grave is a simple one under the open sky.

There are many other graves of his disciples in the compound. One particularly beautiful marble grave is of Bi Mamoola, who died in 1826–27. It has a lovely headstone.

Teliyo'n ka Phatak

This was originally the gateway to the haveli of Syed Muzaffar Khan, an influential Mughal noble from the reign of Emperor Shah Jahan. He held a *mansab* of 5,000, and the title of *Khan-e Jahan*.

There are no signs of the haveli or mansion now, and the gateway was named after the *teli*, or people involved in the trade of oil.

* * *

From Chandni Mahal Police Station to Matia Mahal

Shehr mohabbat ka yun ujda
Door talak taameer nahi hai

Ruined is the city of love and care
Alas! Destroyed beyond repair!

—Kaif Bhopali

There is a small part of the original wall of Shahjahanabad from a road, which goes past the Chandni Mahal police station and Delhi Stock Exchange to Ganj Mir Khan. The police station has been built in the gateway itself.

The Holy Trinity Church

Tucked away behind a board near the Chandni Mahal police station is the Holy Trinity Church. It belongs to the Church of North India, and was built as a memorial to Rev. Alexander Charles Maitland, who died in Delhi in 1894. The church was consecrated in 1905, and is unique for its half-domes.

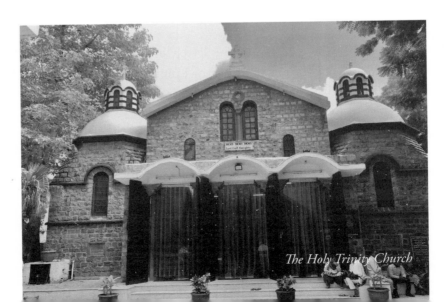

The Holy Trinity Church

Rev. A. Coore designed it. It has a small compound with residences, and a small open space behind which the church stands high. Mr R.V. Smith, the well-known Delhi chronicler, quotes a Delhi Archdiocese publication in which Sir Edward Maclagan (1864–1952), a British administrator, says that there were 120 Catholics in Delhi during Emperor Shah Jahan's reign in 1650. Their number went up to 300 by 1686, when Emperor Aurangzeb was on the throne. Two priests looked after them.

Rang Mahal, Ganj Mir Khan

This is another area in Purani Dilli that gets its name from a lovely palace built by one of the descendants of Bairam Khan, of which no traces remain. There was another Rang Mahal built by Mirza Jamshed Bakht and bought later by Ilahi Bux, the father-in-law of Emperor Bahadur Shah Zafar.

Under the British, it was a *kachehri* or courthouse of the Delhi *tehsil*.

I used to go to the house of the late Prof. Yunus Jaffery who lived here. He always had many stories to share of life before 1947 when there were still havelis here and life was gentler.

Chandni Mahal and Gali Sheesh Mahal

I have often wondered about this beautiful name, which gives its name to the area.

It was a palace built in the reign of Emperor Mohammad Shah and at one time was in the possession of Salim Mirza, son of Emperor Akbar Shah II. It belonged to various members of the Mughal Empire.

The Gali Sheesh Mahal was also named after a palace built in the reign of Emperor Mohammad Shah. Mirza Suraya Jahan bought it.

Bazar Sitaram

Phir iss andaz se bahar aayi
Ke huye mahr-o maah tamaashayi

Spring has come again in such a manner
That the sun and moon have become spectators.

—Mirza Ghalib

I walked through this bazar with Abu Sufiyan, the young entrepreneur whose family belongs to Shahjahanabad and has a Mughal lineage, and Ashok Mathur, whose *Kayastha* Mathur family was employed by the Mughals and then by the British. He is the fifth generation to be living in a beautifully maintained haveli in Roshanpura.

As soon as we entered Bazar Sitaram, a dilapidated wall, some rusted iron gates and a huge tree growing inside what seems to be an empty lot came into view. On all sides are small shops.

'This is the Haksar Haveli,' Ashok told me. 'Jawahar Lal Nehru got married to Kamla Kaul in this house.' I wondered why the Haksars or the Nehru family haven't tried to look after the haveli. A local resident joined us and told us that this is 'Nehruji's *sasural*' (Jawaharlal Nehru's in-laws' house): the Kaul haveli, where Kamla Kaul grew up and her baraat stayed. There was a palpable sense of pride in the shared history that they had hosted the first prime minister's wedding.

A big square looms ahead. 'On the right is the area of the Banias and Kashmiris, and on the right the Muslim neighbourhood.' We walked towards the right and I admired a lovely red gate, which – like everything else in this area – had definitely seen better days. We passed by a beautiful stone doorway with floral carvings on the top and two finely sculpted gatekeepers. In front of it were iron rails, piles of wooden boxes and a vendor selling his wares.

Bazar Sitaram
Photo courtesy Jayshree Shukla

'You know, this door was intact a month ago when I passed it,' Sufiyan told me. A crack is clearly visible now. Do we really deserve our heritage, given how uncaring and downright callous we are about it?

During Dussehra a *sawaari* (procession of Lord Ram, Sita and Lakshman) is taken out in this area.

'If Matia Mahal is the place to go to during Ramzan, Hauz Qazi and Sitaram Bazar are a must during Dussehra,' I was told by Ashok.

Ashok described how the sawaari would be preceded by *bhishti*s (water-bearers) who would sprinkle the streets with water for the procession to pass through. They were Muslims, and his grandmother would always send some money as a present for them.

Ashok has many such stories of the days when everyone lived in communal amity and it was pride, their *shehr*, Shahjahanabad, that bound them together.

Kaleshvar Nath Mandir/Chauraasi Ghante ka Mandir

This temple was built under the last Mughals. According to local legend, Lala Sitaram, who owned many shops in this area, built this temple after the appearance of a *shivling* on that land.

Chauraasi Ghante ka Mandir

This temple is in Bazar Sitaram, and was earlier known as Kaleshvar Nath Mandir. Now it takes its name from the eighty-four (*chauraasi*) bells that hang in it, all tied together. These eighty-four bells signify the eighty-four cycles of rebirth that a person goes through to be born as a human being, according to Hindu beliefs.

However, Maulvi Zafar Hasan mentions 104 bells in 1919, and says that these were offerings from the grateful devotees whose prayers were answered by Lord Shiva or Kaleshvarnath. It was believed that Kaleshvarnath's blessings granted children to women who were considered infertile. It is possible that the bells he mentions include the ones offered by devotees after their vows were fulfilled.

The temple has an entire pantheon of images of gods and goddesses in niches around the shivling in the main shrine as well as outside. There are idols of Lord Hanuman, Shri Ganesh, Radha-Krishna, Ram Darbar, as well as of the Devi.

It is a very busy temple, and outside the premises flower-sellers do brisk business in the mornings and during festival times.

VI

CHAWRI BAZAR AND ITS ENVIRONS

Tu wa shokhi o tabassum ba hazaar
Man o ijz o jaan fishaani za sar-e niyaz kardan

Your coquetry, your smile
and your flirtatious way
And me with my head bent
low, to accept whatever
you say.

—Pandit Narain Das Zameer

MATCHLESS TRADING CO.

1730/C, MARKET, LAL KUAN, DELHI-110006

ONE STOP SHOP FOR BAKER'S CONFECTIONERS AND HOME BAKERS

Complete

MATCH

1730/

Ph: 01

Lal Kuan
Photo courtesy Jayshree Shukla

Qazi ka Hauz/Hauz Qazi

This is a bustling city area also called Hauz Qazi.

There used to be a hauz in this area near the Chawri Bazar, which gives it its name. It was constructed on the lines of a baoli and was constructed by Matabarud-Daula in AD 1847. A stream flowed into it, and once that was choked the hauz dried up too.

Hauz inside the Qazi ki Masjid complex

According to *Sair-ul-Manazil*,[66] to the north of Hauz Qazi was the mansion of Raja Jai Singh and Nawab Turk Jang Badal Beg Khan, a *risaldar* (commander of a military troop) in the second half of the eighteenth century. There are no traces of the mansions, but a mosque named Badal Beg ki Masjid exists on a first floor in Lal Kuan area near it and is popular with the local residents who come there to pray.

Another interesting description given is of the house of Bajna, a courtesan, who prepared an idol of 'Deo' and put it in front of her door during the first ten days of the month of Muharram.

Hauz Qazi ki Masjid

Just opposite the Chawri Bazar Metro station outlet in Hauz Qazi is an old, narrow, stone doorway sandwiched between shops and equally narrow buildings. It has a beautiful jharoka on the first floor that caught my eye and we decided to go in.

As the area is full of hawkers, daily labourers waiting to be hired for the day, and commuters, it is easy to miss it. We almost did. I think it was innate curiosity that made me peep in, and it was like entering wonderland. Once inside, we were mesmerized by a pretty hauz and a lovely, functioning masjid. The mosque is private and only for family, but it does not stop outsiders who come in to pray. The inscription on the façade describes it as a mosque belonging to a Chisti family.

I met Abul Hasan. His father's name is Janab Misbah and grandfather's Janab Abul Fatah. His great-grandfather, Mufti Mohammad Abdul Ghaffar, is mentioned as the *mutawali* (hereditary caretakers) in Maulvi Zafar Hasan's book *Monuments of Delhi*. Abul Hasan traced his family lineage all the way back to the Sufi saint Malik Yaar Parran of the Sultanate period, whose dargah is in the Bagh-e Bedil complex near Pragati Maidan. Abul Hasan is fourteenth in the line of descent.

Hauz Qazi ki Masjid

Mufti Mohammad Abdul Ghaffar's father, Mufti Karimullah, rebuilt and extended an old family mosque that already existed in this location built by Nabiullah who was the eighth in line of Malik Yaar Parran.

Nabiullah came to this area and bought a garden here and built a small mosque for his own prayers. The hauz was possibly part of the garden and has an inscription on the wall: The garden of Nabiullah AH 1131 (AD 1718–19)

The mosque, which is very pretty in shades of blue and gold, has an inscription calling it the mosque of the Chistis.

It is a private mosque and is maintained by the family. However, local shopkeepers and people around do come and pray inside.

The family lives on the floors above and around the mosque.

Roshanpura

This was one of the areas where the Kayastha community lived. There were huge havelis belonging to the Mathur families here. Today most of them have shifted out and only a handful of them remain. My friend Ashok Mathur lives here. Ashok asked his nonagenarian father, who has seen life when Shahjahanabad or *shehr* as they called it, still had vestiges of glory, and told me, 'My father says that he's lived himself truly within the walled city – born in 1930 in this haveli made by his father's uncle … times when everything could be counted on fingers … schools, colleges, hospitals … cars, buggies and *ikka*s were used by the rich and *tonga*s by the middle class, with cycles also a possession of luxury … very few private schools but most were run by philanthropic institutions and big industrial houses … He studied in a Commercial School, Charkhewalan and did his B.Com. Honours from Sri Ram College of Commerce (SRCC), both institutions run by Lala Bharat Ram and Charat Ram of the DCM Group. His college campus was those days in Daryaganj, just adjacent to the

faseel (the wall surrounding Shahjahanabad) on which the boys would climb to see the beautiful River Yamuna flowing on what's Bela Road now … informal lifestyles and informal tenancies which later on became a big reason for disputes and neglect of heritage properties.

'He misses his community living and a group of school friends who'd entertain themselves with picnics, enjoying mangoes in Okhla and three compulsory visits in a year to Kalkaji Temple which was surrounded by dense forests of wild berries and *keekar*. There was no Nehru Place, Kalkaji Residential Area in those days, and there was a fear that we

Ashok Mathur's haveli in Roshanpura

must return to the sheher before sunset because the place was often attacked by dacoits. The mode of transport was a tonga only …

'He's lived a life where money wasn't much of a factor … love and respect prevailed … no competition amongst students … *khandaan*s (old families, including extended family) and families had values and individuals lived with principles – a life that's completely fantastic to imagine now…'

Ashok still lives in his ancestral home, and it is an oasis of peace in a dense, concrete jungle.

Chitragupt ka Mandir

Chitragupt ka Mandir

The family deity of the Mathurs is Chitragupt, and there is a small and beautiful temple dedicated to him in the lane. The Kayasthas were the scribes and writers, and most of them very well-versed in Persian and Urdu. The inscriptions on this temple are all in Urdu, which showcases the syncretic culture.

Shah Bola ka Barh

A faqir named Shah Bola lived under a banyan tree in the Mughal era, and it is from him that this area got its name. There's still a tree there under which vendors sell tea and chaat but no signs of any grave that I could make out.

Nai Sadak: Egerton Road

This road connects Chandni Chowk to Chawri Bazar. It was built after 1857 when the British remodelled the streets of Delhi to make it easy for troops to patrol. It is now a wholesale book market.

Chawri Bazar

This bazar extends from behind the northern wall of the Jama Masjid till Qazi ka Hauz in a straight line.

Though there are many versions for how the name came about, the most credible is that it was very wide or *'chawda'*, which got corrupted to *chawri*.

This used to be a double-storey bazar, with traders, darners, *halwai*s, paper-sellers, braziers, etc.

On the top floor lived the *arbab-e nishat* (Classical dancers and singers) and *tawaif*s (courtesans). These were the days when the courtesans were the repositories of art, culture, classical music and dance. Boys from genteel families were sent to their salons to learn social etiquette and manners.

From dusk till midnight, the bazar would be full of people – all the young sprigs of Delhi, the lovers of poetry, music and beauty would dress up and come here for the evening *mehfil*s presided over by these ladies.

Flower-sellers would be standing here selling garlands of white buds and crying out to passers-by that their flowers were guaranteed to rejuvenate the most jaded of senses.

The rich and famous would arrive in their horse-driven carriages and later in their motor cars. From one corner, one could hear the tabla beats, from another the tinkling of the *ghunghroo* bells or some divine voice singing a ghazal. Everyone who passed by would be enchanted and keep gazing at the upper floors. The regular visitors would go to their favourite *kotha*, but the newcomers would be attracted by what they felt was the most alluring sound.

All this changed after 1857.

Chawri qaaf hai ya khuld o bareen hai Rasikh
Jamghate hooro'n ke, pariyon ke pare milte hain

O Rasikh Chawri is either Caucasus ot the heaven itself
The flocks of damsels and fairies are everywhere.

—Rasikh[67]

Courtesans allowed their salons, known as *balakhana* or *kotha* (because they were on the first floor with ground floor being shops), to be used as meeting places for the 'rebel sepoys', and helped pass on messages. They spied on their British clients, encouraging them to talk, and relayed information to the sepoys.

When the British were punishing the perpetrators of the Uprising, the might of their wrath also fell on the courtesans. It was then that they discovered that the courtesans were in the highest income brackets, owning huge properties and enjoying an elevated status in society.

Just confiscation of property was not enough – the most attractive of the *tawaif*s were sent to British garrisons to service the troops there. The tawaifs who excelled and contributed to classical music, dance and the Urdu literary tradition, and were considered an authority on etiquette, now became common prostitutes.

The *arbab-e nishat* or Kathak dancers and classical singers were now the 'nautch girls' (from word *naach* or dance).

In the present day, Chawri Bazar is no longer a paradise on earth and is an overcrowded street with electric wires hanging down dangerously from the poles. It is a wholesale market, selling paper items such as wallpaper, stationery and wedding cards, as well as hardware. In fact, I went there to buy all the hardware when I was doing up my house. It is also very popular for its chaat shops.

Masjid Ruknud-Daula/Nawab Wali Masjid/Paththar Wali Masjid

As one walks from Chawri Bazar metro station towards Jama Masjid, there is such a crowd in the Chawri Bazar lanes that one keeps their eyes peeled straight ahead to avoid banging into someone. It's easy to miss this exquisite mosque on the first floor on your left unless you know about it and look up. This is the Ruknud-Daula Mosque.

It was built by Nawab Ruknud-Daula, the prime minister to Emperor Akbar Shah II, in AH 1222 (AD 1807) under Sheikh Pir Baksh as the architect. This exquisite masjid was known earlier as Nawab Wali Masjid after its builder's name. Later it became famous as Paththar Wali Masjid, perhaps because of its beautiful sandstone façade.

It was renovated by Nasiruddin Ahmed Khan, grandson of Ruknud-Daula in AH 1332 (AD 1913) under the supervision of the architect's grandson. The *katba* (inscription) was inscribed by Faiyyaz Khan, a sculptor.

The family shifted to Hyderabad sometime in the nineteenth century, and the late Imam Nuruddin (imam of the mosque) told me that the mosque was entrusted into the care of a Lalaji (he didn't know the name) and till

Masjid Ruknud-Daula

recently he was the one who took care of it. Now the Delhi Waqf Board has taken over.

The beauty of this mosque lies in its stone carvings. They have all been carved in the main stone itself and not added from on top. It is simply breathtaking and one has to go there and see it for oneself to believe that such exquisite work was done in India. The flowers were carved out from the slab of stone itself and one can imagine the painstaking work involved.

The *qibla mehrab* (niche in the wall denoting the direction of Mecca towards which Muslims pray) inside has again been carved out of the main block and, as Imam Nuruddin had said, might have taken a couple of months.

On my first visit I met Imam Nuruddin, who had been leading the prayers in this mosque, has been here for over forty years. He lived nearby and is a darner by profession. He showed me his work and as you can see the work is so skilled that there are no traces of the darn from on top. Sadly, he passed away a few years ago.

I had put up photographs of this mosque on my blog and got a message from his great-grandson, Jamaluddin Ahmed Khan:

> Ruknuddaula was my great grandfather. He and his son Ziauddaula were the prime ministers of the Mughals. During the Mutiny, Ziauddaula lost his sons because they were at the forefront of the mutiny. They were hung at the Khooni Darwaza. His youngest son as a child was taken in disguise by his maid to Hyderabad. There in Hyderabad, Nawab Bashiruddin Ahmed Khan grew up and returned to Delhi to claim his property that was confiscated by the Britishers.
>
> Ruknuddaula built this mosque in the middle of the then red light district to encourage people to go to the masjid and pray, as opposed to getting involved in immoral activities such as prostitution.

Charan Das ki Baghichi

Behind Chawri Bazar, tucked away in a lane, is a small but beautiful temple dedicated to *Sant* Charan Das.

Originally named Ranjit Singh, the saint was born near Alwar in Rajasthan in 1706. He moved to an area of Fatehpur Beri (today's Chattarpur) and started accepting followers. He was a follower of the Bhakti movement. He and his followers, called *Charandasi*s, did not believe in caste system. They also did not marry and adopted *chela*s or disciples.

Emperor Mohammad Shah held the saint in great esteem and gave him an endowment of four villages for the maintenance of his sect.

The mandir is dedicated to Radha-Krishna and has an appealing dome topped with an upturned lotus. The inside of the dome is gorgeously ornamented.

I met the extremely affable and hospitable devotee, Man Singh Chola who related a very interesting story of how the saint performed a miracle of saving a boat carrying a marriage party, caught in a storm. He told me that the temple is very popular with the Khatik sect who live near Ajmeri Gate and even today bring the newly wed couples to the temple for the saint's blessings. They are mostly in the business of wholesaling of fruits though the younger generation is now entering private and government service. The saint is said to be an avatar of Lord Krishna.

Charan Das ki Baghichi

Lal Kuan

Dikhai diye yun ke bekhud kiya
Hamein aap se bhi juda kar chale

She appeared in such a way that I lost myself
And went taking away my 'self' with her.

—Mir Taqi Mir

Lal Kuan was named after a red sandstone well that was situated there.

Mubarak Begum ki Masjid

As you go from Hauz Qazi towards Lal Kuan, the first thing that strikes you is a brightly painted red mosque set on a first floor on the left. There are three arches and a single hall.

It is indeed striking, and as I climbed up the steps on a Friday when the congregation was praying, it was full of men. Above their heads I could see the three domes and the marble inscription on the façade of the main arch:

Mubarak Begum built this mosque, which is superior to the arched sky.
Its dignity is not less than that of Jerusalem; call this a second Jerusalem.

The chronogram yields the date AH 1238, which translates to AD 1822–23.

I did not miss the irony of men praying there, for Mubarak Begum, a dancing girl, was the mistress of Sir David Ochterlony, and this mosque was colloquially called the *Randi ki Masjid* or the Whore's Mosque in the nineteenth century. Today it is addressed by its proper name of Mubarak Begum ki Masjid, and I am glad she has received her due.

Sir David was Delhi's first British Resident and lived like the Indian aristocrats of Delhi. Mubarak Begum built this mosque after his death when she inherited his property.

The bottom floor has shops that would once have paid for its maintenance; today it is under the Delhi Waqf Board who look after it.

Mubarak Begum ki Masjid

Zeenat Mahal

This was the palace belonging to the youngest and favourite wife of Emperor Bahadur Shah Zafar. It was her special and personal retreat. The emperor is said to have spent time here too.

As befits the *Malika-e Dauran* or chief consort of the emperor, it was a beautiful and majestic building of red sandstone built in AD 1846.

On the arch of the gate was the inscription with the chronogram composed by Emperor Bahadur Shah Zafar, which read the year 1846:

O Zafar, Zeenat Mahal erected a matchless palace; the suitable date of erection became 'This house of Zeenat Mahal'.

Zeenat Mahal

After the Revolt of 1857, this mahal was given to the Maharaja of Patiala as a reward for siding with the British.

During the Second World War, the British rented it and converted it into a food ration office. Later, a government school rented it.

In 1974, it was declared unsafe, and the government acquired it and demolished the main part of the mansion.

Today, except for the sad remnants of the imposing vaulted red sandstone gateway and the rooms above, nothing much remains. The entire compound, as in other havelis, has been taken up with small residences.

Gunjan Hassan, co-founder and director at Zoberry Foods Pvt. Ltd, visited it often as a child. Her maternal grandmother lived in one of the havelis. She describes a lively neighbourhood with many residents belonging to different religions. One of the features of these houses here was the fact that they had wide staircases that, according to her grandmother, were a boon as a *janaaza* (bier) could be taken down them easily.

VII

KHARI BAOLI AND ITS ENVIRONS

Kabira khada bazaar mein,
maange sabki khair
Naa kaahu se dosti, naa kaahu
se baer

Kabir, standing in the bazaar
prays for all,
Neither enmity or over-
friendliness with anyone
at all.

—Kabir

Khari Baoli

Khari Baoli

There was a medieval mosque in Koocha Nawab Mirza – from the reign of Sher Shah, AD 1539–45, and adjoining its north wall was this Khari Baoli. As the water was brackish, it became famous as *Khari Baoli* (pronounced as *khaari*).

The baoli hasn't sustained, but the name has. Shops and houses have taken over the location. Khwaja Imad-ul Mulk Abdullah built a well here in AD 1545, and after six years, in 1551, he converted it into a baoli. When Emperor Shah Jahan built Shahjahanabad, this became a part of the city.

Nothing remains of it except a copy of the inscription on it, as Sir Sayyid Ahmad Khan recorded it in *Asar-us Sanadid*.

Bazar Khari Baoli

This is said to be the biggest spice market of Asia. The entrance to the spice market is through an old gateway that probably belongs to Sarai Bangash, a sarai that was built in the later Mughal era.

Bazar Khari Baoli

Khari Baoli

The Red Fort

The magnificent Jama Masjid

Photo courtesy Jayshree Shukla

View from the Jama Masjid

Fatehpuri Masjid

Rukn-ud Daula Masjid

Moti Masjid

Sirhindi Masjid

Musamman Burj

Zeenat-ul Masjid

Sufi Sarmad ka Mazaar

Gurudwara Sis Ganj

Photo courtesy Abu Sufiyan

Naya Jain Mandir

Radha-Krishna at the ISKON temple in Vakil Pura

The Rang Mahal

Qudsia Bagh

St. James Church

The Anglo-Arabic School

Tazia procession in front of the Jama Masjid

Photo courtesy Jayshree Shukla

Those were the days of Puraani Dilli

Bazars of Shahjahanabad

The Flagstaff Tower

Kallu ki Nahari

Photo courtesy Jayshree Shukla

Bashiruddin Ahmad Dehlvi writes that the area 'is [in] the control of Lala Narain Das and is used as a godown and shops of grain trade. Its darwaza, which is on the road towards Bazar Khari Baoli, is very majestic. It is actually a building but called a darwaza and in front of it is an octagonal courtyard. There is no trace of the sarai.'

Today the Gadodia Market, built by wealthy merchants in the 1920s, is accessed through this darwaza. It is a three-storeyed building built around a courtyard, with another building inside the courtyard.

It is worth climbing up to the top of the building as it offers a view of the Fatehpuri Masjid and Chandni Chowk.

St. Stephen's Church

A road from Fatehpuri Mosque, going past Khari Baoli, goes on to the Old Delhi Railway Station. This is called the Mission Road, after the Cambridge Mission of India, an Anglican Christian missionary initiative that was led by graduates of Cambridge University. It was established in the mansion of Nawab Bahadur Jung, that was bought by the mission at a throwaway price of ₹12,000 after the Uprising when the British confiscated it. The St. Stephen's Hospital was started here.

St. Stephen's Church was built on Mission Road by the Society for Propagation of the Gospel, which was supported by the Cambridge Mission. Built at a cost of ₹18,500,

St. Stephen's Church

the foundation stone was laid by the Bishop of Calcutta in 1865. It was ready within a year. It is built in the Romanesque style and has a tall four-faced bell tower on one side with a bell hanging from it. It is red in colour and can be seen from far off.

The inside of the church is very peaceful and spiritual. Tall arched windows allow sunlight to come in. Above the altar is a quote in Urdu from Isaiah 6:3:

Quddoos Quddoos Quddoos Khuda Wanda rabbul afwaj

Holy, holy, holy is the Lord of Hosts (army of angels)

Towards the back, below a beautiful round stained-glass skylight, is an inscription in Urdu from Matthew 21:13:

Mera ghar dua ka ghar kahlayega
Magar tum issue dakuo'n ki khoh banaate ho

My house shall be called a house of prayer
But you make it a den of robbers

Sirhindi Masjid

Sirhindi Begum, wife of Emperor Shah Jahan, built this mosque in 1650 when the city of Shahjahanabad was being built. It was originally just outside the Lahori Darwaza, which was demolished after 1857, and is now on the Khari Baoli Road leading on to Sadr Bazar.

As it is known today as Lal Masjid or Lahori Gate Masjid, I had a hard time finding it. It is thanks to Rameen Khan, a heritage enthusiast who compared the lithograph in *Asar-us Sanadid* and found it, that I discovered it.

Sirhindi Masjid

Sir Sayyid Ahmad Khan had described it thus: 'Though this is a very old mosque, it has been so strongly built that it can last till doomsday!'

It is possibly because of the strong construction that it is still standing today, as a railway track running behind it must be sending vibrations to its foundations all the time.

It is built completely of red sandstone and has three domes that are painted white. As the walls and arches of the mosque are painted red, it looks very striking. It had an attractive courtyard that was encroached upon, and only an abbreviated courtyard with a small space for walking and taps for ablution exists today.

In the medieval era, the *sarai* of Marvah Ikram was located near it, and so it saw great movement of people. Today too there are many hawkers outside, and the shopkeepers and workers of the area assemble here for prayers.

A small madrassa for young boys is being run in the premises, and rooms have been built near the entrance for them to stay in.

VIII

CHANDNI CHOWK

Dil mera jalwa-e aariz ne
behalne na diya
Chandni Chowk se zakhmi ko
nikalne na diya

My love-struck heart has no
respite from her beauty's spell
The wounded couldn't
leave Chandni Chowk to
recuperate well.

—Anonymous

A house in Chandni Chowk
From ASI Archives (Felice Beato, 1858)

Princess Jahanara Begum was born 21 Safar, AH 1023 (AD 1614), on a Wednesday, when her father, still a prince, was on a campaign to conquer Chittor. Her grandfather Emperor Jahangir celebrated her birth.

She was very well-educated in religious as well as classical literature, and was well-versed with Persian and Arabic. She was her father's favourite. When her mother died, she had willed half her property to Princess Jahanara and divided the rest amongst the others. Princess Jahanara Begum was given the highest honour at the age of seventeen, and she became the Badshah Begum of the kingdom.

When Prince Aurangzeb won the war of succession, Princess Jahanara spent the years in isolation and captivity with her father in Agra Fort.

She left this world on 3rd Ramzan AH 1092 (5 September AD 1681), and was buried in the grave she had made for herself, in Hazrat Nizamuddin's dargah in Delhi.

She was a prolific builder and built the Chandni Chowk, Begum ki Sarai and Begum ka Bagh between Fatehpuri Masjid and the Red Fort.

Masjid Fatehpuri

Also known as Nawab Fatehpuri Mahal Begum, this mosque was built by one of the wives of Emperor Shah Jahan, in AD 1650, when Shahjahanabad was being built. It is situated at the end of Chandni Chowk.

It is next to Khari Baoli bazar, and so the entrance is always crowded, but once inside it we get a sense of peace. Apart from the main entrance on the east, there are two other doorways open on the north and south. These doorways with their arched entrances and parapets have obviously seen better days. Shops on the outside flank the doorways.

Fatehpuri Masjid

As one steps into the courtyard, the first thing that catches the eye is the pretty white dome with its longitudinal green stripes and green lotus finial. Originally these stripes were black. A masonry finial crowns it. Though the dome is not of marble but red sandstone, it has been plastered so beautifully that it gives the impression of being marble from far. Red battlemented parapets run all along the roof in front of the dome.

The mosque is built of red sandstone, and its unique feature is that it is the only medieval mosque with a single dome, flanked by two 80-feet-high towering minarets on both sides.

The mosque itself is built on a plinth of 3½ feet. In the centre is a lofty archway with two wings that have three scalloped arches on each side. The central mehrab (in the direction of qibla) is very deep and high, giving a beautiful appearance to the interior of the mosque. The pulpit next to the mehrab used to be the only piece of marble in the mosque, but today the mehrab and the wall has all been cased with marble.

A mukabbir, or platform for repetition of the imam's words, was added later in front of the main arch so that those in the courtyard could also hear and follow him during congregations.

There is a huge oblong tank for ablution in the courtyard that used to be fed by the famous Faiz Nahr in the Mughal era. A red sandstone enclosure next to it has graves of religious leaders who lived, prayed and taught in the mosque.

It has three doorways, and the main door (facing east) was aligned with the Lahori Darwaza of the Red Fort. During Emperor Shah Jahan's reign, the nobles had to dismount here and walk up to the Red Fort. This was the main reason for Emperor Aurangzeb to build a barbican here as it was a long distance off and inconvenienced the nobles.

Two other doorways open on the north and south.

The rebels in the Uprising used it as a space for living and consulting, and after the fall of Delhi, British troops were stationed there. Post-1857, the British confiscated it, and the courtyard and surrounding galleries and arcades auctioned at a cost of ₹29,000 to Lala Chunamal, a rich merchant of Delhi. The Muslims were in no position to buy it as after 1857 they had been dispossessed and displaced.

In 1873, Anjuman Rashideen Sulah Kul applied for return of the mosque. The British government agreed and tried to buy it back, calculating 5 annas per 100 rupees as interest on the original sum, at the cost of ₹110,000. In addition, a piece of land in Palwal was offered. However, Lala Chuna Mal refused it.

Later, when Muslims were pardoned for their role in the Uprising and allowed to re-enter Shahjahanabad after the Delhi Darbar in 1877, the British gave Chuna Mal four villages in exchange for the mosque and bought back the mosque. The building was thus returned to the Muslims and brought back into use as a mosque.

The shops that had been built in the mosque courtyard were evacuated. The flooring was repaired. Two galleries were added in the twentieth century where a madrassa used to function. It was so well made that it seems as if it was all built at the same time.

Hazrat Meeran Shah Naanoo aur Hazrat Shah Jalal ke Mazaar

Hazrat Meeran Shah Nanoo was a contemporary of Hazrat Kalim-ullah Jahanabadi, and he hailed from Thaneshwar. After coming to Delhi, he settled

Hauz and Mazaar

down in a room of the mosque. He died at the age of eighty and was buried in the courtyard of this mosque.

Another grave here is that of Hazrat Shah Jalal, who was the khalifa of Hazrat Naanoo Shah, and he spent his whole life in prayers in this very room.

The graves of Mufti Muhammad Mazhar, Maulana Muhammad Musharraf Ahmad and Maulana Dr Muhammad Sayeed are also in the mosque compound.

Ghanta Ghar

This was once the famous Chandni Chowk with tree-shaded avenues and shops. After the 1857 Uprising, all the trees were cut and the roads planed. Not a single tree was left to provide shade to shoppers.

In the centre of Chandni Chowk, the Delhi Municipality built a clock tower in the 1870s, at an estimated cost of ₹28,000.

The Indian Tricolour was hoisted on the Clock Tower on 15 August 1947, replacing the Union Jack that used to fly there. It collapsed sometime in the 1950s. The Ghanta Ghar was right in the middle of the Chandni Chowk street near the the Town Hall.

There used to stand a bronze statue of Queen Victoria in front of Town Hall and that was replaced by one of Swami Shraddhanand after Independence.

195

Chandni Chowk

Princess Jahanara Begum designed this in AD 1650 as the most beautiful market square in the world. It was a 480-yard-long market with a 100-square-yard square, with a square pool in the centre. This square is called Chandni Chowk. It had shops selling unique objects d'art, textiles, attar, hookah bases made from porcelain or glass, wine cups, gems and jewellery. The shops themselves were scented with the finest perfumes, with bolsters and brocaded cushions lining the walls, and shopkeepers who bent deeply from the waist to present their salaams.

In *Asar-us Sanadid*, Sir Sayyid Ahmad Khan says, 'It's beyond my ability to describe its beauty and attraction. The evenings are magical here with the youth, princes and nobles coming here for an evening stroll and entertainment … There are very attractively built shops on both sides of the chowk, which sell all kinds of wares. There is nothing in the world, which is not sold here.'

Today it is a congested, overcrowded market with a divider instead of the stream that flowed here, and it is difficult to imagine that it was ever so beautiful.

Chandni Chowk as seen from the Fatehpuri Masjid

Princess Jahanara Begum ki Sarai/Town Hall

A beautiful sarai, perhaps the most beautiful of its time in India, was built near the Chandni Chowk, or Moonlit Square in AD 1650. The emperor's favourite daughter wanted to perpetuate her memory.

Bernier writes:

> The caravansary is a large square with arcades, like our Place Royale, except that the arches are separated from each, other by partitions, and have small chambers at their inner extremities. Above the arcades runs a gallery all round the building, into which open the same number of chambers as there are below. This place is the rendezvous of the rich Persian, Usbec, and other foreign merchants, who in general may be accommodated with empty chambers, in which they remain with perfect security, the gate of the caravansary being closed at night. If in Paris we had a score of similar structures, distributed in different parts of the city, strangers on their first arrival would be less embarrassed than at present to find a safe and reasonable lodging.

It was built on a square of 186 yards with two grand gateways. The southern gateway opened into Chandni Chowk, and the northern into the Begum ka Bagh.

One entered into a courtyard in which there were two wells and a mosque. All around the courtyard was a double-storeyed building with bastions on its corners. There were ninety rooms on both levels, with a balcony running around it on the top floor and a terrace on the first. This can only be seen in Mazhar Khan's illustrations. After 1857, the British government demolished it; a Town Hall was built in its place later.

This sarai had two Darwazas, with the southern one opposite Chandni Chowk and the northern Darwaza a gateway into the Bagh. It had two big wells and a masjid inside the courtyard. There was a double-storeyed building around the courtyard and travellers would come here in huge numbers. Vendors had their shops here for their use.

Town Hall is a huge hall built between 1860–65. It was a yellow-painted brick structure originally called 'The Lawrence Institute', after John Lawrence, the lieutenant governor of Punjab province. It had a literary society, chamber of commerce and museum. In 1866, it was bought over by the municipality and turned into the Town Hall.[68]

Begum ka Bagh/Queen's Gardens/Gandhi Maidan

The Begum ka Bagh was built by Princess Jahanara Begum in Chandni Chowk. It was a very eye-catching and appealing, 970 x 240-yard bagh. It had many pavilions and cupolas for sitting and enjoying that were demolished in 1857 itself.

The canal used to flow through it. It had beautiful mansions, pleasure gardens and *baradaris*.

Gandhi Maidan

The original pieces of the elephants standing in front of the Qila's Dilli Darwaza were assembled and kept here. A photograph by Beglar in the British Library shows the much-patched-up elephants.

It was renamed Queen's Garden after 1857, and a statue of Queen Victoria used to stand here. Today a statue of Mahatma Gandhi stands here, and it is known as Mahatma Gandhi maidan.

Jhajjarwala Shiv Mandir

This temple was built by Hardev of Jhajjar and is known as Jhajjarwala Temple. When coming down Chandni Chowk from Fatehpuri Masjid, it's on the left side, opposite the Parathe Wali Gali.

The Shiva Temple has a shivling and statues of Parvati, Ganpati, Kartikeya and Nandi. There are also statues of Ganga and Hanuman in the niches.

Just down the lane is a Radha-Krishna Temple, also called the Jhajjarwala Mandir.

Jhajjarwala Shiv Mandir

Baptist Church

Baptist Church

This is on the main Chandni Chowk Road and is a functioning church built in the style of European architecture. The Baptist Missionary Society of London bought some land in the southern part of the Red Fort in 1792 and built a church on it. This was destroyed during the 1857 Uprising and the present church in this location was then built in 1860. It has beautifully inscribed verses from the Bible in Urdu.

Khooni Darwaza

Today the Lal Darwaza of Sher Shah Suri's reign and city Shergarh near Feroz Shah Kotla has earned this distinction, but under the Mughals there was another Khooni Darwaza. I am writing it down because when reading texts from the late eighteenth and nineteenth centuries, one gets confused. This Darwaza no longer exists.

This was at the entrance of Dariba bazar and was built in the later Mughal period. When Nader Shah invaded India in AD 1739, it was in front of this darwaza that the massacre of the residents of Delhi took place.

Sunehri Masjid

Alexander Cunningham, the grand old man of ASI, wrote:

Some buildings may be remarkable only for their historical interest, but they are worth preserving on that account alone, although they may be otherwise insignificant. Such, for instance, is the small mosque of Raushanuddaulah in the Chandni Chauk of Delhi, where Nader Shah sat for several hours while plunder and massacre were going on all around him.

The history of Nader Shah by Abdul Karim says that a rumour had been spread in the city that Emperor Mohammad Shah had assassinated Nader Shah in the citadel. The *Qazilbash* or soldiers of Nader Shah were attacked by the citizens of Delhi, and it is said that about 3,000 were killed. By midnight, the report of these happenings reached Nader Shah who at first disbelieved it. The orderly he sent to inquire was murdered. Then Nader Shah ordered 2,000 *jazarchee*s to occupy the gates of the Fort and fire into the crowd. For a while, the disturbance abated, but by morning it started again. He rode out of the Fort to the Roshan-ud Daula mosque, and ordered that no man dressed as a Hind (Indian) was to be spared.

Sunehri Masjid

Michael Axworthy has written:

On the morning of 22 March (1739) Nader mounted his horse and rode from the palace to the Roshan-od-Dowala mosque (the former name of Sunehri Masjid). As he arrived there with his men about him, some people threw stones from balconies and windows around the mosque, and a shot was fired, killing an officer beside him. He had already made up his mind, but this final insult may have added fury to Nader's frustration. He went to the roof of the mosque and stood by the golden domes, looking out over the houses, shops and roof of the Chandni Chowk district. He ordered that no one should be left alive in any part where any of his soldiers had been killed, and then drew his sword as a signal that the massacre should begin.[69]

From 7 a.m. to 4 p.m., Delhi was given up to massacre. Emperor Mohammad Shah, alarmed at the reports that reached him, sent a messenger to Nader Shah begging for forgiveness. It is said that the invader spared the people of Delhi only for the sake of Mohammad Shah.

Another account says that Mirza Mehdi, the physician of Nader Shah, was seated on the steps of the mosque when Asif Jah, the prime minister of Emperor Mohammad Shah, came with a petition to beg for mercy. His sword was hanging in his neck in surrender and he was bareheaded. When Asif started reading the long petition, Mirza Mehdi said that by the time he finished reading it, the whole of Delhi would be wiped out, so he should be brief. Asif Jah asked him for mercy and that he should do what he considered best. Mirza Mehdi took him into the presence of Nader Shah who then forgave the citizens of Delhi, and the soldiers immediately sheathed their swords.

Emperor Mohammad Shah held a feast for Nader Shah in gratitude. It was in this feast that Nur Bai, the Mughal emperor's favourite courtesan, presented a song for the Persian king. Nader Shah was enchanted by her and wanted to take her back to Persia with him. Nur Bai used her wits to escape that fate.

Today, unless you know about the Sunehri Masjid and are actively looking for it, you will never notice its tarnished golden domes.

This mosque is an oblong of 48 feet by 19 feet; it stands on a masonry platform from the level of the road, which it overlooks. There is a grill on its unpretending gateway. Eight narrow steps lead up to the courtyard. There are three arched entrances to the mosque, which are normally kept locked and opened only at prayer times. They lead to three rooms. Three gilt domes cover the three rooms, the centre dome being larger than those on the side.

There is encroachment from all sides. The stairs leading up from the courtyard of the mosque lead up to a warren of rooms, which are occupied. I climbed it up thinking I could go up to the roof and landed inside someone's room instead.

Gurudwara Sis Ganj

This gurudwara was built in AD 1675 on the spot where Guru Tegh Bahadur was executed on the orders of Emperor Aurangzeb on his firm refusal to convert to Islam.

Gurudwara Sis Ganj

Gurudwara Si Ganj

The famous *kotwali* Chabutra (courtyard) of the Mughals where the Guru was imprisoned is now the *langar* hall of the gurdwara. The Northbrook Fountain is built on the spot where the Guru's associates, Bhai Mati Das, Bhai Sati Das and Bhai Dyala, were tortured and killed. There is now a museum on Sikh history here, built in their memory.

The kotwali was again the scene of some horrific events in 1857. It was on this Chabutra that the bodies of Emperor Bahadur Shah Zafar's sons and grandsons were displayed for three days after Major Hodson shot them dead. Later, a gallows was put up here by the British, and long lines of condemned

Indian men stood here waiting for their turn to be hung, seeing the agony of the men dying before them.

Northbrook Fountain/Bhai Mati Das Chowk

It was built in 1872–76 at the cost of ₹10,000, paid for by Lord Northbrook.

    This place is now called Bhai Mati Das Chowk to honour the Sikh martyr who was executed at this spot on Emperor Aurangzeb's orders. A railing encloses the fountain itself and a small shrine to the martyrs has been built facing the gurudwara.

Northbrook Fountain/Bhai Mati Das Chowk

Gauri Shankar Temple/Appa Gangadhar ka Mandir

Next to the Shri Digambar Jain Mandir is the a beautiful marble temple famous as Gauri Shankar Mandir, also famous as Appa Shankar Mandir because Appa Shankar, a Maratha Brahmin in the service of the Scindhias, had this built. This is important as it is the only monument built by the Marathas during their brief supremacy in Delhi. The temple is dedicated to Gauri Shankar (Parvati and Shiva). There are other shrines too devoted to Ganesha and Radha-Krishna.

It is a very busy temple, with flower-sellers selling flower baskets to be offered at the shrine. One climbs up the marble stairs and enters a large courtyard behind which are the main shrines. At all times one can hear the peeling of the bells and the chants of the devotees.

The shivling here is said to be 800 years old.

Shri Gauri Shankar Mandir

Shri Digambar Jain Lal Mandir

Urdu Mandir/Lashkari Mandir/Shri Digambar Jain Lal Mandir

Shri Digambar Jain Lal Mandir is the oldest and best-known Jain temple in Delhi. It is directly across the Red Fort at the beginning of the Chandni Chowk area. Its red *shikhar*s or steeples can be seen from afar, and it is a must-visit. One must remember that it has timings and is *closed* between 11.30 a.m. and 6 p.m and then again at night.

There is a beautiful marble *manstambh* (pillar) at the entrance. The ground floor has administrative offices and the main temple is on the upper floor. In the mornings it is full of devotees who come to seek blessings before heading to work. There are many shrines on the top floor with the idol of Lord Mahavira in the central one. The old Tirthankar idol is kept in a side chamber. It is beautifully built and maintained.

When Emperor Shah Jahan built the Qila-e Mubarak, he also invited several Agrawal Jain merchants to come and settle in the city and granted them some land south of the Chandni Chowk, around Dariba Gali. He had many Jain soldiers in his army too.

One of the Jain soldiers kept an idol of Tirthankar Parsvnath in his tent, which was opposite the Fort's Lahori Gate. This idol was from AD 1491, and all the Jain soldiers worshipped it. The idol was kept in a small tent, and because it was a temple belonging to the army camp – it was called Urdu Mandir (as this area was called Urdu Bazar camp market) and also Lashkari Mandir, or Army Temple.[70] Later the Agrawal Jain community acquired the three marble idols and built a temple over it on the same spot as the tent in approximately AD 1656. It's a highly venerated temple.

Shahjahanabad was also called 'Urdu-e Mualla' or Exalted City, and the language was known as *Zabaan-e Urdu-e Mualla*. The word 'urdu' as used to denote a language was a development that occurred only after 1857, when the British tried to divide the populace on linguistic lines by using Persian script and words for Muslims, and Sanskritized Hindi and Devanagari script for Hindus. Till then, it was Hindavi/Rekhta/Hindustani that was the language for common people.

In 1800–07, Raja Harsukh Rai, the imperial treasurer, obtained imperial permission to build a temple with a shikhar in the Agrawal Jain neighbourhood of Dharamapura, just south of Chandni Chowk. This temple, known for fine carvings, is now known as the *Naya Mandir* (New Temple). Its red walls also gave it the name Lal Mandir.

According to legend, Emperor Aurangzeb once gave orders that no drums should be beaten here, but the sound of drumming continued. Nobody could be seen beating them. The emperor went himself to ensure that no one was beating them, and found no one there, while the sounds continued. Probably spooked, he immediately gave orders that the temple drums could be beaten at all times without any restriction.

A new marble shikhar was built in 1935, but the three idols are still kept in the sanctum sanctorum of the old temple. The main idol of Shri Parasnath dates back to AD 1548. There is a bird hospital within its compound in a building behind it, which is very popular with bird lovers.

IX

LANES LEADING OFF FROM CHANDNI CHOWK

Zindagi yun bhi guzar hi jaati
Kyun tera raahguzar yaad
aaya

Life would've passed anyhow
Why did your road come to
my mind?

—Mirza Ghalib

Delhi Bank, later Lloyd's Bank
From ASI Archives

Ballimaran

When going from the Digambar Jain Lal Mandir towards Fatehpuri Masjid, towards the end of Chandni Chowk, on the left, there is a signage with *Ballimaran* written on it. It is popular because this area houses Ghalib ki Haveli.

This area had residences of many rich and important nobles, particularly Hakim Ajmal Khan and the nawabs of Loharu. There are two theories related to its name, one being that there was a stream flowing into it and people needed oars (*balli*) to navigate. The second version is that oarsmen or makers of oars lived here. Bashiruddin Ahmad Dehlvi gives a list of huge havelis in the area and doubts the second theory.

It was an area famous for its Hakims, and the famous Hakim Ajmal Khan lived here in Sharif Mahal.

Today this area is teeming with restaurants and optical shops.

Sadiah Aleem, a journalist, spent her childhood in this area. She reminisces:

> The Ballimaran of my childhood was the Ballimaran of beautiful arches and open roofs breathing in the fresh air. It was the place where life was actually alive … where sounds of azaan would mingle with cooing of the doves and the bells tied around the neck of goats. The Ballimaran of my childhood was also the wood stove of my grandmother where she would cook apple preserves, kheer

and various types of curries for us. This was the place where two diyas with neem and rose petals would be lit to collect the soot to make the kajal which would smile in my grandmother's eyes.

Today Ballimaran is famous for Ghalib's Haveli, but when I was a child there was a shop selling wood and charcoal where a man in a white *banian* and blue *tehmat* would be sitting on a huge wooden settee smoking a huqqa. Next to him was his pet ram that would flirt with the goats in the lane ... The ram had long curled horns and we children would be scared of it. I would venture there only behind the protective presence of my maid.

While she chose wood for the stove I would get a curious sense of pleasure in playing in the charcoal and dirtying my clothes and getting soot in my hair!

That Ballimaran is now only a dream that calls out to me and makes me restless and nostalgic.

Today Hindustani Dawakhana is famous, but for us children it was a series of rooftops we would jump over, playing hide and seek, feeding the monkeys and without a care in the world. Of course, we were always careful not to disturb any jinn whose stories our elders would tell us.

Today Ghalib's Haveli is shining brightly and a proud memorial to one of the brightest jewels of India and indeed the world.

The childish laughter and spooky stories of *Jinn Mamu* have now given way to a wholesale market for spectacles and shoes.

From here we'd sneeze our way through chillies and spices to my paternal grandparents' home in Phatak Habash Khan via Khari Baoli. The narrow lanes would suddenly widen and also fall silent. This area had bigger houses, with floral tiles on their arches. This house had an underground room called *tehkhana* and that would give us succour on burning hot summer afternoons.

This was a mixed mohalla and we had Hindu and Muslim friends who would run all over the rooftops, feeding bananas to monkeys who were considered the embodiment of Lord Hanuman.

At night we would sprinkle the courtyard with water and sleep on charpoys and spend the nights counting stars and finding the rabbit on the moon. Smell of the bela flowers would fill our senses. Those days of innocence, those days of communal harmony and joy keep knocking on the doors of my heart ever so often.

Gali Qasim Jan

Nawab Qasim Jan was an Iranian noble who joined the Mughal court in the reign of Mughal emperor Shah Alam II. He was given the title of Nawab and

Ghalib ki Haveli

he built his haveli in Ballimaran, close to the Qila. Ahmad Baksh Khan, who founded the princely state of Loharu, was his nephew.

A haveli belonging to Haji Ghulam Nasiruddin, famous as Miyan Kale Sahib, the spiritual mentor of Emperor Bahadur Shah Zafar, was located here, and the area was called Ahata Kale Sahib. Mirza Ghalib lived in Ahata Kale Sahib for some time. During the Uprising of 1857, he lived in Sharif Manzil as the hakim was a personal physician of the Maharaja of Patiala whose soldiers were fighting on the side of the British and some of them guarded this area.

He shifted to the haveli that is famous as Ghalib ki Haveli in 1865.

The government of Delhi acquired part of the haveli in 1999 and turned it into a memorial of Ghalib. There's a marble bust of the poet in a side room near the entrance and some of his personal items are displayed here. His verses are inscribed on the walls, and it has become very popular with tourists. The rest of it still houses small shops.

Ladliji ka Mandir/Bada Mandir

A road going into Katra Neel from Chandni Chowk houses many important and historic temples. This beautiful mandir is in the second lane in Ghanteswar Gali.

The Ladliji ka Mandir was built in AD 1756 by Naval Goswami Pradyumanji. Though he established the statues of Radha and Krishna there, he laid emphasis on the worship of Ladliji or Radha, hence the name Ladliji ka Mandir.

Radha's image is of brass and Krishna's of black marble. A smaller image of Lalitaji (one of the nine principal *gopis*/cowmaids and a friend of Shri Krishna and Radha) is kept next to Radhaji.

The ceiling has a beautiful though fading painting on it.

The priest in the mandir was extremely helpful and we had an hour-long spiritual conversation on Shri Krishna, whom I am a devotee of too alongside following Islam as my faith. Shri Krishna had many Muslim devotees, the

Ladliji ka Mandir/Bada Mandir

most famous of them being the famous Urdu poet and revolutionary Maulana Hasrat Mohani who wrote many verses in praise of Shri Krishna. Many Muslims, like me believe that since as per a hadith (saying of the Prophet) Allah sent down 124,000 prophets on earth and at no point was any place on earth without a prophet, that Shri Krishna and Shri Rama are also prophets.

Another devotee had come there from Brindaban as he had been told of this unique temple. He said that apart from Barsana (near Mathura) to which Radhaji belonged, this is the only other temple devoted to her.

It was Radha *Ashtami* (Radhaji's birthday) the day I visited it, hence many devotees had visited the mandir. I also partook of the delicious prasad there.

It is an oasis of peace in a very busy and commercial area and a must visit for anyone seeking peace and some spiritual solace.

Ghanteshwar Mahadev Mandir

Ghanteshwar Mahadev Mandir

A lane going off from Katra Neel is known as Ghanteswar Gali. A little way inside it, on the left of the narrow alley, is a huge marble doorway with two lions on both sides and large bells hanging on top.

Bashiruddin Ahmad Dehlvi talking of its historic past says that the area of Katra Neel used to be known as Vidyapuri, and the old name of this temple was Vishveshwar Mahadev Mandir.

He goes on to say that the shivling in this temple in Katra Neel is ancient, and it is said to be as old as the compilation of the Saubhare Samhita and the Padma Purana that speak of its mythological name.

The original temple is a small, domed pavilion with bells hanging on the side and one big bell in the centre over the shivling. It is a beautiful yellow, with a painted ceiling, but it has been enclosed in a much bigger marble building with images of other gods and goddesses.

Samru Begum ki Kothi/Bhagirath Place

A lane from Chandni Chowk near the huge State Bank of India building leads on to Bhagirath Place.

Today it is the hub of the electronic and accessories market in Delhi known as Bhagirath Place, after Seth Bhagirath who purchased the haveli in 1940. I made several trips to it when I was buying electrical fittings and lamps for my house. In fact, the word 'place' is a corruption of the word 'palace'.

A short trip here and you will never be able to guess that this area, which includes the bank, was once the majestic and grand mansion of a Kashmiri dancing girl who became one of the most important women of her age.

Begum Samru was a fourteen-year-old Kashmiri dancing girl who stole the heart of a forty-five-year-old mercenary soldier, Walter Reinhardt Sombre (which was corrupted to Samru). They lived together for some years and then got married in AD 1765.

Samru had his own private army and he pledged it to the highest bidder. In return for help to the Mughal emperor against the Jats, Samru was given the rich principality of Sardhana near Meerut. After Samru's death, Begum Samru was given the *sanad* to rule Sardhana, and the diminutive begum became one

Samru Begum ki Kothi

of the most formidable fighters of her age. She converted to Catholicism in 1781, three years after her husband's death, and took the name Joanna, after Joan of Arc.

She ruled over Sardhana in the eighteenth and nineteenth centuries. Her hold over her army and her estate was legendary and she even led the forces herself.

In 1787, she rushed at the head of her army to rescue the Mughal emperor, Shah Alam II, who was besieged by the Rohilla chief, Abdul Qadir, in the Red Fort. She outwitted Ghulam Qadir and forced her way into the fort. The Rohilla chief had to concede defeat in front of her superior intelligence and firepower. She was conferred the title of *Zeb-un-Nisa*, or jewel among women, by the emperor. The intrepid begum saved the emperor's life on another occasion and was given the title of *Farzand-e Azizi*, or beloved daughter, which was later converted to a more personalized name: Farzana.

The kothi was a beautiful four-storeyed mansion built on a high plinth, with huge halls and verandas. The garden it was built on was gifted to her by Emperor Akbar Shah II. The garden was a beauty in itself, with its fountains and flowers.

Some businessmen bought it in 1847 and established the Delhi Bank here.

One has to push through overcrowded narrow lanes to reach the building that today houses the Central Bank of India. Shops, labourers waiting for employment and vendors now cover the architect Reghelini's signature double staircase built in a way to resemble a flowing stream. This heritage building is one of the earliest buildings to have Greek pillars. The locals believe that there is a hidden tunnel somewhere that leads up to the Red Fort.

The mansion was made into the Delhi London Bank when the British took over control in 1803. This bank was a scene of fierce fighting and bloodshed during the Uprising of 1857. Its then manager, Mr Beresford, fought valiantly along with his wife, but both were in the end killed by the soldiers along with all the other Europeans present in the bank.

It became the Lloyds Bank later, and the inscription of the name still stands above the shops there.

Today it's in shambles and pains my heart every time I look at it.

Dariba and Kinari Bazar

A road from Chandni Chowk leads on to Dariba and Kinari Bazar. The name of the market known as Dariba was originally named *Durr-e Bebaha* or incomparable pearl. It got corrupted to Dariba. It is now a market for jewellery and wedding accessories. Kinari Bazar next to it is a market for laces.

The Dariba bazar (known as Dariba Kalan) houses some famous mosques built on the first floor, so easy to miss. One such mosque is Sharf-ud

Dariba and Kinari Bazar

Daula mosque built in AD 1722 by a noble, Nawab Sharf-ud Daula, in the court of Emperor Mohammad Shah. One of its dome is missing and as its façade is whitewashed, it is difficult to spot. I had thought it was lost to us, but Rameen Khan discovered it in his explorations.

Another first floor mosque is the Surajwali Masjid, which is very visible as it has a large golden-coloured symbol of the sun on its façade with a verse from *Surah Fussilat* of the Quran engraved on it:

> *La tasjudoo li-shhamsi wa laa lil qamar*
> *Wasjudoo lillaah*

> Do not worship the sun and the moon (for they are mere signs
> of Almighty Allah)
> Worship Allah

Badr-ud-din Ali Khan, a well-known seal engraver of Shahjahanabad, built it in the early part of the nineteenth century.

Naughara

Inside Kinari Bazar is a quaint area with nine houses, known as *Naughara* or nine houses. The lane is a cul de sac. These houses are brightly painted and have very pretty doors with red sandstone bases. It is a popular tourist attraction, and a few of the houses now sport antiques shops.

Jauhri Mandir/Shwetambar Jain Mandir

At the end of the cul de sac of Naughara is a Shwetambar Jain Mandir also known as Jauhri Mandir. Both Bashiruddin Ahmad Dehlvi and Maulvi Zafar Hasan, writing in the early twentieth century, say it is 200 years old. Dehlvi writes that it is said that the Jain community established this temple in Emperor Shah Jahan's era.

As with all Jain temples, this temple too is beautifully painted and decorated. And the shrine here also is on the upper floor to preserve the sanctity of the images.

The priest I met there was a very knowledgeable and friendly person, and he explained to me the difference between the Shwetambar and Digambar sects and the reason why the shrines are on the upper floor.

In the centre of the sanctum is the image of the third Tirthankara Sambhava. There are images of other tirthankaras too: Neminath the 22nd Tirthankara, Vimalnath, the 13th, and Parshvnath the 23rd.

X

DHARMPURA

Lord Mahavira in meditation,
Seated under a tree,
In a posture of his own
With the hands on the knees,
Sitting cross-legged
And the body straight upwards
But the eyes closed
And he lost in a sadhna,
The posture artistic
Which the stone statues trying
to capture them,
As the relics of artistic
excellence.

—Bijay Kant Dubey

Ceiling of Chota Jain Mandir

Dharmpura is the area where the Jain merchants lived and many still do. The area is dotted with beautiful havelis and the most gorgeous temples that are crowded with devotees who visit them before going to work.

Koocha Seth

This has two beautiful mandirs known as Bada Jain Mandir and Chhota Jain Mandir.

Chhota Digambar Jain Mandir

Lala Ishwari Das, who was a treasurer in the Mughal court, helped build this temple in 1840 along with members of the Jain Panchayat.

One enters through a flight of steps into a richly ornamented temple. As with all Jain temples, the painted ceilings are a visual delight.

It is a beautiful temple with twenty-four images of *tirthankaras* in the sanctum behind buff-coloured sandstone arches. It has a domed roof with exquisite paintings and two side rooms that are also profusely decorated. The priest and the devotees were extremely helpful, and though photography is normally not allowed, they gave me permission when I explained I am writing a book.

This temple is unusual as the shrines are on the ground floor. In most other temples, the shrines are on an upper floor and administrative offices on the ground floor.

Chhota Jain Mandir

There are carved creepers and flowers on the walls that add to the beauty.

Bada Digambar Jain Mandir

This temple was built between 1828 and 1834 by Inder Raj ji, who lived in Koocha Seth. The main image here is of Tirthankar Adinathji in black marble sitting on a tiered platform of marble with elegant marble screens and gold-painted decoration on the base.

The shrine is on the first floor and we entered through a marble door set in a porch with a pretty *torana*.

Once again there are exquisite paintings decorating the ceilings. The main colour used is gold, and it gives a golden glow to the whole temple.

Bada Jain Mandir

I visited the house of the main administrator of the temple who is probably a descendant. He was extremely gracious and allowed me to take photographs of this beautiful temple. He lives in an old sandstone haveli dating back to the nineteenth century.

Naya Jain Mandir

Today as one walks around in Dharmpura and Koocha Seth, one can see and understand their importance as traders, merchants and, most importantly, as bankers and moneylenders. The later Mughals were often in their debt. The Jains also enjoyed high positions in the court as treasurers.

One such treasurer of Emperor Akbar Shah II was Raja Harsukh Rai. His father, Lala Hukumat Rai, had been invited to shift from Hisar to Delhi by Emperor Shah Alam II. Harsukh Rai was appointed the imperial treasurer by Shah Alam II, and given the title of Raja. He obtained permission to build a shikhar on the temple.

As a Jain temple already existed, this became famous as the new Jain Mandir or Naya Jain Mandir.

Naya Jain Mandir porch

One enters through a small, brightly painted doorway into a narrow passage and then comes out into the main area. A flight of stairs on the immediate right take you up to an exquisite carved stone porch that must have once been the main entrance. It is kept locked today and one has to walk down the passage to enter from the back nowadays. But don't miss out on this porch as the torana is breathtaking. It was a marvellous adaptation of the wooden toranas that were used extensively in stone as decorative pieces.

In the Naya Jain Mandir, as Fergusson[71] comments, 'It was left for a Jaina architect of the end of the 18th or beginning of the last [19th] century, in the Muhammadan city of Delhi to suggest a mode by which what was only conventionally beautiful might really become an appropriate and really constructive part of lithic architecture.'

The back of the strut is filled with pierced, foliaged tracery.

Once you go to the back, you can climb up the stairs into the main temple on the first floor. There are galleries on three sides, and the main shrine is on a raised plinth.

The sanctum is breathtaking in its richly decorated walls, arches and ceiling. The tiered and raised marble platform with inlay work is a piece of art. On it under a canopy sits Lord Adinatha. His image is made of Makrana marble.

There are two halls on either side. In the hall on the left is a *vedi* with 1,008 images of the Tirthankars. In *Bharat ke Digambar Jain Tirth*, Balbhadra Jain writes that initially there was only one *vedi*, but after the Uprising of 1857 more were added to accommodate the images that had been saved during that period. There are also some priceless manuscripts housed in the temple.

No electricity or diyas are allowed in this mandir. As per legend, whenever any attempts at lighting were made, they were magically snuffed out. Narender Jain from Mahabir Pershad & Sons, whose family has been living in Dharmpura for generations and have patronized and visited the temple through the ages, says that the temple does not open in the evenings because the light attracts mosquitoes and other flying insects. To prevent them from dying, as insects are attracted to light, which is said to be a cause of their death, the temple is only open in the morning, when there is natural light.

It is an extremely peaceful place to sit and pray in. As I sat outside, one of the devotees explained the concept and principles of Jainism to me. Every time I visit a religious monument, it is these conversations with the priests and devotees that I cherish, for they are extremely enlightening.

Muhalla Khajoor ki Masjid/Panchayati Jain Mandir

There is not much information available on this temple, but Maulvi Zafar Hasan describes a Jain temple in Muhalla Khajoor ki Masjid, which is the area where the Panchayati Jain Mandir is located. According to him, an officer in the Commissariat Department of Muhammad Shah, named Ayamal, who had incurred the displeasure of his master, was afraid that his house would be confiscated. So, he dedicated his property to an image of the Tirthankar that he had there.

Whatever the reason, it is a beautiful and very richly and profusely decorated mandir with 200 images in it.

Once again the shrines are on the ground floor but on a raised plinth.

*Muhalla Khajoor ki Masjid/
Panchayati Jain Mandir*

Shri Digambar Jain Meru Mandir

Lala Mehar Chand built this double-storeyed temple in 1845. It is a visual depiction of the Nandishvara Dwip the eighth island in Jain cosmology.

The temple is entered via a beautiful carved sandstone doorway with painted wooden doors. The main shrine is on the first floor and is profusely decorated with paintings on the walls and ceilings.

Meru Jain Mandir

XI

SHAHJAHANABAD
KE KOOCHE, KATRE
AUR MOHALLE

*Nikalna Khuld se Adam ka
sunte aaye hain lekin
Bahut be-aabru hokar tere
kooche se hum nikle*

We have heard about Adam's
expulsion from Heaven
I leave your street with even
more humiliation.

—Mirza Ghalib

Entrance to Hakeem Ahsanullah Khan ki haveli

The walled city was divided into various areas, some based on class and some on occupations. A *koocha*, which means corner, is where the alleys meet. The alleys in turn become *katra*s or residential quarters. A *gali* is an alley and a *mohalla* is a large residential area. I mention a few of each to give the readers a sense of Shahjahanabad.

Koocha Faulad Khan, another congested mohalla, was named after Faulad Khan, the son of Habsh Khan, kotwal of Delhi under the Mughals. It is now the centre of a thriving bakery business.

Koocha Chela'n

This was the koocha in which the disciples of Emperor Shah Jahan had their residences. The word Chelan comes from *chela*, meaning disciple or *mureed*. Emperor Shah Jahan is considered a wali (friend of Allah) or Sufi saint and Sarthak Malhotra has found it spoken in terms of the abundance. The Taj Mahal has brought into local peoples lives. Locals believe both the emperor and Mumtaz Mahal were Sufi sants and celebrate their was every year. The *urs* (death anniversary of a Sufi saint) of Emperor Shah Jahan is celebrated every year. I attended one in 2015, where he is honoured as a Sufi saint.

Koocha Ustad Hamid

The famous Shahjahani architect lived in this lane and so it got its name.

Koocha Chelan

Silversmiths used to live here. All that remains is a rather beautiful gate, with cusped arches, eaves and spandrels, which has clearly seen better days.

Koocha Ustad Hira

This was another famous Shahjahani architect whose name was given to the area he lived in.

Koocha Bulaqi Begum

This is in Dariba Kalan and is named after a Mughal prince, Mirza Bulaqi Gorqani.

Naato'n ka Koocha

This is near the Town Hall. Bashiruddin Ahmad Dehlvi writes that it had a mixed population of Hindus and Muslims. *Nat* is the name for the roadside gymnasts and artistes who stayed here. Today, like the rest of Chandni Chowk, it is a wholesale market for clothes.

Kabil (Qabil) Attar ka Koocha

This was next to the Queen's Garden too on the right side. People who made *topis* (caps) and sold clothes and cloth material populated this.

Koocha Ghasi Ram is another koocha that falls on the right as one walks towards Fatehpuri Masjid.

Koocha Rahman

Actually called Koocha Rai Man, this was the property of Hakim Hafiz Mohammad Ajmal Khan. Dentists and artists populated this area. It was built in the later Mughal period.

Maulvi Jameel ur Rahman Sahib, who taught Arabic at St. Stephen's College in the early twentieth century, also lived in this koocha.

Today the entire Ballimaran area and most of the koochas that come out of it are famous for the optical shops selling spectacle frames. There are a number of old mosques mentioned in this area by Maulvi Zafar Hasan, such as Oonchi Masjid, Peepalwali Masjid and Anarwali Masjid. But most mosques have been built anew and very little remains to identify them.

Bashiruddin Ahmad Dehlvi describes an Ek Burj ki Masjid near the entrance of the koocha, which Mohammad Zafar, a shop owner in Koocha Rahman, tells me has been rebuilt into a big structure to accommodate the faithful. He knows that its historic name is Ek Burji Masjid, but says he has heard it called the Hauz Wali Masjid from his father and grandfather. It has been rebuilt into a tall modern structure, and the hauz after which it was named no longer exists.

Twenty-seven-year-old Sadia Syed, a freelance content writer who lives in this area, is a descendant of the famous Mughal-era painter Mazhar Ali Khan. She describes her childhood and the journey of her family. It is while

Koocha Rahman

talking to her that I got a real sense of loss and the revival of memories of Shahjahanabad.

Her maternal grandmother told her stories of her paternal grandfather, Nawab Ahmed Ali Khan, who was the son of Mazhar Ali Khan. Nawab Ahmad Ali Khan got married seven times as his six previous wives couldn't bear him an heir. His seventh wife, Musharraf Begum, bore him a son, named Mohammad Bakhtiyar. When Mohammad Bakhtiyar was seven years old, Nawab Ahmad Khan passed away. The young boy was the sole heir to his father's vast properties in Gurgaon and Ballabhgarh. The extent of his properties can be assessed from the fact that he owned fifty-two wells! This was at the turn of the twentieth century, and after the death of her husband many started eyeing her property. Fearing for the safety of her son, Musharraf Begum burnt all the property papers and came to live in Koocha Rahman, which was part of her trousseau. She somehow managed to bring up her son. Mohammad Bakhtiyar had six daughters. He spent his whole life working for Kanjimull jewellers (the shop still exists in Connaught Place) as a translator and dealing with the British customers. He lived a life of penury. His eldest daughter, Nur Jahan Begum, is Sadia's maternal grandmother. Even after her marriage, her mother spent her life with her mother and in very straitened circumstances. Sadia says she found it unimaginable that their ancestors once lived a life of luxury. She would find it hard to reconcile their present circumstances to the photographs of Nawab Ahmad Ali Khan sitting with *morchal* (fly whisks)-wielding attendants, like a lord.

She says that people talk of the *kamaal* (perfection/wonder) of Shahjahanabad, but all she sees around her is the *zavaal* (decay) and the evanescent nature of life.

Her words struck a chord with me, for that is exactly how I feel when I visit the once-imperial city that is now an urban nightmare of crumbling houses, hanging wires, potholed roads and dirty, crowded lanes.

It is difficult to maintain a heritage structure, and as Sadia says, many are being seduced into handing over heritage structures to builders who give one floor to the family and sell the rest. The huge havelis that were the pride of Shahjahanabad have now been replaced by tiny flats one on top of the other. The result is not only loss of heritage buildings but also a sanitation nightmare.

She says that unlike other children, because of the lack of space and public places in the walled city, she was deprived of outdoor activities. She could not go out in the crowded lanes and cycle or play with other children.

Sadia studied in Ramjas College and realized that most people saw Shahjahanabad as something to look down upon: a backward area where narrow-minded people live.

She made it her life mission to showcase her heritage, along with Abu Sufiyan and his Purani Dilli Walon ki Baatein. They both connected to their roots through that. A speciality of Delhi was the Begumati Zabaan used by the ladies of Shahjahanabad. This was a very idiomatic language and one that has almost been lost. Sadia is reviving this language through the PDWKB Facebook page, where she doubles as Winki Phuppoo, posting short, humorous scripts on daily life.

Like many others in Shahjahanabad, she realizes that education is the key to progress. As she says, had Mohammad Bakhtiyar's daughters been given a basic education, they would not have been in the straitened circumstances that they find themselves in today.

Today their heritage is just stories of the glory days and nothing else.

Shahjahanabad ke Katre, Haveliyan aur Galiyan

Katra Adina Beg Khan

This was built in the later years of Mughal rule, and is near Lal Kuan. A doorway with the name Phatak Adina Beg still exists. As with the rest of the katras in Lal Kuan, it is now a densely populated area with small residences and shops inside the doorway.

Gali Batasha

One end of this gali is in Khari Baoli and the other in Naya Bans. It is the place where pickle and raw jaggery are sold. *Batasha*s and candy toys, etc., are made here, hence the name.

Katra Nawab Loharu

This katra in Ballimaran must once have been a splendid sight given the importance of the Nawabs. Today it is again full of optic shops selling or trading in spectacle frames, and one school. A gateway that is partially consumed by the rising level of the lane leads to a Nawab Gate and then to the Nawab ki Haveli, which is a three-storeyed house built around a courtyard. The traders are using the rooms on the ground floor as warehouses for the spectacles. One Mohammad Aslam Sahib lives there with his brother. He knows that it is a historic building, and his family has been living there for 150 years.

The arches on the rooms on the ground floor are beautifully decorated with stucco. The giveaway as in most old houses is the red sandstone eaves that talk of a past.

Katra Neel

This was the area where the Khatris and the well-to-do people who had followed Emperor Shah Jahan to Shahjahanabad lived, writes Bashiruddin Ahmad Dehlvi. He adds that there are two plausible reasons for the name: one is that the *khatri*s or trading community named the place they lived in after Neelkanth or Lord Shiva, and the other is that indigo traders lived here.

Today it's a very busy and crowded cloth market. Dehlvi had mentioned that this place has many temples, and as I asked for the temple of Neelkanth I

Katra Neel

realized that this is true. I found the Ghanteswara Temple in a lane branching off from it, as well as the Ladliji ka Mandir. At the end of the main lane of Katra Neel on the left hand is a Shiv temple, with a shivling set under a red sandstone pavilion.

Haveli Hisamuddin Khan ka Phatak

Hisamuddin Khan Haider was a nawab from Lucknow, and he built this in the last years of the Mughal rule. His sons, Muzaffar-ud Daula and Nawab Hussain, held high posts in the court of Emperor Bahadur Shah Zafar. Mirza Nawab Hussain was the *nazir* (bailiff) of the Qila.

Haider Quli Khan ki Haveli

Haider Quli Khan held the post of Commander of the Artillery under Emperor Mohammad Shah, and his haveli is in this area too.

Baradari Nawab Wazir

This was a pavilion or baradari near Phatak Sadat Khan where Nawab Wazir had his haveli. The original name of Nawab Wazir isn't known, but it is possible that Abul Mansoor Safdarjung Nawab Wazir of Awadh may be the person in question.

Mori Darwaza

This was demolished after 1857, but the area still bears the name. It's near Hamilton Road.

Gali Teliya'n

There is a huge darwaza here with rooms for sitting on either side. It was part of Nawab Wazir's haveli. It is said that Nawab of Awadh gave this haveli to a singer.

Some very interesting names of which I don't know the origin are Gali Mem Wali (after a European lady?) on Lal Kuan, and Gali Chuiyya Mem near Chitili Qabr. Then there was Koocha Gila, Malliwara (named after gardeners), Kucha Maidagaran (flour merchants locality), Kucha Itteran (perfume-sellers locality), *Farrashkhana* (where those who made carpets and tents lived). I recently came across Gali Chabuk Sawar, an area where probably recruiters of horse-breakers lived, and Gali Mashalchiyan, where the torch-bearers lived. A mosque still functions there, called Masjid Mashalchiyan.

A leisurely walk around Shahjahanabad is very rewarding as one comes across very quaint and descriptive names of people who lived here once upon a time. It is beyond the scope of this book to describe them all.

Havelis of Shahjahanabad

Along with the Qila-e Mubarak or Red Fort as it is now known, the city of Shahjahanabad was also being built with mansions, gardens, boulevards and magnificent gateways during 1638–48. Important princes and nobles were given land to build their mansions inside and outside the walled city.
Stephen P. Blake, in his book, *Shahjahanabad: The Sovereign City in Mughal India 1639–1739*, reconstructs a typical mansion of an important personage based on contemporary accounts: 'A thick wall of stone and in some cases even a moat surrounded the haveli or *nasheman* (mansion or seat). A lofty gateway (also called the Naqqarkhana) housed the soldiers of the daily guard and the drummers, trumpeters, and other household musicians. A large forecourt surrounded by a row of rooms under an arcade lay immediately aside.'

Shahjahanabad Ke Kooche,
Katre aur Mohalle

He goes on to say there would be stables, apartments for the household staff, storerooms, workshops, etc., needed to make life comfortable for the great man. The living quarters themselves would be divided into public and private spaces. The private spaces would be off limits for all but the prince, women, children and servants. These apartments would be elaborately furnished with silk and brocade curtains and cushions, fine carpets and chandeliers, and beautifully designed with gardens, fountains, pools and canals.

A mosque and a hammam were essential Mughal features in all great houses. There would be underground rooms called *tehkhana*s for escaping the heat of the summers. I remember a tehkhana in my grandmother's ancestral house in Moradabad and many cool summer afternoons spent there.

The public space would have an audience hall or *diwankhana*, and near it a library.

A noble's house would have a 4-inch cotton carpeting on which a *chandni* or pristine white cloth covering would be spread, and in winters, silken carpets, writes Bashiruddin Ahmad.

There would be a few couches covered with floral brocade on which the man of the house and his guests would sit. The owner of the house and his chief guest would lean against the bolsters, while there here would be cushions for the other guests to sit against.

There are various-sized niches from the roof till the dado, which are decorated with vases bearing fresh flowers.

The roof is profusely decorated with paintings or stucco work, but images of living beings is avoided as per Islamic laws which forbid it.

Swapna Liddle, convenor of INTACH, Delhi chapter, tells me, 'I have been seeing Shahjahanabad closely over the last twenty-five years, and the most worrying development has been the rapid decline and disappearance of its old havelis. The history and identity of the city, as well as the way of life it represents, dwells in these courtyard homes. Their loss is the loss of the soul of Shahjahanabad.'

These havelis have long since been destroyed, partitioned, built upon or reduced to warehouses. Shahjahanabad has very few old families staying there, as most families left it because of the congestion and dirt, and the problems of commuting, there being no space to drive a car through these narrow lanes, or park those sedans inside or outside. The once beautiful city has been reduced to more or less a commercial centre full of shops and warehouses.

Ashok Mathur, my friend in Roshanpura, tells me,

I have always called this city a civilization … wherein everything from markets to residential havelis to institutions of learning, etc., was given proper, defined areas. Different communities and castes amongst the Hindus were given areas that could make them live amongst their own communities as well as with others. Both at the micro and the macro levels, co-existence prevailed ... it was still carried on till some years ago when too much of commercialism and expansion of Delhi began happening, taking the toll on all old and organized commercial and residential institutions. Haphazard, unauthorized construction and the demolition of heritage sites took place without any checks ... it goes on even today ... Old Delhi became a milking cow for all.... Without giving any importance to preserving our heritage, with the demolition and expansion, the true Delhi-wallahs started moving out, giving up that space to others who came in with no sense of heritage and culture. It not only took a toll on architectural structures, but it also wiped away a whole lifestyle of the Purani Dilli Wale – on language, food, mannerism, *tehzeeb*, *liyaqat* ... and we evolved with nothing except the loss of all that... Today I stand almost alone as one of the old Mathur families whose numbers can be counted on fingers of one hand, residing in a place which had almost all the havelis belonging to them ... I live struggling to manoeuvre through unmanaged traffic, squatters on the road, and the dearth of civic amenities under which the city is reeling towards its death ... No one in the administration seems to bother about the residents any more ... Very unfortunate times ...

Ashok Mathur's pain reminds us why it is important to record our heritage. Following are names of some of the other havelis, which are now destroyed, or at most only their gates remain.

Masjid Qutbuddin//Uonchi Masjid,
Gali Shah Tara

Mahabat Khan ki Haveli

Near the Masjid-e Abdun Nabi was the haveli of a very important Mughal noble, Mahabat Khan. Bashiruddin Ahmad Dehlvi describes it as being to the left of the mosque of Sheikh Abdun Nabi, across a road. He says it was a magnificent haveli in its time, with two lofty darwazas, domed buildings, courtyards with arcaded galleries running around them. It was quite an extensive building with two separate blocks and rooms on all four sides in the area of what is called the ITO (Income Tax Office) today.

In all probability, the Police Headquarters and the Income Tax Office have come up on its site. I am only making a mention of it here as a record since Mahabat Khan was an important Mughal noble.

Prince Dara Shukoh's Haveli

> The wise see not a second in essence
> We and you are mere calling cards
> See One contained evident in many

See One hath formed in shapes many
Prince Dara Shukoh
    (translated from Persian by Gyani Brahma Singh Brahma)

Emperor Shah Jahan's favourite son Prince Dara Shukoh built his haveli here when the city was being constructed. It was called Manzil-e Nigambodh, after the ghat on which it was located. As the heir and favourite of his father, Prince Dara must have been given the land of his choice. He chose the piece of land near Nigambodh Ghat. He built his magnificent mansion at the cost of ₹400,000, between 1639 and 1643.

Since this was along the river, it would have had its own boathouse and boats, which would have given the prince easy access to the Qila. Today all that is left is a colonial building with Ionic pillars, but the mansion in its prime would have looked very different.

It stands to reason that Prince Dara Shukoh probably held his religious discourses and wrote his famous philosophical treatises in this area. I can't even dream of trying to guess how many precious books his library had.

It was in Manzil-e Nigambodh that part of the important translation of the Upanishads into Persian took place. Many Brahman priests and Sanskrit scholars were involved in it here and in Banaras. It was finally published in AD 1656 as *Sirr-e Akbar* (the greatest mystery).

This was taken by Bernier to France where it reached Anquetil Deperron, who translated it into French and Latin. The Latin version reached the German philosopher Arthur Schopenhauer, who was greatly influenced by it and called the Persian Upanishad 'the solace of his life', which awakened an interest in post-Vedic Sanskrit literature amongst the European Orientalists.

Though *Sirr-e Akbar* has survived, Manzil-e Nigambodh, mentioned in the book's preface, according to Prof. K.R. Qanungo, has been lost, and all we have is a building known as Dara Shukoh's library on Delhi's Lothian Road inside Ambedkar University. Even the prince's name is not spelt correctly both here and on the road in Delhi named recently after him.

Emperor Shah Jahan visited his son Prince Dara in this palace twice – once on 2 March 1654 and again on 23 February 1655.

One can only imagine the grandeur of this mansion, which must have been second only to the Qila itself.

Unfortunately only some parts of the original structure are present at the back for those who care to take the trouble to go there. The cusped arches and columns stand a mute witness to the ups and downs of fate.

But why did it fall into such bad times?

Since Prince Dara Shukoh himself was disgraced and killed by his brother Emperor Aurangzeb, his possessions would have been downgraded too.

After Prince Dara Shukoh's death, Prince Muazzam, Emperor Aurangzeb's son and successor, lived in this mansion.

Blake says that since it was damaged in 1739 during Nader Shah's raid on Delhi, it was probably divided into two.

In 1743, Safdarjung, son of Sa'adat Khan gained the use of this palace from Emperor Mohammed Shah in exchange for an offering made by him.

Between 1803 and 1842, the British Residents used it as a Residency.

Sir David Ochterlony, also known as Akhtar Looney, was the first British Resident to occupy this palace. He lorded it there, living more like a nawab than a British officer. When he was living in it as the Resident, he gave it a colonial façade, and we see beautiful Corinthian pillars adorning the building. The rooms also bear his stamp.

It is only if one goes to the back that one can see the remains of Mughal architecture in the rooms below. Even these are being renovated so one doesn't know how long that will remain. The delicate pillars are lying in debris.

From 1842 till 1858, it housed the classrooms of the Delhi College and the residence of the Principal, which had expanded and shifted to this new premise from its old building near Ajmeri Gate, after a grant by Nawab Itmad-ud-daula, the Wazir of Awadh.

In 1857, this building suffered great damage, and the principal of Delhi College, J. Taylor, was killed. After 1858, a district school was established here whose principal was Ram Chander.

This served as a government high school, and there is an inscription here that is responsible for the fallacies leading to its name, put up in the school in or after 1904, which said this building was Dara Shukoh's library made in 1637.

Kutubkhana Dara Shukoh, successor of Shah Jahan – 1637
Makaan Maskan of Ali Vardan Khan Mughal Viceroy Punjab – 1639
Sir David Ochterlony's Residency – 1803
Government College – 1804–1877
Madarsa Zila – 1877–1886
Municipal Board School – 1886–1904

Its present falling ceiling, peeling paint and general look of an uncared-for, un-looked-after building is a sad reminder of the tragic life of the intellectual prince to whom Hindustan owes a lot for encouraging debate on religion and getting many of the Hindu sacred texts translated into Persian and therefrom into other European languages.

Sa'adullah Khan ki Haveli

Sa'adullah Khan was the wazir of Emperor Shah Jahan, and the man under whose supervision the Red Fort and Jama Masjid were constructed. His haveli was situated south of the fort. There was also a Sa'adullah Khan Chowk in front of the Fort. No traces remain of either.

Ustad Hamid Lahori ki Haveli

Ustad Hamid Lahori, the chief architect of Red Fort, had his mansion near the Jama Masjid area, and a mohalla still exists in his name there.

Ghasi Ram ki Haveli

Ghasi Ram, an astrologer in Emperor Shah Jahan's court, had an impressive haveli in Koocha Ghasi Ram, named after him. All that remains is the koocha of the same name.

Kalan Mahal

This was a mahal built to accommodate Emperor Shah Jahan when he came to Delhi while the Qila-e Mualla was being constructed.

It was once an imposing mansion, but it greatly deteriorated under the later Mughals, and after the Uprising of 1857 it was bought by Lala Chunamal for a song.

This later became Model School and then a residential area.

There used to be a magnificent Imli Mahal here, but it doesn't exist now.

Kalan Mahal

Munshi Bhawani Shankar ka Makaan/Namak Haram ki Haveli

This huge haveli was in Koocha Ghasi Ram, built in the later stages of the Mughal era.

Munshi Bhawani Shankar, was a very prosperous and important man when the Marathas ruled over Delhi. He was a bakshi of Gwalior, and once the Marathas gained control of Delhi, they sent him here. Munshiji betrayed the Marathas to the British, and his services were terminated by the Marathas. The Marathas gave him the name *namak haram* or traitor, and so his mansion became famous by that name.

The munshi was very upset and complained to the British, who later gained control over Delhi and issued an order that no one should call him or his house namak haram. But the locals refused to listen to it and the name stuck. The British gave him a pension.

Today, the haveli has been broken down into several shops selling wood and wood coal, and only a small part of the haveli is still used for residential purposes.

It is in a shambles and I felt a strong urge to use a hosepipe on its once intricately carved stone gateway.

Sir Sayyid Ahmad Khan ki Haveli

Az Naqsh wa nigaar-e dar wa deewar shikasta
Asaar-e padeed ast sanadeed-e ajam ra

The marks and engravings on the ruined walls and gates
(They are) the remnant signs of Persia's ancient monuments
—Urfi

For four years I was engrossed in translating the two editions of Sir Sayyid Ahmad Khan's book on Delhi: *Asar-us Sanadid*. In pursuance of that,

I visited each and every monument that he has listed in both. Though he talks only of 130 monuments in the second book, in the first there is a detailed description of almost every building present in Shahjahanabad in 1847.

In that he described the haveli of his maternal grandfather, Nawab Dabir-ud Daulah Marhoom: 'Towards Faiz Bazar is the haveli of Nawab Dabir-ud-Daulah Amin-ul-Mulk Khwaja Farid-ud-din Ahmed Khan Bahadur Masleh Jung. This haveli used to belong to Nawab Mehdi Quli Khan and was bought by him after his death.'

Sir Sayyid's mother Aziz-un-Nisa, was the eldest daughter of Khwaja Farid. Khwaja Farid's family, originally from Iran, had migrated to Delhi two generations earlier. Sir Sayyid Ahmad Khan's grandfather was Mughal aristocracy, and was given the title of *Jawwad-ud-daula*, as well as a mansab of 1,000 infantry and 500 cavalry, in the reign of Alamgir II.

Sir Sayyid inherited this title at the age of nineteen after his father, Syed Mohammad Muttaqi Khan Bahadur, who held the mansab and title before him, passed away.

Sayyid Muttaqi was a mystically inclined man with an uncertain income as the Mughal Empire was on the decline and his pension would be irregular and at times less than the assured amount.

His ancestral mansion was near Jama Masjid, and had suffered in the various attacks on Shahjahanabad in the eighteenth century. At the time of his marriage to Aziz-un-Nisa, it was unfit for living in and perhaps he lacked the resources to repair it.

Prof. Iftikhar Alam Khan in his book, *Sir Syed: Daroon-e Khana*,[72] refutes the common perception that Sayyid Muttaqi moved in with his father-in-law and writes that after his marriage to Aziz-un-Nisa, he moved in to a new house built for his wife in the precincts of his father-in-law Khwaja Farid's palatial mansion, known as Haveli Mehdi Quli Khan. A road separated the two havelis.

Sir Sayyid Ahmad Khan was born there on 17 October 1817.

Sir Sayyid Ahmad Khan ki Haveli

Anyway, as part of my research, I went to Faiz Bazar that is now Daryaganj and into the road named after him, Sir Syed Road, to find his haveli. I had already received many emails from Aligarians living abroad about the pathetic condition of his haveli, so I was more or less prepared to witness degradation, but even then it came as a shock.

The Faiz Bazar area was once the pride of the Mughal Empire, and that is why Nawab Dabir-ud-Daulah had his haveli there. It is now, as in fact is most of Shahjahanabad, a little better than an urban slum, with hanging wires and encroachment and dirt.

The entrance to this haveli, which must once have been a grand gateway, is now encroached on by a shop selling bags. The half that was approachable was whitewashed, and one could see the *lakhori*[73] bricks and the grime of ages. If there were any *naksh-o nigar* (ornamentation) here earlier, they had faded away with time. The entrance was occupied by a number of goats, and I had to jump over them to cross over to what must have once been a deorhi. Today it has a couple of doors.

Where was the Naqqarkhana? Were the goats today's musicians?

An open door showed an *aangan* (courtyard) and some arched doorways. The present owner of the house was gracious enough to call us in and offer us tea, but he denied that it belonged to Dabir-ud-Daulah or Sir Sayyid. He himself had bought it from a Jameela Khwaja after the Partition.

The portion of the haveli that was on the street has long been demolished. All one can see after this darwaza are rows of very ugly flats and then another grand darwaza.

This time around, the darwaza was not encroached, but it had a fruit stall in front of it. When we entered, we found similar scenes of encroachment and crumbling heritage.

Hafiz Javed who lives in this part of the house also denied that this was Sir Sayyid's haveli and said it was restricted to the part we had entered earlier.

After this darwaza is a Khadija hospital, and then a cut in the lane. Locals tell me that this haveli probably existed all the way till this hospital.

Since everyone denied that this was Sir Sayyid's haveli, I came back to my trusted source: *Waqiaat-e-Darul Hukumat Dehli* by Bashiruddin Ahmad Dehlvi, written in 1919.

Dehlvi in fact writes about the haveli here as being two. One he identifies as belonging to Sir Sayyid, which at that point belonged to his grandson, Ross Mahmood. They are, however, one, as the other house was later inherited by Aziz-un-Nisa, who was Sir Sayyid's mother.

Bashiruddin Ahmad Dehlvi identifies the house near Auliya Masjid as near the Phool ki Mandi. In turn, he identifies the Mandi as near Tiraha Behram Khan. This is a point where three roads go off in three different directions from an ancient pipal tree. This tree still stands, and there are still some flower-sellers who have put up their small stalls on its roots.

The first road from here goes to Jama Masjid and then on to Dilli Darwaza; the second goes to Faiz Bazar on the left, and the third one goes on to the Phool ki Mandi.

His house is near Auliya Masjid near Tiraha Behram Khan, which was inherited by his grandson, Ross Mahmood.

That is exactly where we were standing. Bashiruddin Ahmad Dehlvi goes on to write that:

Near the Auliya Masjid is the house of his maternal grandfather Nawab Dabir-ud-daula. He was a very important and wealthy nobleman. He had gone to the Shah of Iran's court as the ambassador of East India Company. He was appointed the Prime Minister of Emperor Akbar Shah II. He was killed during a riot in Bombay.

Now contrast this to the house that Sir Sayyid stayed in for seven months in London. Goodenough House in London bears a plate with English heritage, saying:

Sir Syed stayed at Goodenough House in London for seven months during his trip to England (1869).

While researching, I came upon many articles that describe the efforts and meetings of AMU alumni and officers with Delhi government officials to convert the haveli into a museum after Sir Sayyid's home. We have sadly failed, and seeing the number of pigeon hole flats, shops, people living here, I don't hold out much hope of anything happening in the future either.

This is the man who had spent so much time in lovingly describing and documenting Delhi's monuments.

Razia Begum ki Haveli

Near the Chawri Bazar metro station is a house known by the grand name of Razia Begum ki Haveli. It belonged to Razi-un-Nisa Begum, the daughter of Nawab Qamruddin Khan, a noble from the reign of Emperor Mohammad Shah. There was a gateway that led into a haveli, and koocha named after a corrupted version of her name: Rajna Begum.

Nawab Qamruddin Khan's haveli, according to Maulvi Zafar Hasan, extended as far as Ajmeri Gate and afforded accommodation to his family and descendants. What remains now are the koochas named after his daughters.

Nawab Qamruddin Khan had three daughters – Razi-un-Nisa Begum, Shah Tara Begum and Fath-un-Nisa Begum. A large part of the area from Hauz Qazi to Ajmeri Gate belonged to the nawab sahib, and the three sisters had their havelis in close proximity. All three sisters had koochas named after them.

Abu Sufiyan and I visited the haveli of Razi-un-Nisa Begum to find it in a completely ruinous state and occupied by rickshaw-wallahs. It has been divided into many parts and a number of families live here. I met Raje Lal who is in his nineties and he told me that he and his ancestors have been tenants in this haveli for many decades. He mentioned that his father and grandfather before him also had lived here. So it is probably safe to say they have been here from the late nineteenth century, when most of the old aristocracy fled Delhi in the wake of the Uprising of 1857. The entrance of the haveli is the only testimony to its erstwhile grandeur.

According to Shama Mitra Chenoy,[74] Nawab Qamruddin Khan's haveli was occupied by the powerful Mughal General Mirza Najaf Khan (1723–82) between 1779 and 1782 when he was the *wazir-e mutlaq* (regent), and after his death by his sister Khadija Begum. Others occupied the parts where Qamruddin Khan's daughters lived. Nawab Badal Beg, an influential nobleman from the late eighteenth century, took over a major portion of it. A mosque called Badal Beg still survives in Hauz Qazi.

Badal Beg's haveli was taken over by Hakim Ahsanullah Khan, the wazir and physician of Emperor Bahadur Shah Zafar. The entrance to the area known as Lambi Gali is next to the old Excelsior Cinema (now closed).

The inscription on the haveli of Hakim Ahsanullah Khan had been composed by Mirza Ghalib, but I could find no traces of it. The Hakim Sahib had also built a hammam in the area, but no traces remain of that either.

All that remains are the koochas named after the daughters and the Badal Beg Masjid. The haveli of Hakim Ahsanullah Khan has long since disappeared, and there are houses from the early twentieth century there. One wall had an inscription that it was built by Begum Mahmood-un-Nisa in 1910, with a side inscription saying *Mohsin*.

Chunamal ki Haveli

Lala Chunamal belonged to the khatri caste and was a very rich trader and banker. His haveli is at the beginning of Katra Neel. He made a fortune during the Uprising of 1857 and provided supplies to the British troops. He famously refused to give a loan to Emperor Bahadur Shah Zafar! He bought the Fatehpuri Masjid and some other Mughal buildings after the Uprising.

His haveli is one of the few that have survived, though divided amongst his descendants. I have been inside, and it has been done up very well and showcases many precious artefacts.

After 1857

After the 1857 Uprising, Badar Roo Darwaza and Kelaghat Darwaza were demolished as they obstructed traffic. Kashmiri Darwaza was preserved as a memorial to the 1857 Siege of Delhi.

Calcutta Darwaza had already been demolished earlier. The city wall too had been broken down.

The walled city was divided into two irregular parts by the Chandni Chowk bazar.

A broad new road was taken out in the city's eastern part from Kashmiri Darwaza to Dilli Darwaza, which passed via the old magazine. Another new road was made in the western part, near Lal Kuan bazar, which divides into three near Qazi ka Hauz. One road goes to Ajmeri Darwaza, one goes to

Sitaram Bazar in the south till Turkman Darwaza, and the eastern one goes from Chawri Bazar to Jama Masjid.

To facilitate the movement of troops, a new road called Egerton Road was built which passed in front of Ghanta Ghar and on to Shah Bola ka Barh, opening on to Chawri Bazar. Today this is the hub of stationery and booksellers.

XII

KASHMIRI DARWAZA
AND BEYOND THE
WALLED CITY

Bayaad-e naksh-e imaraat-e
shahr-e yaaran-e bi'n
Ki ein siphir jafa peesha chuun
ba bast o shikast

See the monuments of the
beloved's city
The cruel fate has destroyed
them all.

Kashmiri Darwaza
From ASI Archives (Felice Beato, 1858)

Madrassa and Maqbara of Ghaziuddin Khan/Anglo-Arabic School

Ghaziuddin Khan Nizam-ul Mulk, a descendant of the famous Sufi, Sheikh Shahabuddin Suharwardi, built this madrassa in AD 1710 outside Ajmeri Gate.

Ghaziuddin was an eminent noble of Emperor Aurangzeb's reign. His original name was Mir Shihabuddin Siddiqi, and Emperor Aurangzeb gave him the title of Ghaziuddin Khan. His son was Asif Jah I, the first Nizam of Hyderabad.

It's a beautiful building built in the Indo-Saracenic style and was built by him as a madrassa to impart learning.

It was a very popular custom to build a madrassa, masjid and tomb for self in those days, and this is the style that Ghaziuddin Khan also adopted.

It is a double-storeyed red sandstone building. The entrance itself is very grand – a lofty central arch flanked by three arches on either side. It is three aisled as was the classic style of that time. Past the entrance, one steps into a serene courtyard facing a grand mosque next to which is the mausoleum complex.

The mosque has some of the most stunning red sandstone screens I have seen. It has a double *chabutra* or platform on both sides. The lower chabutra is open. Three marble domes surmount the mosque, with the central one being larger and higher. There are lovely cupolas on the main arch and sides. There used to be a *tehkhana* 36.7 feet long and 40.9 feet wide under the upper northern platform of the mosque.

Anglo-Arabic school

There are galleries on the sides, which were built for the ulema and students. Later reconstruction by the college and school has added more rooms for classes and students.

To the south of the mosque is a marble enclosure measuring 17.7 x 14.8 feet, with beautifully carved, 9-feet-high marble screens. Two arched doorways with screen doors are built in the north and south to enter the enclosure. The north doorway is near the mosque, while the south faces the college and has two marble steps leading up to it. Slim marble minarets on both sides surmount these. Minarets are also built on the corners and on the central screens on east and west, totalling twelve. Since these were very delicate, some have broken.

The flooring is marble too, and is raised. The enclosure contains three graves, and the central one is of Ghaziuddin Khan himself. To the right is that of Chin Quli Khan Nizam-ul Mulk (founder of the Asaf Jahi Dynasty), and on the left is his grandson, Ghaziuddin Khan II. There are other graves outside the enclosure belonging to the family.

A second beautiful sang-e bassi or salmon-coloured sandstone enclosure was built later. It has the most exquisite carved screens and a marble door on the south for entering. The inner enclosure is kept locked, and one can only peep in from the side screens.

In 1803, after Lord Lake conquered Delhi, there was always a danger of raids by the Marathas who had been defeated by the British. It was considered that such a magnificent building should not be left outside the city walls. Thus, orders were given to demolish it. So another grand darwaza to the madrassa and its adjoining buildings, plus four burjis on the four corners, were demolished. Fortunately for us, the rest of it was too strongly built to be so easily demolished, and a lot of money and labour was needed. So a ditch was dug around it and it was included in the city.

The madrassa closed down in the late eighteenth century and was revived in the nineteenth century by the British as Delhi College.

Delhi College

In 1825, the British opened a college here for imparting Western education.

It was one of the most famous colleges of its time, with fine teachers, and produced some outstanding scholars. Sir Sayyid Ahmad Khan, Maulvi Zakaullah Khan, Deputy Nazeer Ahmed are some of the famous alumni of this college.

The Delhi College was a focal point during the Uprising of 1857, and the Indian sepoys who came from Meerut and those who joined them destroyed most of its excellent library of Arabic and Persian books.

The British police occupied it from 1857 to 1890.

Delhi School was re-established as the Zakir Husain College in 1975 in honour of India's former president, Zakir Husain, and was shifted in 1986 to its present location.

The Anglo-Arab Senior Secondary School runs in the old premises.

Kamla Market/Shahji ka Talaab

This was the location of a large octagonal *talaab* (pond) outside the Ajmeri Darwaza made during the reign of Shah Alam II (1759–1806). Every side of the octagon measured 240 feet. Beautiful concrete ghats were made all around it. It had eleven steps leading down to the water.

The Shahji after whom it was named was Nawab Shadi Khan, who was a resident of Balkh. In Shah Alam II's reign, he came to Delhi and at some point built this talaab. During Diwali, diyas were floated in this talaab.

After the fall of the Mughals, it became a dump yard and a breeding place for mosquitoes. And post-Partition, when the refugees came, the almost defunct talaab was levelled and accommodation for the refugees made here.

Kashmiri Darwaza

Kashmere Gate, near ISBT Metro Station, used to be the entry into the walled city from Civil Lines, where the British families lived. Originally, a single-arched door, so named because it stood on the road to Kashmir, it was enlarged and rebuilt in 1835 by British military engineer Robert Smith.

This area saw fierce fighting both when the sepoys captured it and later when the British retook it. On 14 September 1857, it was the scene of the final assault on Shahjahanabad led by Brigadier General John Nicholson. A plaque installed at Kashmere Gate by General Lord Robert Napier in 1876

Kashmiri Darwaza

commemorates the sacrifices of the British officers who retook the city. The gate itself has been cordoned off with an iron railing. It is now a showpiece, which tells the tale of 1857.

St. James Church

Colonel James Skinner built this church on Lothian Road. Skinner, a mercenary, was the son of a Scottish father and Rajput mother. He was popularly known as Sikander Sahib. He raised an irregular light cavalry regiment known as Skinner's Horse, as it was a regular practice for resourceful men to raise irregular fighting units and pledge them, and themselves, to the various factions that were fighting territorial wars in the eighteenth and nineteenth century. He served with his regiment under Maharaja Scindia initially. When Scindia fought against the East India Company, he joined the latter as he didn't want to fight the British. The regiment is still a part of the Indian Army as 1st Horse (Skinner's Horse). Skinner died and was buried in Hansi (in Haryana) before his remains were moved to the St. James Church.

When he lay wounded in the battle of Uniara in 1800, Skinner had vowed that he would build this church if he survived.

The St. James Church was consecrated in 1836. Built at a cost of ₹95,000 by Colonel James Skinner (1778–1841) from his own funds, it took ten years to build. It was built opposite his haveli and designed by Major Robert Smith, a British army engineer. The architecture is Palladian and the design is on a cruciform plan. The three porticoed porches and the majestic central dome with its ball and cross on top strike the visitor first. The church has spacious, well-manicured grounds. When I visited it, I was in for a treat – the two huge stained-glass windows behind the altar, depicting the crucifixion and resurrection of Christ, are exquisite!

As the uniform of the soldiers of Skinner's Horse was a bright yellow, they were often referred to as the Yellow Boys. It is appropriate then that the church is also painted yellow.

It was at this church that successive viceroys attended Sunday services from 1911, till the Cathedral Church of the Redemption, also known as the Viceroy Church, was built in 1935.

Regular service is held in the church. A sense of peace prevails, but it quickly disappeared for me when I glanced at the plaques on the walls.

The walls bear memorial plaques for the Europeans and Indian Christians killed during the First War of Independence. These include Chimun Lal, physician to the Mughal emperor, who ran a dispensary in Daryaganj, and the Beresford family. George Beresford was the manager of Delhi Bank, which was started in Begum Samru's palace in Chandni Chowk where the Central Bank is located today. He and his wife were killed while trying to stop the Indian sepoys from looting the bank on 11 May 1857. When the Uprising started on 11 May 1857, many British women and children hid here and later escaped from Delhi.

Fraser's Grave

Another important personality buried in front of the church is William Fraser, the Commissioner of the territory of Delhi. He was murdered in 1835. Nawab Shamsuddin Khan, of Loharu and Ferozepur Jhirka, and father of the noted

Fraser's Grave

Mughal poet Daagh Dehlvi, was charged and hanged for his role in the crime. Skinner, whose friend was Fraser, played a major role in catching the assassins. When St. James Church was ready, Skinner shifted his friend's body from the local church to the present location.

The beautiful white marble mausoleum with two lions on either side, which Skinner had built for his friend, was damaged in 1857. Today, a simple grave with the memorial epitaph inscribed by Skinner survives.

The church was damaged during the 1857 Uprising and repaired later. There is an excellent conservation plan in place. INTACH, the Delhi chapter, which is in charge, has been taking remedial action.

Memorial for Those Killed in 1857

There is a slab as a memorial for the Europeans who were killed in 1857 in the St. James Church. It has one inscription in four languages – English, Persian, Arabic and Urdu:

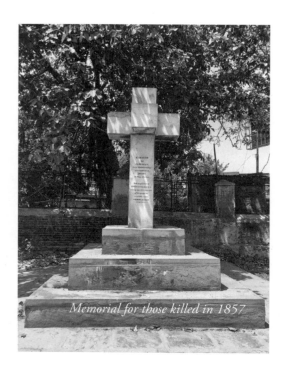

Memorial for those killed in 1857

Sacred to this memory of those who were murdered at Delhi in May MDCCCLBII and in gratitude to God for the mercy in having spared a remnant of his people to erect the cross. [Psalm CTXXEI]

Mr Beresford's family and others killed on 11 May 1857 by the Indian sepoys are buried here.

Skinner Family Cemetery

This is to the left of the church as you enter and is a must-see for its beautiful graves and sepulchres. The inscriptions bear a mix of English and Persian.

Skinner family cemetery

The grave of Alexander Skinner's wife, Alice Anne, or Sardar Bahu, who died at the age of 32 in AD 1881, has a poignant verse in English and Urdu:

Deeply regretted by all
The Lord gave and the Lord hath taken away
Blessed be the name of God
(Job 1.21)
Where the silent willow weeps
A friend, a wife, a mother sleeps
Her infant image here below
Sits smiling at her father's woe
This memorial is erected by her
Disconsolate husband 1884

Delhi State Election Commission Office

St. Stephen's College started life in a small portion of the Shish Mahal in Katra Kushal Rai of Shahjahanabad on 1 February 1881. A school by the same name had functioned there from 1853 to 1854. Reverend Samuel Scott was the founder principal of the college. That part of the building is now occupied by tailors and embroiderers and the rest of the building by tenants. Only a plaque put up recently gives an indication of the important role played by the Shish Mahal in our country's education.

In 1891, the student strength increased to fifty-two, and they could no longer be accommodated in Shish Mahal.

When the need for a bigger building for the college was felt, two sites were proposed: one near Lahori Gate and one near Kashmere Gate. The latter was chosen. This land at that time was valued at ₹5,000.

In AD 1890, the foundation stone for St. Stephen's College was laid by Sir Charles Elliot, then Head of the Public Works Department and later the

lieutenant governor of Bengal. The lieutenant governor of Delhi, Sir James Lyall, inaugurated the new buildings at Kashmere Gate on 8 December 1891. The design was made by Colonel Samuel Jacob Swinton, the chief engineer of Jaipur, and it was built at a cost of ₹92,702.10.

The builders had chosen the Mughal style of architecture as against the prevailing Gothic.

Opposite it is another heritage building which was the college hostel and is now used by the NCC. It was damaged during the work of metro line tunnelling and subsequently repaired by them. It has an inscription, which is very high up on the wall and difficult to read. Since most people are unaware of this building's heritage, I include it here:

This wing of the Boarding House was projected by the Reverend John W.T. Wright M.A. of the Cambridge Mission, Professor in St. Stephen's College from 1883 and Principal from 1898 till his unexpected death at Dalhousie in Sept 1902. It was erected in fulfilment of his purpose by his family and European friends in token of their affectionate regard.

Fakhr-ul Masajid

If Emperor Shah Jahan built the Taj Mahal for his wife, Fakhr-ul Jahan built a mosque for her husband.

> The Fakhrool Musajid was built by Kuneez i Fatima widow of Shoojaat Khan about A.D. 1729, to the memory of her husband who was one of the confidential followers of Nizam of Moolk, Minister of Mohummud Shah. It adjoins the Estate and is nearly opposite to the Church erected by the late Colonel Skinner C.B. and has been of late years repaired at no inconsiderable expense by that distinguished Officer, for the convenience of his followers military and menial. (caption by Sir Thomas Metcalfe, in his *Dehlie Book*.)

> Shujaat Khan's wife was named Kaniz-e Fatima and given the title *Fakhr-ul Jahan* (pride of the world), and this mosque was named after her. Shujaat Khan was posted as commander of artillery under Emperor Aurangzeb, with a rank of 4,000 and 2,500 *sawar*s. He was killed fighting the Afghans in 1675.

Fakhr-ul Masajid

A devout lady, Fatima was disconsolate when her husband died, and thought of no better memorial to his memory than a mosque.

In the painting from the 1840s, you can see that the mosque stands on a platform 8 feet above the ground. Shops now occupy the arches. In fact, it's a very busy road with many shops on either side. It was enclosed on three sides with arcades on its north and south. All these arcades are no more. The mehrab has the kalima *La ilaha illalaah Mohammad ur Rasool Allah* inscribed on it. It's a single aisle mosque with red paint and green doors on either side, which open on to side galleries.

When I visited it on a winter morning, the first thing I saw when I came up the steps to the masjid courtyard was people sleeping under colourful blankets. As everyone's face was covered because of the overhead sun (it was close to noon), I couldn't make out who they were. At first I thought maybe they were homeless people given refuge here. Then my gaze fell on lockers with locks in the side corridor, and the sounds made by us (though I was being very careful and quiet) woke up the sleeping boys.

A little boy about 9–10 years old was peeping from under a blanket at me.

He was little Shahbaz from Haryana. Imam Sahib told me they had all been reciting the Quran at night and had slept at dawn after *fajr* or the morning prayers. These children study in the madrassa here. On my questioning him about the syllabus, the Imam Sahib said these kids learnt Arabic, Quran and Hadith along with Hindi, English, mathematics and other subjects. They appeared for Adeeb and Kamil exams, and later enrolled in Jamia Urdu or AMU for completing their studies.

The dome was banded longitudinally by black-and-white marble, and topped with gilded finials. Now those finials are damaged and drooping. The left wall of the mosque and the colonnade were damaged during the siege of Delhi in 1857. A cannon ball dismantled the pavilion of the minaret on its northeastern corner. The famous Sikander Sahib or Colonel James Skinner who built the St. James Church opposite the mosque had the mosque repaired. It is said that one of his wives was Muslim and came here to pray.

Behind the mosque is the Delhi Nigam office, which was the original site of Hindu College. It was built on land donated by Rai Bahadur Sultan Singh. The college moved from here years ago and these buildings are now abandoned, exposing the mosque's rear.

Hindu College

This is the building where Hindu College started off, before shifting to the University of Delhi campus, and still bears the inscription. It is near the old St. Stephen's College building.

This was not built for the college but was originally Colonel Skinner's residence. Rai Bahadur Sultan Singh bought it from the family and donated it for the purposes of the college.

It is now the Delhi Nigam Office and the old buildings have been ruthlessly demolished. An octagonal room remains in a depressing state, walled up on every side, but its pillars tell a story of a different beautiful past.

Telegraph Memorial

This was the nineteenth-century telegraph, which played an important role in 1857.

The story of Delhi in 1857 may have been very different had it not been for the quick thinking of two young signalmen, William Bendish and J.W. Pilkington, posted in the Telegraph office on Lothian Road, near St. James Church in Old Delhi. Before fleeing, they managed to send a brief warning of the disaster to 'Umballa' (Ambala), late in the afternoon. The signallers were able to report only that Europeans 'had been killed' before they signed off.

There is a memorial erected to them just outside the office, in what is now a filthy area, used by locals to relieve themselves.

Telegraph Memorial

The memorial reads something on the lines of:

Erected on 19 April 1902 by the members of the Telegraph Department to commemorate the loyal and devoted service of the Delhi Telegraph Office Staff, on the eventful 11 May 1857.

On that day two young signallers, William Benedish and J.W. Pilkington remained on duty, till ordered to leave, and by telegraphing to Ambala information of what was happening at Delhi rendered invaluable service to the Punjab government. In the words of Sir Robert Montgomery, 'The electric telegraph has saved India.'

Most of the words have faded, and only 'The electric telegraph has saved India,' can be read clearly.

The telegraph that they sent was:

Dated 11th May 1857
We must leave office. All the bungalows are being burnt down by the sepoys of Meerut. They came in this morning. We are off, don't roll today. Mr. C Todd is dead. We think he went out this morning and has not returned yet. We heard nine Europeans were killed. Good Bye.

Magazine

On Lothian Road, the remains of a munitions magazine are still visible. Its two gates are opposite the Telegraph Office. This area saw great excitement and bloodshed at around 4 p.m. on that day and lived to tell the tale.

This magazine was probably built on the grounds of Prince Dara Shukoh's haveli, and many tunnels were found here when it was being built.

The Central Telegraph Office stands on some of the area of the magazine. It was the biggest British arsenal in north India. When Sir Charles Napier was the commander-in-chief in India in the 1840s, he got the bulk of the artillery inside shifted to another magazine on the Ridge. He felt that a loaded arsenal so close to the Mughal Qila and far away from the British cantonment was unwise. But much of the gunpowder was left for making cartridges and was supplied to other magazines. Some cannons were also left here. It is this that was exploded on 11 May 1857.

Metcalfe had asked Lieutenant George Willoughby, the officer-in-charge, to secure the main munitions magazine and under no circumstance let it fall in the hands of the sepoys. At around 4 p.m., when Willoughby realized that the sepoys had brought ladders to scale the walls after having failed to

Magazine

batter the gates down, he gave orders for the munitions to be blown up. A spectacular display of fireworks soon lit up the Delhi sky. The British officers watching from the Ridge knew that Delhi was lost. The Indian sepoys were angry at being deprived of ammunition, though another smaller magazine had fallen into their hands.

The emperor and the courtiers in the Fort were shaken up since as pensioners of the British they had not seen any action before this.

When the magazine exploded with all its ammunition, around 25 sepoys, 400 onlookers and nearby residents were among those killed – there was flesh flying everywhere. But Willoughby and two of his fellow officers miraculously escaped.

A plaque commemorating the British officers is installed on the magazine gate.

Oldest English Cemetery/Lothian Cemetery

This is a five-minute walk from Kashmere Darwaza near the post office. If one goes by the tombstone on the grave of one Thomas Dun, Colonel James Skinner built it in 1808.

Lothian Cemetery

Dargah Panja Sharif

This dargah has a few relics of Hazrat Ali including a *panja* (palm) imprint on stone. It is a big compound with many graves in it. Once upon a time the entire area was owned by the dargah, but now the dargah is confined to its building, and all around are narrow alleys with shops. It is a focal point of Shia activities during the month of Muharram and many *majlis* (religious assembly to mourn Imam Hussain) are held here. It is quite spacious inside. Most of it has been renovated over the years.

Dargah Panja Sharif

Shia Jama Masjid

Shia Jama Masjid, Hamilton Road

A chance remark by Prof. Yunus Jaffery that Ghalib had written the *katba* (inscription) for the Shia Jama Masjid took me in search for it. I hunted for the location on the Internet. All I could find was Shia Jama Masjid at Kashmere Gate, which was woefully inadequate considering how crowded the place is. It doesn't help that it's totally overshadowed by its more famous namesake, Delhi's Jama Masjid.

Anyway, we finally found it after much asking for directions in the area. The keyword turned out to be Moharram, as the 10th Moharram procession starts from there. The mosque built in 1841–42 stands on a raised platform, and seventeen stone steps lead up to it. Its court was enclosed on the east by an arcade and on the west by the mosque proper, writes Maulvi Zafar Hasan in 1919, but today there is just a single-hall mosque with a small courtyard.

The reason I couldn't find it online is because its original name is Hamid Ali Mosque on Hamilton Road. The katba written by Mirza Ghalib translates as:

> Itmaduddaula, through whose excess of generosity the Red Sea is
> as a pint before the palm of his hand

The perspicuous Hamid Ali Khan who on account of his purity sees the secrets of eternity within his mind

Erected in Delhi an auspicious mosque which should become a place of worship for young and old

Ghalib the nightingale who has his nest in Tuba [tree in Paradise] sang out after the manner of poets

A second Kaba has appeared in the world; the year of erection is 'Kaba resembling'

Under the supervision of Maulvi Tegh Ali – the year 1257 (AH).

Ghalib was a Sunni Muslim who had great faith in Hazrat Ali and the *ahle bait* (family of the Prophet), and as such must have written this inscription with the chronogram. Itmad-ud-Daula Hamid Ali Khan was the prime minister of Emperor Bahadur Shah Zafar.

This is the main hall. There used to be a *qullatain* or small tank at the far-east corner of the mosque. Now there are some taps for ablution, an alcove for the rosaries and *sajdahgaah*s (clay tablets used by Shias for *sajda*), an alcove for the Quran, a Rajasthani chapter on the façade. A piece of the *faseel* (wall) survives opposite the mosque, desecrated by bills and posters.

Metcalfe House

Sir Theophilus Thomas Metcalfe built this magnificent mansion near the Kashmiri Darwaza. He was the British Commissioner of the Mughal Court and held the title which translatated as: the just ruler, dispenser of justice, the ruler of the time, the Nausherwan of the age, founder of justice, of just disposition, the most honourable person of the government, custodian of the country, the exalted son and most beloved of the emperor, Sir Thomas Theophilus Metcalfe Baronet Bahadur Firoz Jung Sahib Senior, resident of Dar-ul-Khilafat Shahjahanabad.[75]

The mansion is built in a huge compound near the River Yamuna. There were many houses inside the compound. It was built for comfort and was very grandly made. It was built on a plinth and had underground cellars – *tehkhana*s – for keeping cool in summers.

These were used for hiding the British in 1857.

His son was the Joint Magistrate of Delhi in 1857. The mansion was looted in 1857 and the son somehow escaped.

This is now the office of DRDO.

The entire road from Kingsway station to Delhi is dotted with colonial buildings, which were inhabited by Europeans, and they had trading shops there.

Nicholson Cemetery

Brigadier General John Nicholson was the British hero who breached the Kashmiri Darwaza and area around it in September 1857 and won back Delhi. He entered from the walls near the Kashmiri Darwaza while another British regiment managed to enter Shahjahanabad from the Badar Roo Burj and the third came in from the Kashmiri Darwaza itself. The third regiment marched up all the way to Jama Masjid, killing everyone who opposed them in their wake.

Nicholson went in himself with a smaller contingent of troops towards Lahori Darwaza as he was expecting a fourth regiment to enter from that side. But the fourth regiment was repelled and Nicholson headed instead towards the Kabuli Darwaza, where a narrow lane went towards Lahori Darwaza. The 'rebels' as the Indian sepoys were called by the British were lying in wait there, and though he attacked them twice he failed. The third time he led the attack himself and was shot in the chest. This was 14 September 1857.

He alternated between life and death for nine days in excruciating pain and died on 23 September, but by then he had heard of the British success. He was thirty-five years old and was buried in the cemetery now known by

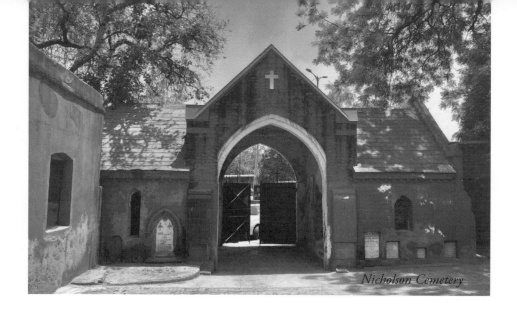

Nicholson Cemetery

his name. His tombstone was made from a marble slab on a garden seat in the Qila-e Mubarak's Mahtab Bagh.

Interestingly, due to his bravery and swordsmanship, a religious cult grew around him called the 'Nikal Seyn', and his followers considered him an incarnation of Lord Vishnu. His regiment allegedly picked up flowers from his grave, gave up soldiering and returned to their villages.

This does not mean he was a model officer as far as Indians were concerned, for he held the 'natives' in deep contempt and favoured torture as a weapon of war.

A statue was made of him in a very warrior-like pose with a naked sword, which used to stand in Qudsia Bagh, facing the Kashmiri Darwaza. It was later shipped to his hometown in northern Ireland.

Ludlow Castle

Named after Samuel Ludlow, the Residency Surgeon whose home it was, it became the Residency. In 1857, it was the residence of Simon Fraser, the British resident, who was one of the first to be slain by the Indian sepoys who had come from Meerut.

Ludlow Castle
From ASI Archives (Felice Beato, 1858)

It played an important part as the site of a battery in the Uprising of 1857, then later became the Delhi Club and then a school. In 1960, the old building was demolished and the school expanded. The No. 2 battery during 1857 was adjoining its wall.

Maqbara of Princess Zeb-un-Nisa Begum

The tomb of Princess Zeb-un-Nisa Begum, the eldest daughter of Emperor Aurangzeb, was in the Tis Hazari Bagh near the Kabuli Darwaza of Shahjahanabad.

Her birth in 1638 to the then Prince Aurangzeb and his wife Dilras Begum was celebrated with great pomp and show in the Qila. Precious stones and money were distributed to the poor for a long time. She was a Persian and Arabic poet writing under the penname of *Makhfi*, or the concealed one. She died in AD 1702.

The tomb and an adjoining mosque were built in the reign of her father Emperor Aurangzeb. When the British built the railway, it was demolished to make way for the railway tracks. Her mortal remains were reburied in Sikandra in Emperor Akbar's mausoleum. Her tombstone read (this is the translation.):

In the name of Allah, Most Gracious, Most Merciful.
This is the tomb of the eldest daughter of the culpable sinner.
May Lord have mercy on her and protect Zeb-un-Nisa,
 Who was among His pious people
and He calls for her forgiveness and is happy with her.
The date of her death was thus pronounced: 'Enter Paradise.'

'Enter paradise' would be the chronogram yielding the year AH 1113/ AD 1701–02.

Shahi Eidgah

This Eidgaah, which is still in use, was built by Emperor Aurangzeb on a small hillock. It had a courtyard of 550 square feet. There is a mehrab in the wall to point towards the qibla, and a pulpit next to it. It is built on a plinth with steps leading to a grand darwaza.

After the Uprising of 1857, the Eidgaah was confiscated by the British and was released later due to the efforts of a Haji Qutbuddin Punjabi.

Shahi Eidgah

XIII

GARDENS

Across the river
- the king's door -
Shahdara
and to the north
- a garden retreat -
Shalimar Bagh
with GT Road's two millen-
nia old
bitumen cutting through
its skin, within
which a walled city
holds together somehow,
sleeping in,
crushed between Kashmere
and Mori Gate, not far
from a river, which
every year, turns into a pity
you'd have guessed the city
by now, if you're a shrewd
billi -
is it, is it
Lahore or Dilli?

—Akhil Katyal

Qudsia Bagh Masjid
From ASI Archives (John Murray, 1858)

Qudsia Bagh

Nawab Qudsia Begum, wife of Emperor Mohammad Shah, built this garden in AD 1748 on the banks of River Yamuna. It covered a huge area, and is now a smaller park.

Nawab Qudsia Begum's son Ahmed Shah succeeded his father, and she gained a position of power. Formerly Udham Bai, she was a very sharp and intelligent lady.

The decline of the Mughal Empire started in the reign of Emperor Mohammad Shah with Nader Shah's invasion driving the last nail in the coffin.

Nawab Qudsia Begum was a poet and her *takhallus* was 'Ranaayi':

Hum jaante thhe aankh lagi aur sukh huwa
Kambakht kaisi aankh lagi aur dukh huwa

We thought we're about to fall asleep [that made us happty]
But alas! We feel in love [and love deprived us of sleep]

It is said that there was a garden already present here and she built various monuments inside it. She built water channels from the river to flow inside the garden.

The ruins testify to the Begum's taste. The gardens which now host morning walkers were once the scene of the Badshah and his Begum strolling with a huge retinue of servants. The gardens were green, the water flowed in

Qudsia Bagh

channels, fountains spouted, and grand festivities were held here. The palaces were beautifully decorated, with the finest furnishings money could buy. The emperor and his harem, princes, princesses and servants, would come and stay. It would be teeming with khwajasaras, dancing and singing girls, and macebearers and guards. It would be scented by flagons of perfumes, but now it stinks. The royals used this as a rendezvous point.

The garden has a few flowerbeds, lawns, and is very popular with walkers.

Only one darwaza remains of the many that this bagh must have had. This would have been the entrance to the palace. The palace, which has been made famous by a painting of Thomas Daniels, overlooked the river. A mosque in the south-west corner of the bagh was in a garden, which bears mute testimony to 1857. It still stands in its battered condition.

The darwaza is built of red sandstone and originally had beautiful floral inlay work. Now bare stones can be seen. An imam appointed by Delhi Waqf board stays in the ruins near the mosque and it's a functioning mosque. This mosque must have been adjoining a palace and was the private mosque of the emperor and Nawab Qudsia Begum, but nothing remains of that.

The river, which flowed next to and nurtured it, it has moved away in anguish and a dirty *naala* has taken its place.

Qudsia Bagh Masjid

A magazine was built in the Bagh in 1857, and that is why it fared so badly. The two batteries were Martyr Battery and Siege Battery. The openings into Badar Roo Burj, also known as Moira Bastion in official papers, and Kashmiri Burj (originally Ali Burj) were from this garden.

Its fortune can be seen from the fact that it was renamed Nicholson Gardens and now there were plans to rename it MM Aggarwal park after the city commissioner a few years ago.

Roshan Ara Begum's Grave Pavilion

Roshanara Bagh

The foundation of this garden was laid in 1650 when Emperor Shah Jahan was building Shahjahanabad. Emperor Aurangzeb's younger sister Princess Roshanara Begum built this garden. She had sided with Emperor Aurangzeb in the war of succession and gained favour when he ascended the throne.

She died in AD 1671 and was buried in a simple grave in this same garden in a once-upon-a-time beautiful pavilion. The building still stands, but looks very forlorn with its fading paintings and peeling plaster.

A room with marble screens contains the open mud grave, which is without a cenotaph. It was supposed to have a tombstone very similar to her sister Princess Jahanara's, but nothing remains there. The chamber is open to the sky. There was a hauz with fountains, which is now dry and lies a mute witness to time. This leads on to what must have been a grand darwaza but is now unused as the garden is accessed from the road which runs down between the two parts.

In 1917, a cricket pavilion and field was made here – the garden was divided into two by the British. It was named after the deputy commissioner, H.C. Baden, by the Delhi municipality. Today it is famous as the Roshanara Cricket Club.

The part with the grave is a park, popular with walkers and yoga practitioners.

Mahaldar Khan ka Bagh

Mahaldar Khan was a noble from the reign of Emperor Mohammad Shah, and he built this bagh in AD 1728–29 bordering the road going to Karnal.

Its beautiful red sandstone darwaza, which had been reduced to a not so beautiful condition has recently been repaired by the Delhi State Archaeology department. The bagh itself is used by car mechanics as a repair area. The area is called Maharana Pratap Bagh and is on the busy Karnal road.

Muhaldar Khan ka Bagh

There was a bazar too next to the bagh and between the two there was a wide compound in which a *Tripoliya Darwaza* (three-arched gateway) was built. The pair of Tripoliyas still stand. The road under it has been strengthened and is in use.

Shalimar Bagh

This bagh was built in AD 1653 by Emperor Shah Jahan outside the walled city of Shajahanabad and was his first halt when on his way to Kashmir or Punjab.

This bagh had very beautifully built buildings, tanks and canals, with many different varieties of trees out of which a few mango trees were of a variety not available anywhere else. According to Sir Sayyid Ahmad Khan, Emperor Shah Jahan himself named this 'pleasure garden', as in the Hindi language *shala* means window and *mar* means pleasure and luxury. Emperor Jahangir had built a garden of the same name in Srinagar, Kashmir.

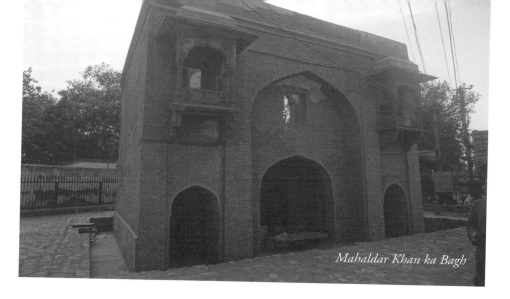

Mahaldar Khan ka Bagh

Today it has become a municipal park where many come to walk and exercise, while the portion with the monuments has been cordoned off with a railing and gate. Once upon a time, Bernier said, it was a fine garden with handsome and noble buildings.

It was here that Prince Aurangzeb held his first coronation and took on the name of Emperor Aurangzeb Alamgir. *Maasir-e Alamgiri* describes this first coronation in this Bagh. As astrologers indicated Wednesday, 31 July, as an auspicious day for the accession, and no time was left to go to Delhi and make preparations for the ceremony, Emperor Aurangzeb stayed for a few hours in the garden of Aghrabad (Shalimar), and sat on the throne at the above mentioned auspicious day. Innumerable presents were given to the nobles, mansabdars and other grandees. As there was no time to read a khutba or strike coins in the new emperor's name, these were done later when he had his second coronation in the Qila-e Mubarak.

Sir David Ochterlony and Lord Metcalfe, Residents of Delhi in the British Raj used it as their summer lodge.

It was damaged during the Uprising of 1857. Today, its Sheesh Mahal is dilapidated and uncared for. The stream is overrun by grass, and the tank is dry.

The gates are kept locked and the guard opens it when requested.

XIV

THE RIDGE

Where the mind is without
fear and the head held high;
Where knowledge is free;
Where the world has not been
broken up into fragments by
narrow domestic walls;
Where words come out from
the depth of truth;
Where tireless striving stretches
its arms towards perfection;
Where the clear stream of
reason has not lost its way into
the dreary desert sand of dead
habit;
Where the mind is led forward
by Thee into ever-widening
thought and action;
Into that heaven of freedom,
my Father, let my country
awake.

—Rabindranath Tagore

British Ammunition store
Photo courtesy Rameen Khan

The Battleground of 1857

It was on the Ridge that the British contingent was stationed from 8 June 1857 onwards, for the siege of Delhi.

The rebels tried to move them from there, but Nicholson came to their rescue. From 7 September to 14 September, they prepared their batteries, and on the 14th attacked the rebels and entered Shahjahanabad. The rebels fought on courageously in the walled city till the 20th, but eventually were routed. On the 20th, the British captured the walled city, and in Diwan-e Khas, they toasted to the health of Queen Victoria.

There are many places where pitched battles were fought.

The Khooni Jheel – so called because several British and Indians died here in 1857

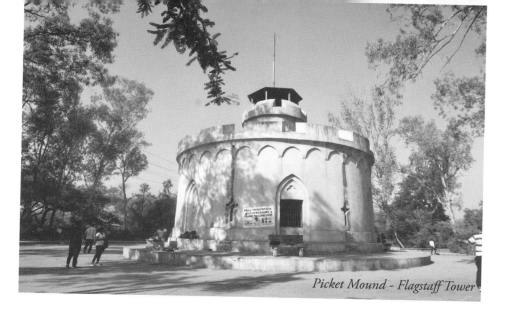

Picket Mound - Flagstaff Tower

Picket Mound (Qurawal ki Tekri)/Flagstaff Tower (Baonta)

Near the Metcalfe house was a brick kiln, which became the picket mound in 1857 for the picket (*qurawal*) of the British army. No traces of it remain.

The Flagstaff Tower is now in the University of Delhi. It was once in complete wilderness at a high point on the Ridge when built by Sir Thomas Metcalfe, the British Resident, in AD 1844.

The Flagstaff Tower is a red-coloured, round tower, which is now enclosed within the university. It was a signal tower, built on a hill. It has three doors with iron grills and a small parapet on top with a small crown – like a roof on top with a wooden cover from where the flag unfurls. It is a one-room building resembling a castle tower.

There are forty steps leading to the top. It has two levels, with the first storey being 22 feet, and the second 16 feet.

Now no one is allowed inside.

Chouburji
Photo courtesy Rameen Khan

Chouburji

It is said that Firoz Shah built this mosque as part of his *Kushk-e Shikar* (hunting lodge), but interestingly it was known as the Baonta ki Masjid, or the mosque attached to the Flagstaff Tower.

It is a double-storeyed building, and Bashiruddin Ahmad Dehlvi writes that on the upper floor there were eight rooms surrounding a larger central chamber. The central chamber had a grave. As I was unable to go up, I can only give his description.

A grave in the courtyard on a high platform gave rise to the speculation that it was built as a mausoleum. It got its name from the four domes on its roof, of which three remain now – lightning damaged the northern one.

This entire area had remains of monuments from the medieval era, but these were all wiped out.

Ashoka's Pillar

This was the second pillar brought by Ashoka and installed here. Shams Siraj Afif writes that Sultan Firoz Shah installed Ashoka's second pillar in his hunting lodge with the same care as he installed the first in Firozabad.

In the later Mughal era, it broke into five parts because of an explosion from a magazine located nearby. Reverend Tieffenthaler, who was in India in 1743–76, has documented seeing the whole pillar.[76]

In 1838, Hindu Rao bought the pillar along with Fraser's mansion, and presented it to the Asiatic Society. The engineer who was given the task of sending the pieces to Calcutta reported that it would be very expensive, and so only those portions of the pillar which had the inscriptions on them were cut and sent to Calcutta.

In AD 1866, it was joined and returned to Delhi and is installed on a platform on the Ridge.

Ashoka's Pillar

Fraser's Kothi/Hindu Rao ka Makaan/Bada Hindu Rao Hospital

This was the mansion of William Fraser who was the British Governor's agent. William Frazer (1784–1835) was the Resident of Delhi from 1830 to 1835. He built the mansion in 1830. It was on a vantage point from where the entire city could be seen, and whichever way the wind blew there was always a cool breeze blowing here.

Nawab Shamsuddin Khan of Firozepur Jhirka and Frazer developed a mutual enmity. According to the British, the Nawab was a charlatan, and because Frazer tried to restrain him, he resented the fact. Indians say that Frazer tried to develop illegitimate relations with a lady who was under the Nawab's protection and in a relationship with him.

It is said that the Nawab hired assassins to kill Fraser. The assassins lived in Bulvemars Ward, which is an alley opening into Chandni Chowk.

Fraser's Kothi – Hindu Rao Hospital
From ASI Archives (Felice Beato, 1858)

They lay in wait for Fraser for a long time but could not find an opportunity to kill him. One day, Fraser had gone to attend a dinner party in Daryaganj in the mansion of the Raja of Kishanganj. It was very late by the time he returned. He was going via Mori Darwaza and here on a bend towards his house a rider overtook his carriage and shot him. He immediately disappeared and could not be caught. He was later traced and arrested and sentenced to be hanged.

They say the actual assassin was lurking in the bushes and ran away to Alwar and was never caught. Nawab Sahib was arrested and produced in court. After a trial, he was sentenced for Fraser's murder, and on 10 October 1835, he was hanged outside Kashmiri Darwaza.

Fraser is buried in St. James Church, and Nawab Shamsuddin in Qadam Sharif.

After Fraser's death, Hindu Rao, a Maratha chief, bought his mansion.

Hindu Rao died before 1857, but this mansion was under the control of his relatives. It came under heavy shelling in the Uprising of 1857 and was greatly damaged. The British confiscated and repaired it. They used it as a pleasure house in the summers.

Now it is a hospital, and though some parts of the original house remain, it has been added on to so haphazardly that it is difficult to make out the original.

I had gone there after reading Prof. Shamsur Rahman Faruqi's *The Mirror of Beauty*, which describes a party held in this mansion and gives a detailed description of the house itself. I was bitterly disappointed.

Kushk Shikar/Jahan Numa/Pir Ghaib

Today Pir Ghaib is the name of a small, damaged, double-storeyed monument. This was once a splendid hunting lodge built by Firoz Shah Tughlaq in AD 1354 on the highest point of the Ridge, to the northwest of the city of Firozabad. It covered a large area and included the present Chouburji Mosque and Ashoka's broken pillar. The remains that stand there today were part of the lodge.

Timur attacked Delhi shortly after the death of Firoz Shah Tughlaq and destroyed this area. His historian Yazdi, as was typical of the flattery of court chroniclers, says that Firoz Shah had named it Jahan Numa because it was written in its destiny that a world conqueror like Timur would bless it with his presence.

Many nobles built their mansions near it once the Sultan started frequenting it.

Sir George Everest used it as a survey station while making his baseline measurements for the Great Trigonometrical Survey, and it was called an observatory. During the Uprising of 1857, it was in the thick of battle as the British were encamped near it.

Initially, the Indian sepoys controlled the Ridge, but they lost it in the battle of Badli ki Sarai in June, giving the British troops a strategic advantage over the walled city during the siege of Delhi. The British troops used Pir Ghaib as an outpost and stationed their heavy battery here.

Pir Ghaib

H.C. Fanshawe says that, 'from the back of the observatory ran the nearest road to the camp from the centre and right of the ridge: this owing to the command which the fire of the enemy had over it, was named the valley of death.'

This entire area has been taken up by the hostels, staff quarters and wings of the Hindu Rao Hospital today. The Pir Ghaib stands within a grilled fence.

The change of name from Kushk-e Shikar to Observatory was due to Sir George Everest, but the present-day Pir Ghaib is very interesting. The monument itself is now a double-storeyed building built of rubble masonry and has steep stairs leading right up to its roof.

On the second floor are two rooms. These rooms have arched openings towards the east and mehrabs in the western wall. A few incised plaster medallions containing names of Allah remain over the mehrabs. Perhaps this area was used as a mosque.

The northern room just above the staircase has a cenotaph that is interestingly placed west to east (contrary to Islamic practices) and has been made there much after the Tughlaq era.

This room is said to have been the *chillahgah* or spiritual retreat of a saint who disappeared mysteriously. This cenotaph was made in his memory and locals gather on Thursday to offer flowers and burn incense sticks. When I went here, I saw oil stains of the lamps. The cenotaph is 6.8 feet x 3 feet and 1.7 feet high, and to the left of this grave are mehrabs of a mosque.

I could not climb up to the roof, but Maulvi Zafar Hasan writes:

> [T]he floor of the southern room is pierced by a circular hole in the centre and directly above this hole there is another in its roof, over which is placed a hollow masonry cylinder 3'2' high and 4' diameter. The cylinder has a segmental opening on the north and south and is covered by a stone slab with a circular hole 4' diameter cut in the centre. Through these holes the sky can be seen from the ground floor.

Perhaps these holes were used for astronomical purposes. I did climb to the roof of the girl's hostel opposite it so I could photograph it and see the roof.

When it was built it must have been much bigger, but now what remains is a 66 feet x 58 feet ruined building, which looks very mysterious and remains one of my favourite Delhi monuments.

Baoli

Just a little way from the Pir Ghaib is a beautiful and quite massive baoli of the same vintage and part of the Kushk-e Shikar. It would have supplied water to the hunting lodge. During the Uprising of 1857, it was the main source of water for the British troops stationed here. It is a rubble masonry structure, and though now the chambers have disappeared, one can see that they must have encircled it.

Baoli

A tunnel was discovered here in the early twentieth century, which, Maulvi Zafar Hasan writes, fostered the belief that it was the same tunnel mentioned by Abul Fazl in *Ain-e Akbari*, made by Firoz Shah and leading from Firozabad (his city) to Kushk-e Shikar. However, he adds that since it is too low and narrow, it couldn't be the one mentioned as that was described as allowing the passage on horseback of Firoz Shah and ladies of his harem.

Mutiny Memorial/Fatehgarh/Ajitgarh

The British government constructed this memorial on the Ridge in memory of their dead. This was the place where they had set up camp during the Siege of Delhi in 1857.

It is an octagonal, tapering tower, 110 feet in height, built on four levels. The top is like a steeple with a 5-foot-tall cross on it. It has a winding staircase inside with seventy-eight steps.

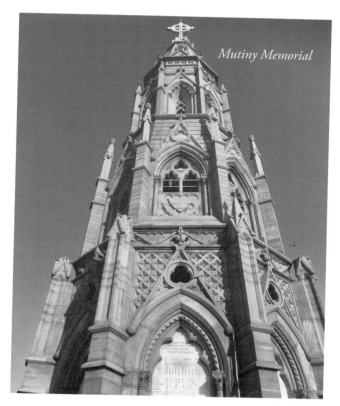

Mutiny Memorial

The bottom level has seven marble slabs, which describe the events of the Siege of Delhi, while the upper levels have windows. Once upon a time, the Qutub Minar could be seen from the upper level!

It has been built on a very high plinth, with two platforms, which is approached by steps.

XV

RAISINA/
JAISINGHPURA/
RAKABGANJ

Sabh meh jot jot hai so-ay
Tis dai channan sabh meh
chaanan ho-ay

Amongst all is the Light —
You are that Light
By this Illumination, that
Light is radiant within all.

Jantar Mantar

This is in the New Delhi that was built by the British as the new capital of India. Most of the old buildings were demolished to make way for the new capital, but a few remain.

Mosque of Abdun Nabi

During Emperor Akbar's reign, in 1575–76, Sheikh Abdun Nabi Numani, who was the *sadr-us sadr* (chief judicial officer), built this mosque in Delhi on the Delhi-Mathura Road.

He was in great favour with Emperor Akbar, who is said to have adjusted the Sheikh's slippers when he took the emperor's leave. He went on many pilgrimages to Mecca. On one of them, the emperor gave him money for distribution to the poor there. On his return he was called to account for it, and when he couldn't he was imprisoned and murdered in 1584–85.

The inscription of this mosque was written by Faizi the great poet, and was removed later and kept in the Red Fort Museum.

This mosque, which today stands at the busy ITO crossing, was made of rubble, and ornamented with coloured tile decoration, which had disappeared by 1919 when Maulvi Zafar Hasan was writing his *Monuments of Delhi*. What we see is its back and large central white dome, behind which is the huge Mahatma Gandhi mural on the Police Headquarters.

The original mosque consisted of three apartments accessed through arched openings.

It is the headquarters of Jamiat Ulema-i-Hind, and they have redone the original structure plus added a triple-wing, three-storeyed hostel to it. This

Mosque of Abdun Nabi
From ASI Archives 1923–24

has formed a square, which is now a cool garden with a pool and fountain, affording peace and tranquillity before one enters the mosque.

Sheikh Mohammad Sahib Chisti Sabri ka Gumbad

> Rise early at dawn, when our storytelling begins.
> In the dead of the night, when all other doors are locked,
> the door for the Lovers to enter opens
>
> —Abu Said Abil Kheir[77]

Near this mosque is the shrine of Sheikh Mohammad Sahib Chisti, who was the khalifa of Sheikh Ibrahim Rampuri. He was a recluse who spent his time in devotion. Though he avoided company, he was of an extremely affable, kind and generous nature. His followers included Mohammad Muazzam, the son of Emperor Aurangzeb.

The Sheikh and his followers built the shrine.

This place is popular as Sheikh Mohammad ki Bain, as there used to be a small lake near this place where he performed his ablutions.

Agrasen ki Baoli

Agrasen ki Baoli

This is one of the most popular baolis in Delhi and is always full of visitors. Though there is no historical reference to support it, it is popularly believed to have been built by Raja Agrasen, an ancient king who ruled over Agra. In the fourteenth century, the Agarwal community who claimed descent from the Raja got it repaired and rebuilt.

It is a large stepped well, built of rubble and dressed stone, on three levels. It has arched rooms on both sides for use by travellers. It measures 129 feet by 24.6 feet at the water level. There is a roofed platform on the northern end that could have been used for seating.

Jantar Mantar

This is an observatory built in the reign of Muhammad Shah by Raja Jai Singh of Jaipur. I describe below the four main instruments from Sir Sayyid Ahmad Khan's *Asar-us Sanadid*.

Jantar Mantar

1. Jai Prakash

This is an instrument to measure shadows. A pillar on the upper level acts as a measuring tool, with a horizontal circumference of 53 feet and 8 inches. Four levels have been built around it, like a well, with one level sunk in the ground and three above the ground. This has been further divided into sixty sections, in which niches have been created, which are left alternatively open or filled up. Circles have been drawn on the inside wall, which have been divided into measurement units for the measurement of degrees, and above, the circles of the circumference and horizon have all been divided.

2. Ram Jantar

This instrument is a raised platform that is positioned towards the north and has four arcs. There are stairs on both sides of the arc so that the effect of the shadows can be studied. Two more arcs have been taken out from below the platform. Each arc used to have measurement units to record the time and zodiac. However, the signs on this raised platform have all been erased now and the arcs are also broken in many places.

3. Som Samrat Jantar

This building is essentially a measuring instrument. A side wall of lime mortar and stone has been built in the middle of an equatorial sundial with a radius of 18 yards. All the measuring units are given on it. On this ramp, there are stairs to climb to the top. Similarly, there are stairs on both sides of the sundial arcs to facilitate the observation of shadows. The units on this instrument have also been ruined.

Sawai Jai Singh invented these three instruments, and that's why they have been given Hindi names.

4. Karah-i-Maqar

Below this observatory, two concave hemispheres have been placed in such a way that the axes of the zodiac are incomplete without each other. The sphere or *karah* is completed only when one half is placed on the other. There are twelve arcs in these spheres. The signs of the zodiac have been divided in such a way that six are filled in and six are empty. There were signs of measurements everywhere, and perhaps it had an axis, but all these have broken and the units have been erased. In every empty arc are stairs that allow one to climb to the top to study the shadows. The diameter of these spheres is 26 feet, and they are very solidly built of lime mortar and bricks.

This observatory was the first of its kind to acknowledge and use the principles of modern English astronomy. Prior to this, the principles of Greek astronomy were in use, which is why this observatory is unique and well-known amongst those built around the same time.

In the fourteenth year of Emperor Mohammad Shah's reign in AD 1731, Raja Sawai Jai Singh sent many mathematicians along with Father Manuel to foreign countries, from where he got telescopes and other astronomical instruments. Until recently, Jantar Mantar was famous for the innumerous protests held near it.

Gurudwara Bangla Sahib

Burn worldly love,
rub the ashes and make ink of it,
make the heart the pen,
the intellect the writer,
write that which has no end or limit.

—Guru Nanak, Sri Guru Granth Sahib[78]

One of the most popular and beautiful places of worship, Gurudwara Bangla Sahib is situated in the heart of present-day Delhi: Connaught Place, on the intersection of Ashoka Road and Baba Kharak Singh Marg. It gets its name from the fact that it was originally a bungalow or *bangla* of Mirza Raja Jai Singh II of Amber, the commander-in-chief of Emperor Aurangzeb's army. Its original name was Jaisinghpura Palace.

Fourteen days before his death, the seventh Sikh Guru, Guru Har Rai, had chosen and installed his younger son, Guru Har Krishan (July 1656– March 1664), who was five years old at the time, to succeed him.

The elder son, Ram Rai, disputed the right to accession and went to Emperor Aurangzeb for arbitration. Emperor Aurangzeb issued a decree

Bangla Sahib

summoning Guru Har Krishan to his court at the instigation of Ram Rai. The task of persuading him was given to Mirza Raja Jai Singh who sent his minister, Paras Ram, with a *parwana* or epistle.

Guru Har Krishan, though he had taken a vow never to appear before the emperor, saw an excellent opportunity to dispel the misconceptions created by his brother's followers and boost the morale of the Sikhs, and decided to go to Delhi. His mother, Diwan Dargah Mull, Bhai Gurditta Ji, Gurbaksh Mal and Bhai Mati Das accompanied him. They left Kiratpur in the second week of February 1664.

On the way, he stopped at Dyalpur where his sister lived. Many devotees came to meet him and be blessed. A Brahmin named Pandit Chandu Lal lived in that village. He was very proud of his lineage and knowledge. He taunted the young Guru, asking him what he knew of old religious books, as he sat on the throne of Guru Nanak. Guru Har Krishan called a water carrier, Chajju Ram, and asked him to explain the gist of the Gita to the pandit. To everyone's astonishment, Chajju Ram gave an extremely cogent commentary on the sacred book. The wise Guru made his point that knowledge is not the property of any one caste and can be acquired by anyone seeking it. The pandit became a disciple of the Guru after that.[79]

Mirza Raja Jai Singh was asked by the Sikhs to protect the young Guru from any harm. The Raja made elaborate arrangements to look after the young Guru and he was a guest of honour in Jaisinghpura Palace. His devotees flocked to visit him here and though he stuck to his vow of not meeting the emperor, Prince Muazzam, son of Emperor Aurangzeb, visited him. Prince Muazzam was very impressed and praised the Guru to his father.

According to Zafar Hasan, Emperor Aurangzeb tested the intelligence of the young Guru in various ways before deciding in his favour. One of them was asking him to recognize the empress among a number of ladies, all similarly dressed. Guru Har Krishan immediately pointed his finger at the empress!

The actual story is that it was Raja Jai Singh who asked him to identify his queen, Anand Kaur. The Guru earned the name of Bal Mukund or Child Krishna with his sagacity, piety, and gentle and steadfast behaviour towards all.

Based on the Guru's growing popularity amongst the Sikhs who came from neighbouring areas in huge crowds to meet him, and reports by Prince Muazzam, Raja Jai Singh and local Sikh leaders, Emperor Aurangzeb dismissed the claim of Ram Rai, but did not openly announce the claim of Guru Har Krishan.

The Guru continued staying in Delhi and helping all who came in touch with him. During that time, there was an epidemic of cholera and small pox in the city. The young Guru moved around fearlessly amongst all the people afflicted by it, tending to them, irrespective of religion. He went with medicinal herbs and his physicians to wherever the sick were, and the Muslims of Delhi nicknamed him *Bala Peer* or Child Saint.

When Emperor Aurangzeb insisted he come to the darbar, the Guru shifted out of Jaisinghpura and went to live near the River Yamuna in a place now known as Gurudwara Bala Sahib. Though he later returned to the palace, he only agreed to stay in it at night. When Emperor Aurangzeb fixed the date of his coming to the Darbar as 28 March, the Guru gave his last sermon and withdrew to an inner apartment of the palace, signifying his refusal to comply with the emperor's orders. He later contracted small pox and tragically left this world on 30 March 1664 at the young age of 8.[80]

His devotees accompanied his funeral bier, and his last rites were conducted by Bhai Gurudittaji on the same spot where he had pitched his tent near the Yamuna.

A memorial was built on the premises of Jaisinghpura Palace in the young saint's memory. The tank or *sarovar* in the premises is said to be holy as the Guru sanctified it. It is believed to have curative powers and people treat its water as *amrit*, or nectar. During the epidemic itself, thousands are believed to have been cured by this water.

In March 1783, Maharaja Baghel Singh, a Sikh general who led the Sikhs against the Mughals, established his camp in the suburbs of Delhi. He built four gurudwaras to commemorate the visit of Sikh Gurus to the city. He built a Gurudwara at the site of the bungalow where Guru Har Krishan had stayed: the present Bangla Sahib. He built Bala Sahib at the site of the cremation of the infant Guru.

The other two were the Gurudwara Sis Ganj at the site of the execution of Guru Tegh Bahadur, and Rakabganj Gurudwara to mark the site of his cremation.

Later, the devotees of Guru Har Krishan constructed a tank 225 x 235 feet, with an 18-foot-wide *parikarma* or circumbulatory path, and a 12-foot-wide veranda along its three sides.

The Delhi Sikh Gurudwara Management Committee runs a hospital in the basement of the Gurudwara building.

The building itself is very beautiful and its golden dome and finial can be seen from far away. The main hall is large and simple, with the shrine with the holy Guru Granth Sahib.

A lofty standard or Nishan Sahib is also installed in the compound.

There is a Khalsa School for Girls inside the gurudwara, as well as an Art Gallery named after the Sikh General Sardar Bhagel Singh who supervised the construction of Sikh shrines in Delhi in 1783 during the time of Shah Alam II.

There is a huge *langarkhana* where free food is distributed to all who come here regardless of caste, creed or religion. The Sikh community have no parallel when it comes to *sewa* or service. They do it selflessly and diligently. Thousands volunteer in the kitchens and cook for the devotees. I count myself lucky as having partaken of the langar, which is a very blessed experience.

My son used to miss home-cooked food when he first went abroad. In Germany, he found the love and home-cooked food in a gurudwara's langar and was blown away by their warmth.

The main celebrations in the Gurudwara Bangla Sahib take place on the birth anniversary of Guru Sri Har Krishan Sahib and the death anniversary of Maharaja Ranjit Singh.

Gurudwara Rakabganj

To protect their right to wear their caste-marks and sacred threads,
Did he, in the dark age, perform the supreme sacrifice.
To help the saintly he went to the utmost limit,
He gave his head but never cried in pain.

—Guru Gobind Singh[81]

Guru Tegh Bahadur, the ninth Sikh Guru, had undertaken extensive tours of Punjab to instil confidence in the Sikh and Hindu community against the religious persecution being carried out by Emperor Aurangzeb.[82]

It was a matter of time before Emperor Aurangzeb summoned Guru Tegh Bahadur to Delhi. He was apprehended in Agra along with a band of his devotees and brought before the Qazi's court in Delhi. He was kept in custody in the Kotwali for eight days, and tortured to show miracles, accept Islam or court death. He chose the last. Guru Tegh Bahadur was sentenced to death and executed on 11 November 1675.

Khushwant Singh writes that though Emperor Aurangzeb was not present in Delhi at that time, there is little doubt that it had his tacit approval.[83]

Before his body could be quartered and put on public display as ordered by the kotwal, it was secreted away at night under the cover of a storm by two of his devotees, Bhai Lakhi Shah Lubana and Lakhi Shah. They took his body to their house in Raisina village, built a pyre inside it and set the whole house on fire. The ashes were collected and cremated at the same spot.

His head was taken to Anandpur by Jiwan Singh, Bhai Nanu and Bhai Uda, and cremated by his son Guru Gobind Singh.

Gurudwara Rakabganj

Gurudwara Rakabganj marks the place of the cremation of Guru Tegh Bahadur's body, and was built by Baghel Singh in 1783.

Baghel Singh applied for 100 *bigha*s of land to Emperor Shah Alam in the village of Raisina where the Guru had been cremated. He wanted to build a house for mendicants and plant a garden around the Gurudwara. The land was granted by a *farman* dated 1st Moharram in Shah Alam's 29th regnal year (17 October 1787).

Raja Swarup Singh of Jind constructed the present building.

It is a beautiful two-storeyed building adorned by a central dome, and small, domed cupolas stand on the four corners of the platform. It is identical from all sides and has steps leading up to the platform on which the Gurudwara stands.

A sense of calm and peace prevails here.

XVI

FESTIVALS IN THE RED FORT UNDER THE MUGHALS

Jhoola kinne daalo hai
amriya'n
Baag andheri taal kinara
Mor jhinkare
Badal kaare
Barsan laage
Boondein phuniya'n phuniya'n
Jhoola kinne daalo hai
amriya'n
Sab sakhi mil gayi
Bhool bhulaiyya'n
Bholi bholi dole
Shauq rang saiyya'n

Who has put up the swing
on the mango tree?
The orchard is dark, the
peacock dances at the edge of
the lake,
Black clouds splatter rain-
drops softly.
Who has put up the swing
on the mango tree?
All our friends have gathered
at the maze,
Shauq, they all swing inno-
cently.
Who has put up the swing
on the mango tree?

—Bahadur Shah Zafar

Photo courtesy Jayshree Shukla

Diwali

Diwali was known as the Jashn-e Chiragha'n under the Mughals and was celebrated with great enthusiasm. The Rang Mahal in Red Fort was lit up with diyas on Diwali as can be seen in a painting of Emperor Mohammad Shah Rangeela celebrating Diwali outside the palace with some ladies. The emperor was a poet and Rangeela was his nom de plume.

The Mughal emperor was weighed in gold and silver, which were distributed amongst the poor. It is said that some Mughal ladies would climb to the top of the Qutub Minar to watch the lights and fireworks. Fireworks under the supervision of the *mir atish* would be ignited near the walls of the Red Fort. And a special Akash Diya (Light of the Sky) was lit with great pomp, placed atop a pole 40 yards high, supported by sixteen ropes, and fed on several maunds of *binaula* (cottonseed oil) to light up the darbar.

Dussehra

The enthusiastic participation of the Muslims in the Hindu religious festivities celebrated under the patronage of the Mughal kings reflected the prevalence of a composite culture in medieval India, where social and cultural interaction between the two communities flourished at various levels, enriching both.

Maheshwar Dayal's book, *Aalam Mein Intekhaab: Dilli*, published in 1987 by Urdu Academy, describes the history, traditions and culture of Delhi from Mughal times to date. One of the things that fascinated me was the

Sawaari of Lord Rama, Sitaji and Lakshman taken out even today in Shahjahanabad

book's description of the celebration of festivals in the walled city, particularly Dussehra and Ramlila.

After Emperor Shah Jahan shifted the Mughal capital from Agra to Delhi and established the walled city of Shahjahanabad, he extended his patronage to celebrations of various important Hindu festivals observed by his army and people. Dussehra was one such festival, which was established for the Hindu soldiers of his army, on the banks of the River Yamuna, behind the Red Fort.

The Mughal emperors consolidated their rule in India with inter-religious marriages, intermingling with the local rulers and populace and adopting local customs, often mixing time with theirs, which had come from Central Asia and Persia.

Ramlila, an important part of the Dussehra celebrations, is a theatrical enactment of the Ramayana, narrating the story of the triumph of good over evil. The first Ramlila Committee in Delhi was established by Emperor Bahadur Shah Zafar, and it continues to exist till date.

Mirza Qateel in his Persian book, *Haft Tamasha*, written in the eighteenth century, says that the Hindus and Muslims celebrated Dussehra and Ramlila together with great gusto. In the markets and chowks of Delhi, huge effigies of the demon-king Ravana made of cardboard and paper were erected. In Ravana's stomach, an earthen vessel containing sherbet was placed, and small children dressed up as Lord Rama came and fired arrows at this vessel. Huge crowds would gather to watch this spectacle.

Another tradition in those days was the distribution of sherbet in earthen cups called *kulhad*s to everyone. People drank the beverage as a symbol of victory over Ravana – the red-coloured sherbet signifying Ravana's blood. A very big fair was held on the banks of the Yamuna, which drew crowds from far and wide. According to Dayal, on the morning of Dussehra, the Mughal emperor would hold a darbar, or the royal court, at the Red Fort. In accordance with tradition, the bird Neelkanth (Indian roller), which signified victory and success as per Hindu traditions, would be set free in front of the emperor. In fact, it is called the Dussehra bird in folklore. In addition to this practice, a falcon was brought to perch on the emperor's hand. According to Timurid traditions, the falcon symbolized victory and success. This is a classic case of adopting and adapting to local customs.

The emperor on Dussehra rewarded the courtiers and citizens in his darbar. In the evening, the *darogha* (in-charge) of the royal stables had the horses decorated with henna on their hooves and designs on their forehead, and they were bedecked with jewellery. They would then be taken to the Red Fort and paraded under the *jharoka* (window). The emperor would inspect them and reward the grooms for the best-decorated horses. Beautifully adorned horses and elephants would also be taken to the havelis (mansions) of the nobles and rewarded suitably.

During the nine days preceding Dussehra, called 'Navratri' or nine nights, barley would be sown in small boats. On the day of Dussehra, old and young alike would decorate their caps, turbans and ears with barley sprigs, as it was considered auspicious. Since Persian was the court language and widely understood, the quatrains of Tulsi Das's Ramayana would be recited in Persian for all to enjoy and understand. Verses would be composed in Urdu and Persian for the occasion.

Ramlila would be enacted everywhere, and people dressed as Lord Rama, Sita, Lakshman and Ravana were taken around on chariots. Every day there would be new tableaus in the procession. When Lord Rama's exile was enacted, a boat with a boatman would ferry Lord Rama, Sita and Lakshman across Shahji's pond (a symbolic Ganga) near the Ramlila grounds. After 1947, the pond was filled up to make way for Kamla Market. During the day, children would dress up as Rama and Sita and enact the Ramayana. In the evenings, enormous crowds of Hindus and Muslims, men and women, young and old, rich and poor would gather at the Ramlila grounds to watch the plays there.

Holi

Holi would be celebrated on the same scale as Eid in the Red Fort or Qila-e Mualla. It was called *Eid-e Gulabi* or *Aab-e Pashi* (Shower of Colourful Flowers), with everyone joining in.

There would be *mela*s or fairs behind the Red Fort on the banks of the Yamuna. A huge crowd would gather from the fort till Raj Ghat. The *dhaf, jhanjaen, nafiri* (tambourine, cymbal and trumpet) would be played, and nautch girls would dance. Groups of travelling musicians and artistes would gather under the Red Fort and display their tricks and talents. The mimics would imitate the emperor, prince and princesses too, and nobody would take offence. The queens, princesses and noble women would be sitting in their jharokas (overhanging enclosed balcony) and enjoying the entertainment. The emperor would reward these artistes handsomely.

At night, there would be a grand celebration of Holi in the Red Fort, with singing and dancing throughout the night. Famous courtesans from throughout the country would come here. The most popular song would be Emperor Bahadur Shah Zafar's 'Horiyan'. Bands of entertainers would go around Shahjahanabad entertaining the aristocrats and the rich in their havelis. There would be much good-natured leg-pulling with the slogan, *'Bura Na Maano, Holi Hai!'* (Don't be offended, it's Holi!).

Children would also go around entertaining elders with their acts. At night there would be *mehfils* (soirees) in the walled city, with the aristocrats, traders and shopkeepers all enjoying themselves.

Bahudar Shah Zafar (1775–1862) would join the celebration with great gusto and enthusiasm and mingle with his subjects. He wrote a song for the occasion:

Kyun mo pe maari rang ki pichkaari
dekh kunwarji du'ngi gaari

Why have you squirted me with colour?
O, Kunwarji, I will swear at you!

Bhaaj saku'n main kaise moso bhaajo nahin jaat
thaa'ndi ab dekhu'n main baako kaun jo sun mukh aat

I can't run, I am unable to run
I am now standing here and want to see who can drench me.

Bahut dinan mein haath lage ho kaise jaane deoon
Aaj main phagwa ta sau Kanha faita pakad kar leoon.

After many days have I caught you, how can I let you go?
I will catch you by your waistband and play Holi with you.

'Shokh' rang aisi dheet langar sau khelay kaun ab hori
mukh meedai aur haath marore karke woh barjori

Who can play Holi with such a mischievous Kanha!
My face you have coloured and my wrist you have twisted in
your playfulness.

Note: Shokh was the penname of emperor Bahadur Shah Zafar when
writing in Punjabi and Braj Bhasha.

Jam-e Jahanuma, an Urdu newspaper, wrote in 1844 that during the
days of the Mughal Emperor Bahadur Shah Zafar, special arrangements were
made for Holi festivities, and goes on to describe the frolicking and exchange
of colour made from the tesu flowers.

Raksha Bandhan

The Mughal Empire in the eighteenth century was mostly run by powerful
ministers, who put puppet kings on the throne and removed them when their
usefulness was over.

Emperor Aurangzeb (1659–1707) was succeeded by his son, Prince
Shah Alam, who took the title of Bahadur Shah I (1702–12). After him came a
succession of emperors, some of whom sat on the throne for just a few months.

In 1754, the great grandson of Emperor Aurangzeb, Mohammad Aziz-
ud-Daulah, became the eighteenth Mughal emperor to sit on the Mughal
throne. He was chosen from among the many princes living in the royal palace
and placed on the throne with the title Alamgir II (2 June 1754 – 29 November
1759) by Imad-ul-Mulk.

Alamgir II was the reigning Mughal monarch only in name, with all
powers vested in the hands of his wazir, Ghazi-ud-Din Imad-ul-Mulk.

Attacks and plunder by the Afghan ruler Ahmad Shah Abdali had
considerably weakened the Mughal Empire. There was chaos everywhere,
and Imad, suspecting the emperor to be in touch with the Afghan ruler and
plotting to cast the Wazir aside, decided to get rid of Alamgir II altogether.

Imad did not have the courage to eliminate the emperor inside the fort, so he devised a clever idea of drawing the Badshah out.

Alamgir II was a very pious man and had great faith in Sufi faqirs (mendicants). Whenever he heard a faqir had come to Delhi, he would call him to the fort, and if the faqir didn't come, the Mughal emperor would himself go and meet the Sufi.

Imad-ul-Mulk spread the rumour of a very esteemed faqir coming for a visit to Delhi, and staying in Firoz Shah Kotla, and who would not go out to meet anyone. As these rumours were cleverly fed to the emperor, his anxiety to meet the faqir kept growing.

One night, the Badshah said, 'I will go and meet him.'

When he reached Firoz Shah Kotla, the wazir said, 'Jahanpanah, the faqir will be very upset upon seeing your retinue. You should go in alone.'

The Badshah ordered everyone except an eunuch to wait near the entrance and went in alone.

As soon as he set foot inside one of the rooms in the Kotla, he was attacked by the wazir's men and brutally killed. The emperor's body was thrown into the Yamuna.

The wazir came out of the mosque and told the royal retinue: 'The Badshah is sitting with the faqir and has asked me to bring a piece of paper from his khwabgah. You all stay here; I will just be back with that paper.'

He disappeared from there after that.

Meanwhile, a Brahmin lady (named as Ram Kumari in *Dehli ki Aakhri Shama* by Farhatullah Baig) was passing by. She was on her way for the early morning puja at the Yamuna, which flowed under the Firoz Shah Kotla. She saw a mutilated dead body that had floated back to the riverbank and recognized it as that of the emperor.

The Mughal emperors always enjoyed the goodwill of their subjects – Hindus and Muslims alike. She immediately went over to the emperor's lifeless body, sat down there and kept his head on her lap, and crying softly, waited for dawn.

At dawn, she was joined by other worshippers of the Yamuna. They all sat with their dead emperor till help arrived.

Hours passed. When neither the Badshah nor the Wazir came back, the royal retinue got worried and went into the mosque. They found it empty and started running around in search of the emperor.

They found his slain body under the wall of the mosque with the Brahmin lady guarding the corpse. The royal retinue brought the dead body back and after the ritual bath buried him in Emperor Humayun's tomb.

The next emperor, Shah Alam II, called Ram Kumari, the Brahmin lady who guarded Alamgir II's body, and declared her his sister. He rewarded her generously.

After that, on every *Salona* (as Raksha Bandhann was called) festival, she would come and tie a *rakhi* of pure pearls on Shah Alam II's wrist. Accompanying the rakhi would be lots of sweets. In turn, he would gift her clothes and gold coins, as was the norm.

Until the last Mughal emperor, Bahadur Shah Zafar, hadn't been exiled from the Red Fort, this practice continued, with women of Ram Kumari's family coming to tie rakhis on the wrists of the Mughal emperor and other princes.[84]

Eid-ul Fitr

The Islamic calendar is a lunar one, so as soon as the month of Ramzan would be about to end, the emperor would send dromedary riders to look out for the moon. Depending on when the moon was sighted, Eid would be celebrated on the 29th day or 30th day.

Under Emperor Shah Jahan, the Eid prayers were offered in the Jama Masjid, but Emperor Aurangzeb built an Eidgah in Paharganj and later Mughal emperors went there.

Photo courtesy Anjum Alam

On the day of Eid, after eating vermicelli cooked in milk and wearing new clothes and sprinkled fragrant perfume, the men left for the *Shahi Eidgah* in Paharganj in carriages and palanquins or on foot.

After the Eid prayers, the emperor would felicitate the imam before he read the *khutba* (sermon). After the khutba was delivered, people would greet one another with embraces. Guns would be fired in celebration of the moment.

The Badshah would then return to the Fort.

He would hold court in the Diwan-e Khas on the Takht-e Taoos and receive offerings and hand out garlands and turban ornaments to the various princes and nobles.

In *Dilli ka Aakhiri Deedar*, translated as *City of My Heart* by this author,[85] Syed Wazir Hasan Dehlvi writes that, 'Every corner of the city celebrated during Eid. Residents consume hot *kachoris* and kababs bought straight from the shops. Some meet their friends, while some walk around and take in all the sights. Kites of various shapes soar in the sky.'

To date kachoris are sold in the lanes of Shahjahanabad during Eid.

Eid-uz Zuha

On Eid-uz Zuha or the festival of sacrifice too the same protocol was followed, but here there was an addition of animal sacrifice. The emperor would sacrifice a camel in the Shahi Eidgah. He would hold court and there would be celebrations in the Fort and city.

Nauroz

Nauroz or the Persian New Year was celebrated by all the Mughal emperors with great enthusiasm. The Qila would be decked up, and beautifully decorated tents and awnings would be put up.

A colour would be decided by the royal astrologers, and everyone in the Qila would wear that colour, including the emperor.

A special darbar would be held and offerings made to the emperor. The grand Mughals had been weighed on Nauroz, and the gold and silver distributed to the poor.

Later, in the afternoon, boats decorated with the colour of the day would ply in the River Yamuna with royal passengers out to enjoy the day.

XVII

FOOD OF
SHAHJAHANABAD

*Kiya kaamil hame'n ik umr
mein soz-e mohabbat ne
Huye ham aatish-e gham se
kabab aahista aahista*

I was whole, after burning in
love for a lifetime,
The fire of love, it grilled
my heart like a kabab on
slow fire.

—Wahshat Raza Ali Kalkatvi

Today Old Delhi or Shahjahanabad is famous for its food. Most of the recipes are traditional and have been handed down over generations by the cooks who once cooked in the royal kitchens of the Mughals. The emperor, princes and nobles appreciated art for its own sake, and culinary art was one of the most appreciated genres.

The Mughals came in touch with the Portuguese via trade routes and later in Emperor Akbar's religious discussions in Agra and soon the influences started creeping into the former's kitchens. Items such as potatoes and tomatoes were introduced into the royal food. Perhaps the most important aspect was the introduction of chilli that is such an essential ingredient in nahaari.

As described in Munshi Faizuddin's *Bazm-e Akhir*, mealtimes were elaborate affairs. Once the emperor signalied that the food should be laid, the superintendent of the royal kitchens would send the food in sealed dishes to prevent poisoning. Female attendants would bring the baskets on their heads. Food was laid out on a piece of leather covered with a white cloth called dastarkhwan. The emperor would set out a portion of the food for the poor before starting.[86] The emperor like all of us even today would begin the meal by invoking God's grace and end by thanking Him for His Blessings.

Emperor Shah Jahan liked to enjoy his food and spent long hours at the dastarkhwan.[87]

After the fall of Delhi in 1857 and the exile of Emperor Bahadur Shah Zafar, many of these master chefs or *rakabdar*s in the royal kitchen found themselves without patrons, and set up roadside stalls in the walled city to make ends meet. They sold delicious wares on the roadside or on the steps of Jama Masjid.

One of these cooks was Ghummi Kababi, described by Ashraf Subuhi Dehlvi in his book, *Dilli ki Chand Ajeeb Hastiyan*. As long as Ghummi was alive, there was no better kabab being sold. To add to this was the bonus that Ghummi himself was an extremely entertaining man who was single-handedly trying to preserve the Mughal legacy. His salesmanship and his conversation style were refined, and memories of the gracious past bringing back memories of the musical tones of the residents of the Qila. Now we no longer find that language or the food that Miyan Ghummi cooked. The cooks these days pass off limp chillies and burnt meat as food!

As Ghummi would often mutter:

Aji woh din lad gaye jab Khalil Khan fakhta udaya karte thay

The glory days have gone when all the lovers of spicy conversation and kababs would stand there the whole night

The popular vegetarian dishes were *puri sabzi* (deep-fried wheat bread and a potato dish), *puri halwa* (deep-fried wheat bread with a halwa made from semolina and various types of savouries such as *pakoras* (fried gram balls), *andarsa* (rice flour and sesame seeds). The famous *chhole kulche* that are associated with Delhi today came after the Partition brought by the refugees from Pakistan.

I mention here only a few popular Shahjahanabad dishes.

Kababs

Since the discovery of fire, whole animals or chunks of meat were cooked on open fire. At some point in time, early men and women learnt to pierce pieces of meat with wooden sticks to prevent them getting burnt – thus grilled food was invented.

The popular *seekh kabab* originated in Central Asia and comes from the Turkish word *shish kabab*, which literally means 'skewer' and 'roast meat'.

There is a legend that Turkish soldiers would grill meat in open fields using their swords as skewers in their camps at night during their invasion of Anatolia. Though they did not invent the shish kabab, as Homer's Odyssey refers to meat cooked on skewers in an open fire.

For the Central Asian nomad, cooking was not a luxury but a necessity. They would travel with meat pieces and mince, marinated in different spices to tenderize and flavour the meat and cook it in the evening when they camped. Since a lot of meat would be game, unusual smells were also taken care of in the marinating process.

Mongol soldiers too carried on this practice, keeping marinated meat in their saddlebags and cooking it easily and in quick time on fire once they camped for the night. Since they travelled and conquered vast swathes of land, the shish kebab too travelled with them. This practical dish gave rise to exotic kababs of many kinds.

The ones that were served on the royal table as described by Munshi Faizuddin in *Bazm-e Aakhir* are:

- Seekh ke kabab (made by grilling seasoned mince on skewers)
- Shami kebab (made by boiling mincemeat with spices and gram)
- Goliyon ke kabab (round shaped kababs made with coarse meat and deep fried can still be found in the walled city especially during Ramzan)
- Teetar ke kabab (made from pheasant meat)
- Bater ke kabab (made from quail meat)
- Nuqti kabab (these are sweet kababs made by soaking them in sugar syrup)
- Khatai ke kabab (sour kababs).

Ghalib, Mangoes and Kababs

We owe much to Altaf Husain Hali for writing a beautiful biography of the famous poet Mirza Asadullah Khan Ghalib. As someone who loves to eat and cook, for me one of the most fascinating parts of the biography is the description of Ghalib's food habits.

Hali writes that Ghalib's breakfast would be just a glass of almond milk. He was also very fond of meat and ate it for every meal. Hali goes on to write that towards the end of his life Ghalib lost his appetite, but even then a *qorma* made of 250 gm of meat would be served for him at lunch. The meat pieces and the curry would be served in separate bowls. The upper part of the *phulka* (softer, fluffed-up version of the Indian roti) would be soaked in the curry and kept in another bowl for him to eat. There would also be a few paise worth of *dahi* (curd) in a bowl. Sometimes, there would be the yolk of an egg in another bowl.

In the evenings, he would eat shami kababs or seekh kababs. He had a small appetite but he was very particular about what he ate. Mirza Ghalib always lived in straitened conditions and, one day, when the *dastarkhwan* (tablecloth) was set for his lunch, it was full of crockery, but the food that was put on it was very meagre. He smiled and said, 'If you go by the plenitude of crockery, then my dastarkhwan seems like that of Yezid, but if you go by the quantity of food, then it that of Bayazid.'

Yezid was the second caliph of the Umayyad Dynasty, famous for his impiety and persecution of Hussain ibn Ali, the grandson of the Prophet (PBUH), leading to his eventual death in the battle of Karbala. Bayazid Bastami was a famous ninth-century Persian Sufi known for his piety and asceticism.

When we talk of summers in India, we think of mangoes. And when we think of mangoes, Dilliwalle must think of Mirza Ghalib. He was extremely fond of mangoes, and in summers his friends would send him different varieties of the fruit from their orchards, but the bard could never have enough of mangoes.

A famous anecdote describes an occasion when Ghalib was strolling with Mughal Emperor Bahadur Shah Zafar and some of the emperor's companions in the Bagh-e Hayat Baksh or Mahtab Bagh in the Qila-e Mubarak (Red Fort). The mango trees were laden with different varieties of the fruit. They were meant only for the emperor, the princes and the women of the harem.

Ghalib would keep looking at each mango that they passed with great attention.

The emperor asked, 'Why are you looking at each mango so attentively?'

With folded hands, the poet replied with great sincerity: 'My Lord and Guide, some poet once said that every fruit has the name of the person (and his ancestors) destined to eat it written on it. I am looking for the name of my grandfather, father and my name!'

The emperor smiled and had a basket of the choicest mangoes delivered to Mirza's house the same day.

Another anecdote if of the time when once Ghalib was sitting in the veranda of his house with a very close friend of his, Hakim Razi ud-Din Khan, who wasn't fond of mangoes. Just then, a donkey cart passed by. The donkey sniffed at a pile of mango skins lying there and, turning its face away, walked off.

The Hakim Sahib turned towards Mirza and said, 'Look, even a donkey doesn't eat mangoes!'

Ghalib immediately retorted, 'Undoubtedly, donkeys don't eat mangoes!'

One day, Maulana Fazl-e Haq and some other gentlemen were discussing the merits of different varieties of mangoes. Mirza was also part of the gathering. When everyone had given their opinion, Maulana Fazl-e Haq turned to Mirza and asked him for his opinion. The bard smiled and said, 'My friend, in my view, only two things are necessary in mangoes: they should be sweet, and they should be numerous.'

Despite the fact that his friends would keep sending him mangoes as gifts, he was never satiated with his favourite fruit. I dedicate a family recipe to Mirza Ghalib, his love for kababs and mangoes.

Qaliamba is a unique dish that combines shami kabab with unripe mangoes.

Qaliamba (*serves 6*)

Part 1: Shami kabab

> ½ kg minced mutton (should be dry)
> ½ cup chickpea (*chana dal*)
> ½-inch ginger stick (*adrak*)
> 1 onion, chopped
> Seeds of 1 brown cardamom (*badi elaichi*)
> 3 pieces clove (*laung*)
> ½ tsp black peppercorns (*sabut kali mirch*)
> 2 bay leaves (*tejpatta*)

Whole red chilli to taste (*Sabut lal mirch*)
Salt to taste

- Add all ingredients to a pressure cooker and without placing the lid, boil with ¼ cup of water.
- Place the lid and give it ten minutes in the pressure cooker.
- Once done, let it cool down.
- If there is some water left, open and cook till dry. If the paste is not thick enough, the kababs will break.
- Grind to a paste in a food processor.

- Add finely chopped onions, green coriander and green chillies to the mix.
- Make kabab-shaped cutlets out of it.
- Shallow-fry till golden brown. The trick is to fry in very slow heat, with a little oil, a few at a time.

Part 2: The Murabba

250 gm raw mangoes (*ambiyan*)
150 gm sugar
½ cup water

- Peel and prick the mangoes with a fork.
- Cut long, thin slices and throw the seeds (*ghutli*) away.
- Boil the mango pieces with water and add sugar.
- Cook till the syrup becomes thick.

Part 3: Finishing touch

Mint leaves (*pudina*), finely chopped to taste
Green chillies (*hari mirch*), finely chopped, to taste
Place the kababs in a wide vessel.
Pour the murabba over them and cook for 10–15 minutes on very low flame.
Garnish with mint leaves and green chillies and serve.

Nahari

The word *nahar* means early morning, and the name describes the dish. This meat dish was cooked throughout the night and served early morning for the construction workers when Shahjahanabad and the Qila were being built. It is a spicy meat dish that also aids digestion as the water is brackish.

It used to be a purely winter dish, though today it is eaten throughout the year.

In those days, food was supervised by hakims. Emperor Shah Jahan consulted his hakims, who came up with two recipes: for non-vegetarians, a spicy dish called nahari made of buff (buffalo meat) to be eaten *nahar muh* (on an empty stomach) in the morning. And for vegetarians, a spicy combination of *chhole* and *bedvi* (a form of puri) to be eaten in the morning. Nahari was a working-class dish. It does not find mention in the royal menu described in *Bazm-e Aakhir*.

Mutton Nahari (*serves 6*)

(Recipe shared by Mrs Farhat Jahan, who learnt it from her mother-in-law, a descendant of the Mughals. The family is the fourth generation living in Shahjahanabad.)

> 1 kg mutton, preferably shank portion (cut into 8–10 pieces)
> 4 tbsp *ghee* (clarified butter)
> 2 medium onions, finely sliced
> 1 tsp ginger (*adrak*) paste
> 1 tsp garlic (*lahsun*) paste
> 2 tsp coriander (*dhania*) powder
> ½ tsp turmeric powder (*haldi*)
> 3 tbsp roasted gram flour (*besan*; you can dry roast on a griddle or frying pan)
> 3 tbsp nahari masala
> Dough (atta) to seal the degh

Whole spices to make your own nahari masala

    1 tbsp cumin seeds (*jeera*)
    2 tsp fennel seeds (*saunf*)
    1 tsp dry ginger powder (*saunth*)
    5–6 green cardamoms (*hari elaichi*)
    2 black cardamoms (*moti elaichi/kali elaichi*)
    4–5 cloves (*laung*)
    1 bay leaf (*tejpatta*)
    1-inch cinnamon stick (*dalchini*)
    8–10 black peppercorns (*sabut kali mirch*)
    ¼ tsp grated nutmeg (*jaifal*)

Garnish

    1 inch ginger, cut into thin strips
    4–5 stalks fresh coriander leaves
    1 tbsp lemon juice

To make your own nahari masala, dry roast all the whole spices for the masala, cool, then grind them to a fine powder. Alternatively, you can buy readymade masala from a grocery shop.

To make the Nahari curry

Heat ghee in a deep bottom stockpot (preferably a *degh*).

Once the ghee is hot, add the sliced onions and fry till they start to turn brown.

Add the mutton pieces, ginger paste, garlic paste, coriander powder, turmeric powder and salt. Mix well to coat the mutton in ghee and spices. Sauté for five minutes.

Add the nahari masala and eight cups of water.

Mix well, cover seal the vessel with the dough of thick consistency and cook on very low heat for about four hours until the meat is tender.

The way to know that the meat is cooked is when it breaks easily with a wooden spoon.

Dissolve the roasted besan in half a cup of water such that there are no lumps. Slowly add it to the gravy.

Stir to mix it well in the gravy and let it simmer for another 10–15 minutes till the gravy thickens.

Garnish with lemon juice, ginger strips and fresh coriander leaves. Serve hot.

(*Note:* 1 cup = 240 ml; 1 tbsp = 15 ml; 1 tsp = 5 ml)

The word Mughlai for a particular cuisine is actually a misnomer, as actual Mughal dishes were far blander than what we are served under that name.

The Central Asians were nomadic warriors. For them, cooking was on the go. Many a time they would be riding with marinated meat in their saddlebags, which would need less time to cook when they set up camp at night.

What we eat today is an amalgamation of these basic dishes influenced by indigenous and Persian cuisines. In India, most dishes use generous amounts of oil and spices, especially chilli, which is not native to Central Asian food.

When you speak of Mughlai food, you immediately think of the most famous of them all – the korma. Although in the Persian-Arabic script we write it with a 'Q', it is popularly known as Korma in India.

Like the rose, it tastes just as spectacular by any name.

History tells us of a Central Asian dish called *ashqorma/qorma/kuverma*, and it is this dish that was adapted in the kitchens of the Mughal emperors.

There is no mention of Korma in the *Nuskha-e Shahjahani* which has recently been translated from Persian by Salma Yusuf Husain as *The Mughal Feast*. In my conversation with her, she said that it was a later addition. There were several types of korma being served on Emperor Bahadur Shah Zafar's table, including fowl, fish, game meat and mutton korma, so it must have been very popular in the nineteenth century.

Today the korma is a must whether in restaurants or houses.

However, what we eat today was perfected in the kitchens of the Awadh Nawabs with a lot of Persian influence to adapt to Indian tastes. Though in Iran itself, as I found out, the food is quite bland.

Korma literally means braising the meat, and in korma, the meat is braised in oil (traditionally it was desi ghee), yogurt and spices, then simmered in water till tender.

For festive occasions, blanched and finely ground cashews were also used as thickening agents. For everyday use, peanuts can be used as a substitute.

When we were growing up, korma was made only for parties as it involves a tedious amount of roasting of the meat and masalas.

Daily meals at home were primarily Qaliyas, a meat preparation with turmeric and vegetables. We were taught that the base of korma is fried onion paste and yogurt, and haldi is never added to it. Qaliya on the other hand uses haldi and raw onion paste.

My mother hated cooking and couldn't understand my passion for it. Fortunately for my father, who was a foodie, I had inherited my Dadi's (paternal grandmother) skill and passion for cooking. I spent many an hour watching her cook.

In those days we had a *chulha* (coal stove), and on winter evenings, we would gather around it in the kitchen for hot chapattis off the chulha along with Dadi's stories. It was one of those times when I asked her about the inordinate amount of time she was spending on roasting the masala that she gave me the instruction about roasting: *'Masala aise bhuno jaise dushman ka kaleja'* (roast your spices as passionately as if it were the enemy's heart).

It wasn't just a figure of speech, it was the philosophy with which she cooked – she put her heart in it. The trick in cooking any meat dish is in the *bhunna* or roasting of the masala. Too little and it looks pale and tastes insipid;

too much and it will taste bitter. This instruction – not meant to be taken literally – by my grandmother is the story of korma, a dish that is infused with labour, love and passion, but one that delivers magic when done right.

Bazm-e Aakhir has a detailed list of dishes that were cooked for the emperor. It mentions various types of kormas, including of game meat and fowl. Of course, everyone has their own special recipe for korma, but I am including mine.

The royal korma would have included a lot of cream and dry fruits.

I am a foodie and I like to cook as well as eat. Over time I have simplified recipes and realized that regular cooks – for whom these dishes may be unusual – need lots of tips on how to get it right, so I am sharing some of them.

The three don'ts of traditional north Indian Korma:

1. Haldi is not added
2. No tomatoes are used
3. Garnish of coriander leaves is only done on Qaliya, not on Korma.

And the five rules for getting it right:

1. The onions should be finely sliced and fried just the right golden-brown colour. If underdone, the colour and taste of the korma will be pale and dull. If you burn or over-brown the onions, you're back to the dullish brown colour, this time with a bitter taste.
2. Don't add salt till the masala has been roasted as it will splatter.
3. During the roasting process, keep adding dashes of yogurt so that the masala doesn't stick to the pot. The reason hotel korma tends to be so oily is because they add lots of oil while roasting to cut down on time and effort. If you love your arteries as much as you love good food, use yogurt.
4. The meat should be well cut. Trim all fat from it as fat gives it a very oily appearance and taste, as well as an uninviting smell. The best meat is from the shoulder or rump (*raan*).

5.   Open the pot/pressure cooker only when the steam has completely escaped, else the dish will lose colour and the meat will become tough.

Our family recipe for mutton or chicken korma:

Meat or chicken: ½ kg (Vegetarians: I substitute soya nuggets for my daughter who is a vegetarian and it tastes quite good.)

1 big onion: finely chopped and fried golden brown

1 tbsp each of ginger paste and garlic paste

1 tbsp coriander powder, lightly roasted in a tawa or pan. (Keep stirring to prevent burning. Should be removed the minute it changes colour and gives off a fruity aroma.)

1 tbsp garam masala powder (recipe below for those who want to make a fresh batch at home)

2 green cardamoms (elaichi)

3 bay leaves (tej patta)

½–1 tbsp Kashmiri chilli powder (for colour and less spice. You can use regular chili powder if you like spicy food.)

5–7 cashews or groundnuts, lightly roasted and made into a paste with a little water

½ tbsp desiccated coconut, roasted lightly and made into a paste

½ cup yogurt

Salt to taste

½ cup vegetable oil

A pinch of good-quality saffron

For the marinade

2 tbsp yogurt

1 tbsp ginger–garlic paste

A small amount of salt

Marinate your meat in 2 tbsp yogurt, 1 tbsp ginger–garlic paste and a small amount of salt for 2–3 hours. This is particularly important if you are making chicken korma, as the meat is very bland and tasteless.

Heat oil. Add onions to it. Fry till golden brown. Drain and spread on a paper napkin to absorb excess oil. Lightly crush or grind it with a dash of yogurt. Set aside.

Add cardamom and bay leaves to the oil. When they splutter, add the marinated meat, shaking off the excess liquid. Fry on high heat for a few minutes so its juices are sealed inside.

Drain the meat and set aside.

Now add the ginger-garlic paste, coriander powder and the rest of the marinade and chilli powder to the oil. I don't add raw onion paste to my korma as I like light gravy. In case you prefer thick gravy, add 1 small raw onion ground to a paste.

Keep adding dashes of yogurt and stirring till it stops sticking to the sides of the pot and gives off a rich aroma. The gravy should almost glow.

Add ground cashews, coconut, fried onion paste, the garam masala and stir for a bit. Add any leftover yogurt and stir.

Now add the meat, salt to taste, 1 cup water and pressure-cook (for mutton), or cook in a covered pot (if chicken) for fifteen minutes.

If you want it richer, add 1 tbsp of fresh cream.

Soak the saffron strands for a few minutes in warm milk (1 tbsp) and add to the korma.

Garnish with slivers of almonds, serve and feel like royalty.

XVIII

EMPEROR BAHADUR SHAH ZAFAR AND THE SIEGE OF DELHI

Ai vaaye inqalaab zamaane ke jaur se
Dilli Zafar ke haath se pal mein nikal gayi

Curse the tyranny of the rotating wheel of time
Delhi slipped out of Zafar's hands in a moment.

—Bahadur Shah Zafar

Delhi Darwaza of Red Fort

Emperor Shah Jahan entered the Qila-e Mubarak through the gate facing the River Yamuna on 17 May 1648. This magnificent fort in Shahjahanabad (Old Delhi) was to be an enduring symbol of Mughal glory. Though the fort, now called Red Fort, is still a symbol of Indian power, the Mughal legacy didn't last long. The empire disintegrated with the Mughal defeat at the Battle of Buxar in 1764 that established the East India Company in India. The British then got the right to collect revenue from Bengal, Bihar and Orissa.

As mentioned earlier, it was said of Emperor Shah Alam (1759–1806):

Sultanat-e Shah Alam, Az Dilli te Palam

The kingdom of Shah Alam is from Delhi to Palam.

When Abu Zafar Sirajuddin Mohammed Bahadur Shah, better known by his pen name Bahadur Shah Zafar, the eldest son of Emperor Akbar Shah II and his Rajput wife, Lal Bai, ascended the throne, even this didn't hold true.

Emperor Bahadur Shah Zafar was not only an acknowledged Sufi master with several disciples, he was also a poet whose nom de plume was 'Zafar', or victor. He was an unparalleled shot, archer, horse rider and acrobat. At any other point in time, these would have made for a great scholar, statesman or ruler, but he inherited an empire that was his only in name as the British writ ran through it. He was their pensioner. The British Resident in Delhi was responsible for everything that happened in Delhi as well as in the Qila.

By the time the sixty-two-year-old Bahadur Shah II ascended the throne in 1837, the Mughal emperor no longer received *nazr* (tribute), and coins issued under his name had been abolished. The British had also deleted the phrase *Fidwi Khaas* (your special servant) from the Governor General's seal, and even encouraged the Indian princes to do the same.[88]

In 1844, Lord Ellenborough imposed many restrictions on the Mughal emperor. Emperor Bahadur Shah Zafar was debarred from not only giving khilats or robes of honour to his nobles, but also from holding darbar seated on the royal throne. The emperor was debarred from nominating his successor and was asked by Lord Ellenborough to leave the fort and move to Mehrauli where his father Emperor Akbar Shah II had built a palace.[89]

The silver throne which was kept in the Diwan-e Khas was removed and locked up. It was brought out on 12 May 1857 by the sepoys when they crowned him Shahenshah-e Hind. The Diwan-e Aam which had been locked up for thirteen years was reopened after the outbreak of the Revolt in May 1857.

In 1856, Lord Canning wrote to the British Resident of Delhi: 'A lot of the elements of the glory of the Badshahi have finished … It is, therefore, not difficult to think that on the death of the Badshah by just a few lines on paper the title could be abolished.'[90] With the death of Emperor Bahadur Shah II, the royal family would have to vacate the Qila-e Mubarak too.

Pious and spiritually inclined, he spent his time contemplating God and writing *Sufiana kalam* (mystical poetry). Whenever he was implored for help by his subjects, he espoused their cause.

Along with his empire, he had also inherited the national outlook of his ancestor Emperor Akbar, and father, Emperor Akbar Shah II. There are many such incidents described in Zahir Dehlvi's *Dastan-e Ghadar*[91] and other contemporary Urdu books.

Francis Godlieu Quins, commonly known by his penname 'Frasoo', the contemporary European, Urdu–Persian poet in his court, writes: 'The Musalmans, mujahideen and the Hindus – each of these classes have revolted, all of them high as well as low came together.'[92]

He believed in the wisdom that all his subjects were his children, and in fact his last prayer when he left the Qila after the fall of Delhi on the night of 16 September 1857 was:

'Khuda, the Hindus and Muslims of India are my children. Please keep them safe and don't let them suffer for my deeds at the hands of the British.'

(Related by his daughter Kulsum Zamani Begum who saw him praying on his *musalla* the night he left it. This has been included in the story 'Shahzadi ki Bipta' in the book *Begumaat ke Aansoo* which comprises eyewitness accounts recorded by Khwaja Hasan Nizami.)[93]

The Hindu men and women who came to bathe in the River Yamuna every dawn would participate eagerly in the jharoka darshan when the emperor appeared before his subjects in the balcony of the Musamman Burj in the Qila every morning. Only after that would they go home and eat.

Bahadur Shah Zafar condemned the actions of maulvis who tried to divide the populace on religious lines:

Kaho mullah se kiya hum se rindo'n ko padhega
Ki hum Lahaul padh ke teri taqreer sunte hain

Ask the mullah what can he teach one so drunk in love
I hear his speeches with a disclaimer on my lips.

The Indian society of the nineteenth century was living quite happily and in communal harmony, bar a few incidents here and there. When Bahadur Shah Zafar was exiled, there was a palpable sense of loss amongst the Hindus and Muslims alike; they felt as if they had lost their father.

It was in this scenario that, on the morning of 11 May 1857, a group of sepoys from the Meerut cantonment of East India Army came to the Fort demanding the restoration of eighty-two-year-old Bahadur Shah II as the emperor of Hindustan.

'*O Dharma Awtar* (Dharma Incarnate), if you place your kind hand on our heads we shall secure you full-fledged kingship all over Hindustan.'[94]

They appealed to him saying that every proclamation that they had heard so far was in his name: '*Khilqat Khuda ki Mulk Badshah ka Hukm Company ka*' (the Lord's creation, the emperor's country, the company's command).

'But now, the British have been empowered to rule us on your orders. So we have come to you as petitioners, hopeful of justice.'[95]

Initially reluctant, the emperor eventually agreed. On the following day, an unused silver throne lying in one of the rooms of the Fort was dusted and brought out, and Bahadur Shah II was crowned *Shahenshah-e Hind*. The sepoys had already rebelled against the usage of cartridges for the Enfield rifle, rumoured to be laced with the fat of pigs and cows. After killing British officers in Meerut, they escaped to Delhi and succeeded in capturing it.

Bahadur Shah II, though initially hesitant to join the rebel sepoys, soon joined in wholeheartedly and issued a royal farman declaring that it was the imperative duty of all citizens, Hindu or Muslim, to join in the Uprising, appealing to his Hindu and Muslim citizens to oust the foreign oppressor.

On 25 August 1857, Bahadur Shah Zafar issued a proclamation. S. Mahdi Hussain writes[96] that the original proclamation was lost, but in 1858, after Zafar's sentence but before he was actually sent to Rangoon, Burma, his descendant Prince Firoz Shah, who was still at war with the British, issued its replica and thus it became famous as the Azamgarh Proclamation.

It was translated by J.D. Forsythe, the secretary to the chief commissioner of Oude, as the 'Proclamation issued by the Rebels'. It declares that 'as both Hindoos and Mohammadens have been ruined by the oppression of the infidel and treacherous English, therefore it is the bounden duty of all the wealthy people of India to stake their lives for the well-being of the people of India'.

It talks of Muslims rallying under the flag of Muhammad and the Hindus under the flag of Mahavira (used for Hanuman). It goes on to say that the sacred books of Hindus and Muslims have prophesied the end of British rule after this year (1857) and thus, people should remove fear of its continuance from their minds and join in 'our cause'.

(There was a prophecy that 100 years after the Battle of Plassey (1757), the British rule would come to an end.)

The proclamation addresses zamindars, merchants, men of service, artisans and scholars of both creeds, 'Hindoos and Musalmans' (Maulvis and Pandits). This last part is very interesting as it says: 'You are aware that the British are opposed to your religion and as the present is a religious war you should join and gain the good will of the creator, otherwise you will be considered sinners. If you will join us you will receive mafees and land from the emperor.'[97]

So, this was a religious war where Hindus and Muslims, of 'high' and 'low' castes, all fought against the foreign power of the British East India Company, under the banner of the Emperor of Hindustan, Bahadur Shah II (more popularly known as Bahadur Shah Zafar), and fought a common enemy: the *firangi* or foreigner.

However, it is important to note that Bahadur Shah Zafar was not fighting Christians or Englishmen but the British East India Company. 'He (Zafar) opposed the company's paramountcy and the Englishmen as a class enjoying the highest and most lucrative offices in the state,' writes S. Mahdi Hussain.

In fact, Francis Godlieu Quins chronicles that:

Zafar called all the three classes of people (Musalman, Hindus and Mujahideen) to a personal interview, and having taken an oath explained his object. He asked that the Hindus should swear by Ram and the Ganges and that the musalman should swear, each placing a copy of the Quran on his head.[98]

From 11 May to 14 September 1857, Delhi was once again under Mughal rule. This time was, as the saying goes, *'Char din ki chandni, phir andheri raat.'* (Four days of moonlight and then dark night.)

These four months first witnessed the murder of the British by the rebellious sepoys, and then later, retaliatory killings by the British.

Bahadur Shah Zafar personally tried to stop the murder of Europeans under his protection in the Fort. He exhorted the sepoys in the name of humanity and religion, but to no avail. To a man of his temperament, this brutal bloodshed was galling:

Zafar aadmi uss ko na jaaniyega vo ho kaisa hi sahib-e fahm-o zaka

Jisse aish mein yaad-e Khuda na rahi jisse taish mein khauf-e Khuda na raha

Zafar doesn't count human a man, be he a man of understanding and charity
If he doesn't remember God in moments of happiness, or doesn't fear God when angry.

Other 'rebel' leaders too issued proclamations, pamphlets, papers, making a plea for the ousting of the foreign rulers from the Indian subcontinent. 'These pamphlets apart from making a very strong case for Hindu–Muslim unity also sought to revive the notion of Mughal sovereignty.'[99]

During the Uprising of 1857, the British tried their best to disrupt the Hindu–Muslim unity that was very apparent amongst those they called *'baghi'* or rebels.

Colonel Keith Young, Judge-Advocate General of the Indian Army who was present with the British forces on the Ridge in Delhi, regularly sent letters to his wife in the safety of Shimla. This wife published them later as *Delhi –*

1857: The Siege, Assault, and Capture as Given in the Diary and Correspondence of the Late Colonel Keith Young.

On 29 July 1857, he wrote to her:

Camp, Delhi Cantonments, Wednesday, 29th July:

Hodson just now came into our tent and interrupted my writing this. He tells me that a letter has just come in from the city confirming what we had before heard of the dissensions going on, and they seem likely to terminate in something serious at the Festival of the Eed, as some of the Mahomedan fanatics have declared their fixed intention of killing a cow as customary on that day at the Jumma Musjid. It is hoped that they will religiously adhere to their determination, and there is then sure to be a row between the Mahomedans and Hindoos.

Camp, Delhi Cantonments, Thursday, 30 July:

All is quiet in camp, and the mutineers must, I should hope – as we all believe – be quarrelling amongst themselves, and unable to agree to come out and attack us again. The Eed, we trust, will bring matters to a crisis with them, and be the day for a grand row between the Hindoos and Mahomedans.

Camp, Delhi Cantonments, Sunday, 2nd August:

Our hopes of a grand row in the city yesterday at the Eed Festival have not, apparently, been fulfilled – at least the only newsletter received from the city alludes to nothing of the kind. The King had issued strict orders against killing cows, or even goats, in the city, and this, if acted upon, must have satisfied the Hindoos; and instead of fighting amongst themselves they all joined together to make a vigorous attack to destroy us and utterly sweep us from the face of the earth, when it was arranged that the King should perform his evening prayers in our camp!

Bahadur Shah Zafar had foreseen this trouble and banned cow-slaughter in the areas he nominally controlled. In *The Great Uprising of 1857*, Prof. Z.H. Jafri cites that they found several documents in the Mutiny Papers in the National Archives, New Delhi, by Bahadur Shah Zafar and Bakht Khan, the commander-in-chief of the Indian forces, asking the people to desist from cow-slaughter, and to the *kotwal* to capture the cows from the houses of people who might go ahead with such sacrifices. There is evidence to support the fact that the police officers took these orders very seriously and thus prevented any sacrifice of cows by them, which could have led to the trouble that Young and his colleagues were so eagerly anticipating.

Bakr-Eid passed peacefully in 1857, thanks to the wise decisions of the emperor.

When Emperor Bahadur Shah Zafar was put on trial, 'the British prosecutor said that the same mutineers who had objected to the greased cartridges[100] when issued by the British officers, were using and biting the same cartridge when they were firing them against the British officers. The claim was, however, that it was done by them of their own free will, not under coercion.

However, military expert Manimugdha Sharma tells me that only 12,000 Enfield rifles had been sent from England, and no Indian regiment had been issued the Enfield rifle when the Revolt broke out, nor did very many of them actually see an Enfield cartridge, let alone handle it. The above statement just goes to show that the British perception of the sepoys' loyalty to the emperor was very strong.

All the 'rebel' leaders fought under the banner of Emperor Bahadur Shah Zafar, be they Begum Hazrat Mahal, Rani of Jhansi, Maulvi Azimullah Khan, Nana Sahib or Kunwar Singh. There were two banners used by them: one, the green banner of Islam, and the other, the holy *dhwaj*. The Proclamation of Emperor Bahadur Shah Zafar exhorts the orthodox Hindus to raise the banner of Mahavir.[101]

By mid-September, Delhi was back under British control. The Mutiny memorial on the Ridge in Delhi gives a timeline of the Revolt of 1857. The last two lines read:

Capture of the Palace – Sept 19th
City finally evacuated by the Enemy – Sept 20th

Kar chuke tum nasiihate'n ham ko?
Jaao bas naaseho Khudaa Hafiz

Are you done giving me sermons?
O admonisher, stop now! Khuda Hafiz!
— Bahadur Shah Zafar

By 21 September 1857, the British were ensconced in the Red Fort, and the emperor and his sons fled, seeking refuge in Emperor Humayun's Tomb.

The following day, the emperor's close confidant, Mirza Ilahi Bux, disclosed his whereabouts to the British. Major Hodson negotiated the surrender and took his captives back to the Red Fort. On the way, the major ordered Emperor Bahadur Shah Zafar's sons, Mirza Mughal and Mirza Khizr Khan, and his grandson, Mirza Abu Bakr, to descend from the carriage and disrobe. He then shot them dead at Khooni Darwaza near Firoz Shah Kotla.

It is said that after his defeat, Emperor Bahadur Shah Zafar announced:

Ghaaziyon mein bu rahegi jab talak imaan ki
Takht-e London tak chalegi tégh Hindustan ki

As long as there remains the scent of faith in the hearts of the valiant
The sword of Hindustan shall flash from here till the throne of London

The reality was different. The emperor was held prisoner in a dingy room of his ancestral fort during the summer of despair for the residents of

Shahjahanabad (Old Delhi), when numerous residents of the walled city were either killed or rendered homeless.

He had to stay in a small room in one of the new buildings that had come up near the Delhi Darwaza instead of his sumptuous apartments, which were now occupied by the new rulers, the British.

On 27 January 1858, the Emperor of Hindustan was tried for 'rebellion, treason and murder' by a military commission in the same Diwan-e Khas where he used to recite his poems to great applause. On 9 March, it was decided that Emperor Bahadur Shah Zafar would be exiled. Seven months later, he was exiled to Rangoon in Burma with two of his wives, two remaining sons and a few servants.

The emperor was old and had by then become senile from shock. He made no attempt to defend himself. He didn't even have a lawyer. The British prosecutors happily glossed over the fact that in May 1857, Emperor Bahadur Shah Zafar was the de jure sovereign. The East India Company were a de facto power, and thus the sepoys of the Bengal army were legally the subjects of the emperor. He was still considered the emperor by the people of Delhi, and sedition charges against him were baseless. How could he be held for treason against himself? It were the British who were considered usurpers.

Such was the enduring legacy of the unfortunate emperor that on 14 June 1862, four years after his exile, the (British) political agent of Bhopal reported that Zafar's ghazal, *Gayi yak-ba-yak jo hawa palat nahin dil ko mere qaraar hai*, was being sung by minstrels of India.[102] There were fears that if it wasn't banned, it could incite people to another uprising.

In confinement, deprived of pen and paper, Zafar scribbled with charcoal on the walls of his cell verses of sorrow and sadness at the tragic end of the Great Rebellion.[103]

Main woh kushta ke meri lash par ai doston
Ek zamaana deeda-e hasrat se takta jaayega

Ai Zafar, qayam rahegi jab talak aqleem-e Hind
Akhtar iqbal iss gul ka chamakta jaayega

Friends, I am that slaughtered man at whose corpse
a whole world will continue to look with grief and envy.
O Zafar! So long as the country of India endures,
The star of the glory of this flower will shine.[104]

Aftermath of the Uprising of 1857

It is to be hoped that the memories of the martyrs of what is referred to as the First War of Indian Independence will be remembered and their sacrifices honoured.

The year 1857 was a watershed one in the history of India. The British East India Company quelled the mutiny of Indians, thus paving the way for India to become a British colony. The imperial ambitions of the British received a jolt and resulted in many decisions that changed the fate of India.

'Among the many lessons the Indian mutiny conveys to the historian, none is of greater importance than the warning that it is possible to have a Revolution in which Brahmins and Sudras, Hindus and Mahomedans, could be united against us,' British historian George William Forrest mentioned in the introduction of the State Papers soon after the end of the First War of Independence.

Once the British realized that if Hindus, Muslims, rich and poor, high and low castes could get together again, the next time they may succeed in dislodging them, they systematically started a policy of what is now called divide and rule.

According to historian Irfan Habib, it was the largest anti-colonial uprising anywhere in the world. Out of 135,000 native soldiers of the Bengal army, only 7,000 remained loyal to their British masters.

It was the sheer scale that rattled the might of the British Empire, and they struck back with unparalleled cruelty – killing, executing and looting all those whom the slightest shred of evidence linked to the revolt. The brunt was borne by Muslims as they shared the faith of the man declared as Emperor of Hindustan. It was seen as a 'Mohammedan conspiracy making capital out of Hindu grievances'.

Most of the princes and princesses either were killed or died trying to escape, or spent their lives in ignominy and poverty. Many innocents from every site associated with the centres of the Uprising were killed, and Hindustan, as we knew it till 1857, changed for ever.

Queen Victoria was declared the Empress of India, and this set in motion a chain of events that resulted in the drain of wealth from India, bringing it down from being one of the richest economies in the world to being one of the poorest.

Bahadur Shah Zafar, the last Mughal emperor, died at 5 a.m. on Friday, 7 November 1862, and was given a hurried and ignominious burial in Rangoon.

Kitna hai badnaseeb Zafar, dafn ke liye
Do gaz zameen bhi mil na saki ku-e yaar mein

How unlucky is Zafar – for burial
he could not get 2 yards of land in the land of the Beloved.

As Prof. Z.H.Jafri writes, Delhi became an international city and an important centre of knowledge during hey days of India's medieval past. Numerous families of migrants from West Asia, Khurasan and Central Asia brought the elements of higher intellectual tradition and scientific innovations. The city was in the galaxy of major centers of knowledge in the then contemporaneous societies. The scholars of the city were recognized for their expertise and merit in numerous disciplines throughout the Islamic East.

Soon, everything changed drastically in the aftermath of the Great Uprising of 1857. In its aftermath, a 'reign of white terror' led to the systematic destruction of the Indo-Islamic cultural past, the annihilation of an established societal order and almost the total extermination of the erstwhile ruling house(s). One finds a feel of such devastation in the couplets of Bahadur Shah Zafar (d. 1862) himself:

Na tha shehar Dehli wo tha chaman-i Dilli
sab tarah ka tha wahan aman
wo khitab iska toh mit gaya
faqat ab toh ujda dyaar hai

Delhi was not simply a city – a garden it was.
What shall I say of the peace that it had
They have erased all its repute
Now it is simply a place laid waste.

Sir Sayyid Ahmad Khan (d. 1898), an eyewitness and a loyalist, could somehow muster the courage to write *Asbab-e Baghawat-e Hind* in March 1858 itself. It is interesting to point out that there is not a single word in this very incisive pamphlet about the subsequent repression unleashed on the city of Delhi. Sir Sayyid could never think of revising his *Asar-us Sanadid* (first published 1847, reprinted in 1854) as, perhaps, it would have necessitated a description of the havoc caused to the physical and intellectual landscape of the city by the British after 1857.

It was only in AD 1874 that Khwaja Altaf Husain Haali (d. 1914), lamented the destruction in his famous elegy on Delhi by saying:

Mit gaye tere mitane ke nishan bhi ab to
Aye falak iss se zyada na mitana hargiz

Even the traces of the city's destruction are gone
O Heaven! can there be a greater oblivion than that?

Similarly, Maulana Abul Kalam Azad (d. 1958), describing the post-Mutiny city of Delhi, used an Oriental metaphor, for the city being a virtual graveyard of our bygone civilization: *Hamari guzashta tehzib ka qabaristan.*

BIBLIOGRAPHY

Axworthy, Michael. *The Sword of Persia Nader Shah: From Tribal Warrior to Conquering Tyrant*. London & New York: I.B. Taurus, 2009.

Azad, Maulana Abul Kalam. *The Rubaiyat of Sarmad*. Translated by Syeda Saiyidain Hameed. New Delhi: ICCR, 1991.

Aziz, Sadia. 'Mosque, Memory and State: A Case Study of Jama Masjid (India) and the Colonial State c. 1857'. M.Phil Dissertation, University of Delhi.

Beg, Sangin. *Sair-ul-Manazil*. Translated into English by Nausheen Jaffery, edited by Swapna Liddle. New Delhi: Tulika Books, 2017.

Begley, Wayne Edison; and Ziyaud-Din A. Desai, eds. *Taj Mahal: The Illumined Tomb: An Anthology of Seventeenth-Century Mughal and European Documentary Sources*. Cambridge, MA: Aga Khan Program for Islamic Architecture, Harvard University Art Museums, 1989.

Begley, Wayne Edison, and Ziyaud-Din A. Desai, eds. *The Shahjahan Nama of Inayat Khan*. Delhi: Oxford University Press, 1990.

Bernier, Francois. *Travels in the Mogul Empire: A.D. 1656–1668*. Translated and annotated by Archibald Constable. Bombay/London: Oxford University Press, 1916.

Blake, Stephen P. *Shahjahanabad: The Sovereign City in Mughal India 1639–1739*. Cambridge South Asian Studies 49. Cambridge, MA: Cambridge University Press, 2002.

Chenoy, Shama Mitra. *Shahjahanabad: A City of Delhi 1638–1857*. New Delhi: Munshiram Manoharlal, 1998.

Dayal, Maheshwar. *Alam Mein Intikhab Dilli*. Delhi: Urdu Academy, 1978.

Dehlvi, Bashiruddin Ahmad. *Waqiaat-e-Darul Hukumat Delhi*. Delhi: Urdu Academy, 2012.

Dehlvi, Mirza Farhatullah Beg, ed. Rasheed Hasan Khan, *Dehli ki Aakhiri Shama*, New Delhi: Anjuman Taraqqi Urdu (Hind), 2015.

Dehlvi, Syed Wazir Hasan. *Dilli ka Aakhiri Deedar*. Edited by Syed Zameer Hasan Dehlavi, Delhi: Urdu Academy, 2006. (Also see the edition edited by Shahid Ahmed Dehlavi. Delhi: Dilli Printing Press, 1934.)

Dehlvi, Zahir. *Dastan-e Ghadar: Tale of a Revolution*. Translated by Rana Safvi. Gurgaon: Penguin Random House India, 2017.

Elliot, H.M. *Shah Jahan*. Lahore: Sh. Mubarak Ali, 1875. Retrieved from Asia Cornell University Library archive, https://archive.org/stream/cu31924006140374/cu31924006140374_djvu.txt.

Faizuddin, Munshi. *Bazm-e Aakhir*. Edited by Dr Kamil Quraishi. Delhi: Urdu Academy, 2009 (Original edition Delhi: Armaghan, 1885.)

Fanshawe, H.C., *Delhi Past and Present*. New Delhi: Asian Educational Services, 2002 (1902, reprinted).

Faruqi, Shamsur Rahman. *The Mirror of Beauty*. New Delhi: Penguin Books, 2013.

Fergusson, James. *History of Indian and Eastern Architecture*. London: John Murray, 1876.

Gandhi, Surjit Singh. *History of the Sikh Gurus Retold: 1606–1708 C.E.* New Delhi: Atlantic, 2007.

Gorgani, Shahzada Mirza Ahmad Akhtar, *Sawaneh-e Dehli*. Edited by Marghoob Haider Abidi. Delhi: Urdu Academy, 2009.

Gupta, Narayani, *Delhi between Two Empires 1803–1931: Society, Government and Urban Growth*. New Delhi: Oxford University Press, 1997.

Hasan, Maulvi Zafar. *Monuments of Delhi*, Vol. 1. New Delhi: Aryan Books, 2008 (1916).

Hasan, Mohiuddin, *Dilli ki Begamati Zuban*. New Delhi: Maktab Jamia Limited, 2012.

Hearn, Gordon Risley. *The Seven Cities of Delhi*. London: W. Thacker & Co., 1906.

Hussain, S. Mahdi. *Bahadur Shah Zafar and the War of 1857 in Delhi*. Delhi: Aakar Books, 1958.

Hussain, S.M. Azizuddin, *1857 Revisted*. New Delhi: Kanishka Publishers, 2007.

Jafri, Saiyid Zaheer Husain. 'Voices of the Vanquished: The Indigenous Literature in the Rebels' World'. In *1857 Revisited: Myth and Reality*, edited by Kirti Narain and Mohini C. Dias. Mumbai: Himalaya Publishing House, 2008, pp 113–30.

Jain, Balbhadra. *Bharat ke Digamber Jain Tirth*. Nashik: Bharat Varshiya Digamber Jain Tirthkshetra Committee, 1974.

Khan, Iftikhar Ali. *Sir Syed Daroon-e Khana*. Aligarh: Educational Book House.

Khan, Sayyid Ahmad. *Asar-us Sanadid (The Remnants of Ancient Heroes)*. Translated by Rana Safvi. New Delhi: Tulika Books, 2018. Originally published in Urdu in 1867.

Koch, Ebba. *Shah Jahan and Orpheus: The Pietra Dure Decoration and the Program of the Throne in the Hall of Public Audience at the Red Fort in Delhi*. Graz, Austria: Akademische Druck-u, 1988.

Lahori, Abdul Hamid. 'Badshah-Nama', in H.M. Elliot, *Shah Jahan* (Lahore: Sh. Mubarak Ali, 1875). Retrieved from Asia Cornell University Library archive, https://archive.org/stream/cu31924006140374/cu31924006140374_djvu.txt

Liddle, Swapna. *Chandni Chowk: The Mughal City of Old Delhi*. New Delhi: Speaking Tiger, 2017.

Nizami, Syed Khwaja Hasan. *Begumat ke Aansoo*. Translated in English as *City of My Heart* by Rana Safvi. New Delhi: Hachette India, 2018.

Nizami, Syed Khwaja Hasan. *Dilli ki Jan Kuni*. Translated as *The Agony of Delhi* by A. Sattar Kapadia. Delhi: Delhi Printing Press Works, 1922.

Peck, Lucy, *Delhi: A Thousand Years of Building*. New Delhi: Intach Roli Guides, 2005.

Prigarina, Natalia. 'Sarmad: Life and Death of a Sufi', in *Sufism and Irfan: Non-Akbarian Schools*. Russia: Institute of Oriental Studies. https://iphras.ru/uplfile/smirnov/ishraq/3/24_prig.pdf.

Rezavi, Syed Ali Nadeem (transl.). '"The Mighty Defensive Fort": Red Fort at Delhi under Shahjahan – Its Plan and Structures as Described by Muhammad Waris'. *Proceedings of the Indian History Congress* 71 (2010–11): 1108–21. Retrieved from https://www.jstor.org/stable/44147579?seq=1#page_scan_tab_contents.

Safvi, Rana. *City of My Heart*. New Delhi: Hachette India, 2018.

Safvi, Rana. *The Forgotten Cities of Delhi*. Book Two in the 'Where Stones Speak' trilogy. New Delhi: HarperCollins, 2018.

Sanderson, Gordon. *Delhi Fort: A Guide to the Buildings and Gardens*. Delhi: Asian Educational Service, 1914.

Shea, David, and Anthony Troyer (trans.). *The Dabistán or School of Manners: The Religious Beliefs, Observances, Philosophic Opinions and Social Customs of the Nations of the East*.

Translated from the original Persian. London: Walter Dunne, 1901.

Singh, Khushwant. *The Illustrated History of the Sikhs, Vol 1: 1469–1839*. New Delhi: Oxford University Press, 2006.

Smith, R.V. *Delhi: Unknown Tales of a City*. Delhi: Lotus Publishers, 2015.

Spear, Thomas George Percival; Narayani Gupta. *The Delhi Omnibus*. Edited by R.E. Frykenberg. New Delhi: Oxford University Press, 2002.

Stephen, Carr. *Archaeology and Monumental Remains of Delhi*. Ludhiana: Mission Press, 1876.

Suboohi, Ashraf. *Dilli ki Chand Ajeeb Hastiyan*. Delhi: Maktab Jamia Limited, 2011.

NOTES

1. AH is the term used to denote the Hijri year used in the Islamic lunar calendar. It begins from AD 622, the year that Prophet Mohammad and his followers migrated to Medina from Mecca.

2. Inlay work – the insertion of stone on stone in prepared grooves – at the time. This was called parchinkari in Persian and inspired by Persian inlay techniques.

3. Bulbulikhana is an area in Old Delhi near Turkman Darwaza. This is described in *The Forgotten Cities of Delhi*, Part II of the trilogy *Where Stones Speak*.

4. Rana Safvi, *The Forgotten Cities of Delhi*: Book Two in the *Where Stones Speak* trilogy (New Delhi: HarperCollins, 2018).

5. The second month of the solar Hijri calendar, the official calendar of Iran and Afghanistan, used as reference in Mughal-era Persian documents.

6. Syed Ali Nadeem Rezavi, transl., '"The Mighty Defensive Fort": Red Fort at Delhi under Shahjahan – Its Plan and Structures as Described by Muhammad Waris', *Proceedings of the Indian History Congress* 71 (2010–11): 1108–21. Retrieved from https://www.jstor.org/stable/44147579?seq=1#page_scan_tab_contents.

7. Rezavi, 'The Mighty Defensive Fort'.

8. Wayne Edison Begley and Ziyaud-Din A. Desai (eds), *The Shahjahan Nama of Inayat Khan*. Delhi: Oxford University Press, 1990.

9. Begley and Desai, *Shahjahan Nama*.

10. Gordon Sanderson, *Delhi Fort: A Guide to the Buildings and Gardens*. Delhi: Asian Educational Service, 1914.

11. Begley and Desai, *Shahjahan Nama*.

12. Francois Bernier, *Travels in the Mogul Empire: A.D. 1656–1668*, translated and annotated by Archibald Constable (Bombay/London: Oxford University Press, 1916).

13. Rezavi, 'The Mighty Defensive Fort'.

14. Carr Stephen, *Archaeology and Monumental Remains of Delhi* (Ludhiana: Mission Press, 1876).

15. Edited by J.P. Losty, *Delhi: Red Fort to Raisina*. New Delhi: Roli Books, 2012.

16. Ebba Koch, *Shah Jahan and Orpheus: The Pietra Dure Decoration and the Program of the Throne in the Hall of Public Audience at the Red Fort in Delhi* (Graz, Austria: Akademische Druck-u, 1988).

17. 'Long live the Emperor.' In keeping with the secular traditions of the Mughals, the Emperor was called both Badshah (in Persian) and Mahabali (in Sanskrit) as recorded in *Bazm-e Aakhir* written by Munshi Faizuddin in 1885.

18. Ebba Koch, *Shah Jahan and Orpheus*.

19. *The Delhi Guide* by Mr Beresford was written in 1856 and has been quoted by Carr Stephen in *Archaeology and Monumental Remains of Delhi*. I could not obtain a copy of it myself.

20. Gordon Sanderson, *Delhi Fort*.

21. Bishop Reginald Heber, the bishop of Calcutta, came to Delhi in 1824, and has left a valuable account of the fort.

22. Zahir Dehlvi, *Dastan-e Ghadar: Tale of a Revolution*, translated by Rana Safvi. Gurgaon: Penguin Random House, 2017.

23. Wayne Edison Begley and Ziyaud-Din A. Desai, eds., *Taj Mahal: The Illumined Tomb: An Anthology of Seventeenth-Century Mughal and European Documentary Sources*. Cambridge, MA: Aga Khan Program for Islamic Architecture, Harvard University Art Museums, 1989.

24. Bashiruddin Ahmad Dehlvi, *Waqiaat-e-Darul Hukumat Dehli* (Delhi: Urdu Academy, 2012), vol. 2, p. 112.

25. Wayne Edison Begley and Ziyaud-Din A. Desai (eds), *The Shahjahan Nama of Inayat Khan*. Delhi: Oxford University Press, 1990.

26. Ibid.

27. *Mulakhkhas-e Shahjahan-Nameh* (Abridged: *Shahjahan-nameh*) compiled by Mirza Muhammad Tahir Khan Aashna entited Inayat Khan, introduction, editing and annotations by Dr Jameel-ur Rahman, Alhoda International Publishers and Distributors, Centre for Persian Research, Office of the Cultural Counsellor, Embassy of Islamic Republic of Iran, New Delhi, 2009.

28. Wayne Edison Begley and Ziyaud-Din A. Desai (eds), *The Shahjahan Nama of Inayat Khan*. Delhi: Oxford University Press, 1990.

29. Translation by Prof. Sunil Sharma, Professor of Persianate & Comparative Literature, Boston University, Boston, USA.

30. Translated from the original Persian by Ajmal Siddiqui.

31. Translated by Prashant Keshavmurthy.

32. Abdul Hamid Lahori, 'Badshah-Nama', in H.M. Elliot, *Shah Jahan* (Lahore: Sh. Mubarak Ali, 1875). Retrieved from Asia Cornell University Library archive, https://archive.org/stream/cu31924006140374/cu31924006140374_djvu.txt

33. This description is based on an account by Bashiruddin Ahmad Dehlvi.

34. Khan, *Asar-us Sanadid*.

35. As per sharia, a *wuzu* tank should be 2 yards wide and 50 yards long, or 4 yards wide and 25 yards long, or 5 yards wide and 20 yards long — then it qualifies as flowing and not still water. If it is smaller than that, it should have water flowing out of it.

36. Khan, *Asar-us Sanadid*.

37. Carr Stephen, *Archeology and Monumental Remains of Delhi*.

38. Sanderson, *Delhi Fort*.

39. Dehlvi, *Waqiaat-e-Darul Hukumat Dehli*.

40. Edited by J.P. Losty, *Delhi: Red Fort to Raisina*. New Delhi: Roli Books, 2012.

41. Gordon Risley Hearn, *The Seven Cities of Delhi*. London: W. Thacker & Co., 1906.

42. *The Asiatic Quarterly Review*, Vol. 4 (London: East & West, 1914).

43. Sanderson, *Delhi Fort*.

44. Khan, *Asar-us Sanadid*.

45. Rezavi, 'The Mighty Defensive Fort'.

46. Khan, *Asar-us Sanadid*.

47. Translation from Sanderson, *Delhi Fort*.

48. Begley and Desai, *Shahjahan Nama*.

49. Stephen, *Archeology and Monumental Remains of Delhi*.

50. Edited by J.P. Losty, *Delhi: Red Fort to Raisina*. New Delhi: Roli Books, 2012.

51. A *ghat* refers to a flight of steps leading down to a river.

52. A *mannat* is a request to the gods with the promise of a specific action if the wish is fulfilled, for example, I will feed 100 poor people if the baby is a girl, or, if I pass these exams I will never lie to my parents again.

53. Lal, Magan; D. Westbrook, Jessie, *The Diwan Of Zeb-Un-Nissa: The First Fifty Ghazals Rendered from the Persian*. London: John Murray, 1913.

54. Dehlvi, *Waqiaat-e Darul Hukumat Dehli*.

55. Heena Yunus Ansari, 'Indigenous Discourse of the Great Uprising of 1857: A Study of Urdu Weekly Newspapers from Lucknow and Delhi', unpublished M.Phil dissertation, University of Delhi, 2015.

56. Sadia Aziz, 'Mosque, Memory and State: A Case Study of Jama Masjid (India) and the Colonial State c. 1857', M.Phil Dissertation, University of Delhi.

57. Aziz, 'Mosque, Memory and State'.

58. Maulana Abul Kalam Azad, *The Rubaiyat of Sarmad*, transl. Syeda Saiyidain Hameed. New Delhi: ICCR, 1991.

59. Ibid.

60. *The Dabistán or School of Manners: The Religious Beliefs, Observances, Philosophic Opinions and Social Customs of the Nations of the East*, translated from the original Persian by David Shea and Anthony Troyer. London: Walter Dunne, 1901.

61. Natalia Prigarina, 'Sarmad: Life and Death of a Sufi', in *Sufism and Irfan: Non-Akbarian Schools* (Russia: Institute of Oriental Studies), https://iphras.ru/uplfile/smirnov/ishraq/3/24_prig.pdf.

62. Maulvi Zafar Hasan, *Monuments of Delhi*, Vol. 1 (New Delhi: Aryan Books, 2008 [1916]).

63. Dehlvi, *Waqiaat-e-Darul Hukumat Dehli*.

64. Khan, *Asar-us Sanadid*.

65. http://dywa.co.in

66. Sangin Beg, *Sair-ul-Manazil*, translated into English by Nausheen Jaffery, edited by Swapna Liddle. New Delhi: Tulika Books, 2017.

67. Dehlvi, *Waqiaat-e-Darul Hukumat Dehli*.

68. Swapna Liddle, *Chandni Chowk: The Mughal City of Old Delhi*. New Delhi: Speaking Tiger, 2017.

69. Michael Axworthy, *The Sword of Persia Nader Shah: From Tribal Warrior to Conquering Tyrant*. London & New York: I.B. Taurus, 2009.

70. Balbhadra Jain, *Bharat ke Digamber Jain Tirth*. Nashik: Bharat Varshiya Digamber Jain Tirthkshetra Committee, 1974.

   Hasan, *Monuments of Delhi*.

   Dehlvi, *Waqiaat-e-Darul Hukumat Dehli*.

71. James Fergusson, *History of Indian and Eastern Architecture*. London: John Murray, 1876.

72. Iftikhar Ali Khan, *Sir Syed Daroon e Khana* (Aligarh: Educational Book House).

73. *Lakhori* bricks derive their name from the immense quantities (lakhs) in which they were manufactured for building activities during the eighteenth, nineteenth and early twentieth centuries.

74. Shama Mitra Chenoy, *Shahjahanabad: A City of Delhi 1638–1857*. New Delhi: Munshiram Manoharlal, 1998.

75. Khan, *Asar-us Sanadid*.

76. Dehlvi, *Waqiaat-e-Darul Hukumat Dehli*.

77. Translated from Persian by Vraje Abramian.

78. Sri Guru Granth Sahib Quotes, Goodreads blog, https://www.goodreads.com/work/quotes/3298636-sri-guru-granth-sahib

79. Surjit Singh Gandhi, *History of the Sikh Gurus Retold: 1606–1708 C.E.* (New Delhi: Atlantic, 2007).

80. Gandhi, *History of the Sikh Gurus Retold*.

81. Khushwant Singh, *The Illustrated History of the Sikhs, Vol 1: 1469–1839*. New Delhi: Oxford University Press, 2006.

82. Ibid.

83. Ibid.

84. The reign and death of Alamgir II, and the role of Imad-ul-Mulk in the emperor's murder is well-documented. I have taken this story from *Bazm-e-Aakhir*, written by Munshi Faizuddin, a Mughal courtier in 1885. Faizuddin spent a lot of time inside the Red Fort, or Qila-e-Mualla, as he was the attendant of Mirza Ilahi Bux, the father-in-law of Emperor Bahadur Shah

Zafar. This story has also been mentioned by Mirza Farhatullah Beg in his nineteenth book, *Phool Waalo'n ki Sair* who names the lady as Ram Kumari.

85. Rana Safvi, *City of My Heart*. New Delhi: Hachette India, 2018.

86. Salma Yusuf Husain, *Recipes from the Kitchen of Emperor Shah Jahan: The Mughal Feast*. Roli Books, New Delhi, 2019.

87. Ibid.

88. S. Mahdi Hussain, *Bahadur Shah Zafar and the War of 1857 in Delhi*. Delhi: Aakar Books, 1958.

89. Hussain, *Bahadur Shah Zafar and the War of 1857*.

90. Syed Khwaja Hasan Nizami, *Dilli ki Jan Kuni* (1922). Translated as *The Agony of Delhi* by A. Sattar Kapadia.

91. Translated in English as *Tale of a Revolution* by Rana Safvi.

92. Hussain, *Bahadur Shah Zafar and the War of 1857 in Delhi*.

93. Syed Khwaja Hasan Nizami, *Begumat ke Aansoo,* translated in English as *City of My Heart* by Rana Safvi. New Delhi: Hachette India, 2018.

94. Hussain, *Bahadur Shah Zafar and the War of 1857 in Delhi*.

95. Dehlvi, *Dastan-e Ghadar*.

96. Hussain, *Bahadur Shah Zafar and the War of 1857 in Delhi*.

97. Ibid.

98. Ibid.

99. Saiyid Zaheer Husain Jafri, 'Voices of the Vanquished: The Indigenous Literature in the Rebels' World', in Kirti Narain and Mohini C. Dias, eds, *1857 Revisited: Myth and Reality*. Mumbai: Himalaya Publishing House, 2008, pp 113–30.

100. Since the greased cartridges were said to be the immediate cause of the revolt, a long explanation by military expert Manimugdha Sharma:

> The Enfield Pattern 1853 Rifle-Musket was considered an improvement over the smooth-bore muskets that were being used by the East India Company's armies. Infantry regiments were armed with the Pattern 1842 Musket, which was an improvement over the earlier Short Land Pattern Musket or the Brown Bess in terms of the firing mechanism. The earlier Brown Bess was a flintlock musket; the Pattern 1842 was a cap-lock musket. The calibre of both muskets was the same – .75 calibre – and both used round ammunition or musket balls. Rifle companies were issued the

1838 Brunswick Rifle, which had two grooves cut into the barrel and used girdled musket balls. This made for a tighter fit of the round inside the barrel and gave it better accuracy.

But for the round to go in, a lubricated cloth patch had to be used on the cartridge itself. Beeswax was the standard lubricant, but mutton fat and wax were also used. So the Indian sepoys were accustomed to using animal fat on the cartridges. All these cartridges had to be bitten off at one end and loaded with the powder going in first and then the ball. A ramrod was then used to ram the ball down.

The Enfield rifle was the next stage of innovation. It had a cap-lock firing mechanism and had rifling in the barrel. The bullet was not the standard musket ball but a conical bullet called the Minie ball with grooves cut on it and a cap at its end. The cartridge was also different: longer and more cylindrical than the Pattern 1842's cartridge and using three different pieces of paper. The bullet was at one end of the cartridge and that part used to be greased. The loading drill was also different for this one. The non-greased part had to be bitten off and the powder charge poured into the barrel. Then the cartridge had to be reversed and the greased part placed on the mouth of the barrel and the empty casing for powder broken off. The greased part was then rammed down.

At no point was the greased end bitten off. So, there was no way any grease could have entered the mouth of any user.

The grease was made of tallow and beeswax. The tallow was made of animal fat of an unspecified nature. Cow and buffalo fat may have been used, though pig lard was certainly not. Nevertheless, the sepoys were agitated when rumours started spreading from Dum Dum arsenal that taboo fat had been used in making the paper cartridges. Interestingly, none of the Bengal Army regiments had handled any of the greased Enfield cartridges. In fact, no Indian regiment was issued the Enfield rifle when the Revolt broke out; only the 60th Regiment of Foot (the King's Royal Rifles) had been issued those weapons in India at that time, which was a British Army regiment.

However, because of the rumours, the ammunition factories were ordered not to issue greased cartridges. The sepoys were also allowed to use ghee or beeswax to grease the cartridges on their own. They were also allowed to not bite open the cartridge but tear it open – which became a standard regulation from that point for all British and colonial troops. However, this didn't stop the rumours or allay suspicions. When it became evident that they were not getting the greased cartridges, the sepoys started to suspect that even the ungreased paper was greased due to its glossy appearance. Soon after, they started suspecting that cartridges of the old 1842 pattern were also greased when they were clearly not. This shows that facts no longer mattered. The nature of the rumours also changed – from taboo fat in cartridges to taboo bone dust in flour. That shows that the troops were being incited deliberately.

So, in effect, no Indian regiment had been issued the Enfield rifle when the Revolt broke out, nor did very many of them actually see an Enfield cartridge, let alone handle it.

But from February 1857 onwards, seven-member teams from forty-four Indian regiments were taught to handle, load and fire the Enfield. These Indians were given ungreased cartridges and allowed to grease them with any material they preferred.

Nevertheless, it is unlikely, though not impossible, that Indian sepoys used these rifles against the British. The only scenario in which this is likely is if the Indian sepoys raided the training depots and got them or seized them from the 60th Rifles at Meerut. It is also possible that they managed to seize Enfield rounds, but without the rifles, these would have been useless as the Enfield calibre was .577 while the Pattern 1842's calibre was .75. These would also have been useless for the Brunswick rifle, which had a larger calibre of .704.

But the sepoys certainly had no more suspicions about using the paper cartridges for the Pattern 1842 when the Revolt broke out. With the Enfield too, we can assume that they would have had no problem as well. But they were certainly at the receiving end of Enfield fire. And while their own muskets were effective only up to 100 yards, the Enfield was effective up to 300 yards. That made all the difference in 1857.

101. Irfan Habib, 'Remembering 1857', 'Delhi in 1857: Studies and Documents', Indian History Congress, Dept. of History, University of Delhi, 2010.

102. Ibid.

103. Ibid.

104. Ibid.

Note: Handmade maps of Shahjahanabad and Qila-e-Mubarak are at the end of the book.

105. The map of Shahjahanabad is based on the 'Plan of Delhi 1857–58' by William Mackenzie, Edinburgh, c. 1860.

106. The map of Qila-e-Mubarak is based on 'Shahjahanabad Delhi around 1860' in Ehlers E. & Kraft T.(ed.); *Shahjahanabad/Old Delhi: Tradition and Colonial Change*, Delhi: Manohar, 2003.

ACKNOWLEDGEMENTS

The Where Stones Speak trilogy has a special place in my heart as it started me on my journey of writing. I would like to thank each and every person whom I met on this path starting with Asif Khan Dehlvi and every reader who has bought the previous books. I hope you give this book as much love if not more for it's a labour of love.

This is the last book in the series and not only have I evolved in the course of it but so has my writing. This is a living city and I wanted to present the monuments here as living, breathing spaces and thus I ended up taking most of the photographs for it myself. It was a challenging task for I explored the city in rain, sunshine and cold weather armed with my camera and iPhone. On many of the explorations I was accompanied by Abu Sufiyan and on some by Rameen Khan. We climbed up steep and often dark stairs, walked through crowded markets and often I would be so engrossed in photographing that Sufiyan and Rameen would have to pull me to avoid getting hit by oncoming traffic. Nevertheless, it was fun. I had established a pattern: one day a week was for exploring and three days would be for documenting them. I had got some fantastic photos. I wanted to show the worshippers in the mosques, temples and churches for it is they who are the soul of these places. I wanted to contrast them with archival photographs from Archaeological Survey of India (ASI).

But as they say all the plans of mice and men…

Unfortunately my hard disc crashed. I tried every possible way to retrieve them but nothing worked. I called Arcopol Chaudhuri who had edited my earlier books and asked him for his suggestions on how to proceed. I had clicked the same photos with my iPhone as well with the intention of using them on social media once the book was out. Arcopol talked to the art department at HarperCollins India and, much to my relief, I was informed that these days iPhone photographs are acceptable. I had been willing to reshoot but it would have been a waste of energy. So, I hope in this final instalment of my trilogy you will appreciate not only my writing but also my photography skills.

I often feel Shahjahanabad is embedded in my soul and surely there's some past life connection with it because of which it has a special place in my heart. There is something about this walled city, which pulls at my heartstrings, and perhaps that is to do with the people who live there.

This book would not have been complete without them. First and foremost is Abu Sufiyan, who not only accompanied me on my exploration trips but was also generous with his time and knowledge of the city. Similarly, Ashok Mathur a fifth generation Shahjahanabadi who opened his heart and haveli for me and was a great source of knowledge.

It was luck that introduced Rameen Khan to me for he became a comrade in arms and fellow explorer. He discovered monuments I thought had been lost to us and his passion matches mine when it comes to the subject.

Prof. Shamsur Rahman Faruqi has always encouraged, supported and appreciated my efforts in documenting our history and heritage, for which I am eternally grateful. He sent me a message saying that he loved *The Forgotten Cities of Delhi* (book two in the trilogy) but wished there was a map to help explorers.

I turned to urban planner Shubham Mishra and like a true champ and lover of Delhi he agreed to design the maps. In times of digital technology, Shubham has handmade the maps in this book and that makes it extra special. I will be forever grateful to him for adding value to my book.

Jayshree Shukla and her photography are synonymous with Shahjahanabad and I am indebted to her for sharing her photographs with me. Her joy in the walled city she calls her own also matches mine and I love her wanderings in Delhi series, which document Shahjahanabad.

As always Ajmal Siddiqui has been extremely helpful in translating the verses used in this book and in deciphering the chronograms. I will always be grateful for the ways he enriches my life. You are the younger brother I never had, Ajmal.

Saiyyed Zahir Husain Jafri of History Department, University of Delhi, was my class fellow at AMU. He has always stood like a rock behind me and patiently answered each query of mine. Not only did he help me, but he also boosted my confidence. I am fortunate to have a friend like him.

Prof. Ali Nadeem Rezavi, Chairman, Centre of Advanced Studies, Dept. of History, AMU has similarly been a pillar of support filling in the blanks for me, ever so often.

I am grateful to Mr Janhwij Sharma, Joint Director General, ASI for all his help and to the ASI for providing me with priceless images from their archives.

Historian Dr Swapna Liddle, Covenor INTACH, Delhi Chapter was extremely generous with her immense knowledge of the city as she patiently answered my queries.

I am grateful to Syed Mohammed Qasim for having been a part of my earlier books.

Udayan Mitra has supported me throughout the process of writing this book and I hope I justify his belief in me. His gentle, encouraging ways and prompt responses have always increased my confidence. He is a dream publisher to have.

Mriga Maithel is not only a superlative editor but also a wonderful friend and has added so much to this book. Her queries have led me to explore further and further into the past and bring it into the present for the reader.

I am extremely grateful to Tanima Saha for adding so much value to my book and giving it so much love. I have loved working with you Tanima and together I hope we have created magic!

My thanks to the DTP team at HarperCollins India for their superb art work and layout.

I have been working with Bonita Vaz-Shimray since the first book in this series and her value addition to the book is just that – very valuable! I had taken various photographs for the cover, but Bonita wanted that something extra, something more special. She suggested a few possibilities. Armed with that belief that something special awaited us, I climbed up the steep and daunting steps of the Jama Masjid minaret with Nikhil Arora. It is quite a challenging climb for someone my age but one thing that I learnt from Amma and Baba was 'never say die'. Amma would often say to us when we told her not to over exert that, if something is worth doing, it is worth doing well. I realize the meaning of her words now, when I push my boundaries and my children worry.

After a long time on the top of the minaret and shooting some pretty spectacular photographs Nikhil and I started our long descent down. I knew they were spectacular but the X factor that Bonita had asked for was still missing. Just then I saw this turret window and Nikhil captured it. The rest as they say is magic. Thank you Bonita for that belief and for making the cover extra special.

I welcome Nikhil Arora into my family with lots of warmth and love, and special thanks for doing the cover photography.

My children and husband as always have been very supportive of my work and I am able to do whatever I can because of their encouragement.

And last but not the least, a big thanks to William Dalrymple for believing in my work and endorsing the book. Means a lot to me. It was his book *The Last Mughal* that reawakened a desire to write in me. He brought history into the everyday life of people and today many of us who write on the subject owe it to him for paving the way. I remember standing in a long line in the Dubai Literature Festival to get his autograph on it. I had never thought even in my wildest dreams that one day I would have his endorsement on a book I write.

Prof. Narayani Gupta is synonymous with Delhi, due to her large body of work on the city and it means a lot to me that she too has endorsed my book. It feels like I have received a certificate. Thank you for this and your support and encouragement of my writings.

Above all I would like to thank God for everything that I am or have achieved in my life.

ABOUT THE AUTHOR

Rana Safvi is a renowned writer, scholar and translator. She is the author of the *Where Stones Speak: Historical Trails in Mehrauli, the First City of Delhi, The Forgotten Cities of Delhi, Tales from the Quran and Hadith*, and translator of Sayyid Ahmad Khan's *Asar-us-Sanadid* and Zahir Dehlvi's *Dastan-e-Ghadhar*. Her blog, www.ranasafvi.com, is a repository of her writings on Indian culture, food, heritage and age-old traditions. She is the founder and moderator of the hashtag #Shair on Twitter, a forum that has revived popular interest in Urdu poetry in a major way.

Rana is a postgraduate in history from Aligarh Muslim University. She lives in Delhi with her family.

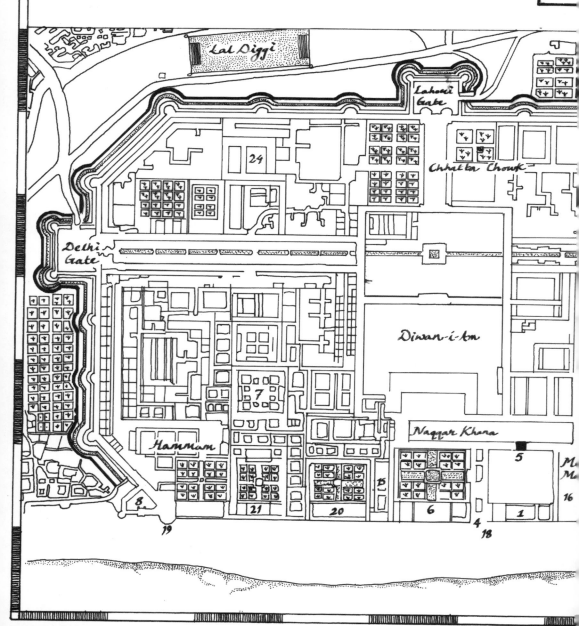

QILA-E-MUBARAK

105

1. Di
2. Za
3. As
4. Mu
5. La
6. Ra
7. Ch
8. Ba

Lal Diggi

Lahori Gate

Chhatta Chowk

Delhi Gate

24

Diwan-i-Am

Naqqar Khana

Hammam

5

M
M

16

8

21

20

15

6

1

19

4

18

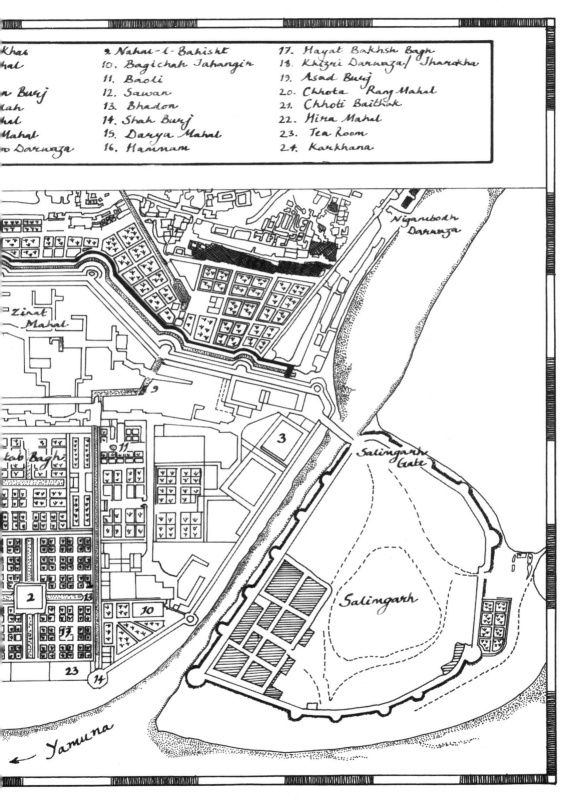

Khas
hal

n Burj
lah
hal
Mahal
o Darwaza

9. Nahal-i-Bahisht
10. Bagichah Jahangir
11. Baoli
12. Sawan
13. Bhadon
14. Shah Burj
15. Darya Mahal
16. Hammam

17. Hayat Bakhsh Bagh
18. Khizri Darwaza/ Jharokha
19. Asad Burj
20. Chhota Rang Mahal
21. Chhoti Baithak
22. Hira Mahal
23. Tea Room
24. Karkhana

Nigambodh
Darwaza

Zinat
Mahal

9

tab Bagh

11

3

Salingarh
Gate

2   13

10

Salingarh

23

14

Yamuna

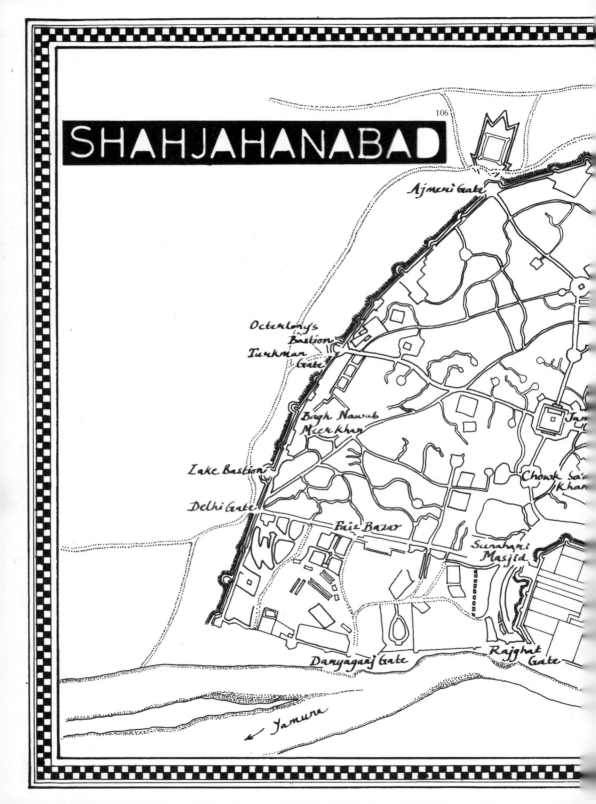

SHAHJAHANABAD

106

Ajmeri Gate

Octerlony's
Bastion

Turkman
Gate

Bagh Nawab
Meer Khan

Lake Bastion

Delhi Gate

Faiz Bazar

Jam

Chowk Sa'
Khan

Sunahari
Masjid

Daryaganj Gate

Rajghat
Gate

← Yamuna

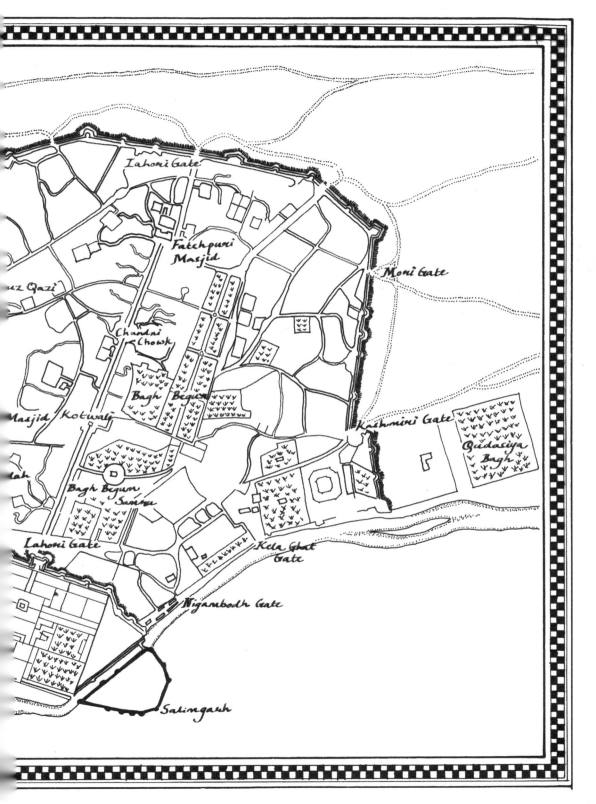